MARGARET ATWOOD
Conversations

Ontario Review Press Critical Series
General Editor, Raymond J. Smith

MARGARET ATWOOD
Conversations

edited by
Earl G. Ingersoll

A Firefly Book

The completion of this collection of interviews was made possible by a
Faculty Research Award from the Canadian government through its
embassy in Washington, D.C. Margaret Atwood, her assistant Melanie
Dugan, and her agent Phoebe Larmore contributed immensely through
their willingness to provide information and their support for the project.
At Brockport numerous individuals provided assistance, especially
librarian Robert Gilliam by locating journals and obtaining copies of the
interviews and Vicky Willis by patiently and conscientiously preparing the
manuscript.

Library of Congress Cataloging-in-Publication Data

Atwood, Margaret Eleanor, 1939–
    Margaret Atwood: conversations/edited by Earl G. Ingersoll.
    (Ontario Review Press critical series)
1. Atwood, Margaret Eleanor, 1939–   Interviews. 2. Novelists,
Canadian—20th century—Interviews. I. Ingersoll, Earl G., 1938–
II. Title. III. Title: Conversations. IV. Series.
PR1993.A8Z468 1990   818'.5409—dc20   89-29944
ISBN 0 920668 80 1

ONTARIO REVIEW PRESS
in association with Persea Books

Published simultaneously in Canada by

Firefly Books Ltd.
250 Sparks Avenue
Willowdale, Ontario
M2H 2S4

A FIREFLY BOOK

Contents

Introduction

TO BOTH ITS champions and its detractors the literary interview has become one of our culture's newest institutions. Its currency has grown with the advancement of communication technology and the ease with which we jet from city to city and continent to continent. It is the product also of our desire to know more about contemporary writers. In contrast to their expatriate forerunners who believed the Great Good Place was London or Paris, contemporary writers are in our midst, appearing on television to promote their books, if they are best-sellers, or visiting college and university campuses to give readings from their work.

One frequent obligation of being "on the circuit" is submitting to interviews which may be broadcast in the area to which writers have come to give their readings or transcribed for publication in literary journals, frequently gleaned by critics and scholars as grist for their mills. Joe David Bellamy, in the introduction to his collection *American Poetry Observed: Poets on Their Work* (1984), has speculated that the literary interview has proliferated to fill a vacuum left by the reluctance of contemporary writers to expend their energies on the kind of literary criticism which in part provided earlier generations of writers with a rationale for their own writing.

To its detractors the literary interview has occasionally been seen as an expression of our fascination with the *personality* of the writer. That fascination often displaces our reading of the writer's work itself. The title of one recent commentary on the literary interview, "Talk Show," typifies the arch attitude of those conservative academics who see many of its expressions as little more than literary gossip and attraction to the writer's life. In his article "Talk Show: The Rise of the Literary Interview" (*The American Scholar*, 1988), Bruce Bawer laments that even at their best literary interviews are not critical essays on the writer's work, and that often they are not at their best because "there seems to be an unspoken understanding among interviewers, editors, and readers that literary interviews should not be held to the same standards of accuracy as, say, literary essays." And "stars" like Truman Capote are allowed to say the most outrageously unfair things about other writers without having to provide evidence for their malicious statements. Without a doubt the literary interview can border on the "talk show"; however, as even Bawer admits some interviews offer insights into writers' work that might be otherwise unrecognized.

Writers themselves have had mixed feelings about the literary interview. All too frequently writers have encountered the literally uninformed interviewer who begins with a comment such as "I've never read
any of your work, Mr. Smith, but I would like to ask you..." Many feel
that the interviewer is bent upon extracting answers that will support
the interviewer's interpretations of the writer's work. Others feel that
the interviewer is seeking to probe the writer's personal life for a biographical explanation of the writer's work. Still others feel that issues
and understandings are too complex to submit to encapsulizing in responses of 100 words or fewer.

Edward Albee speaks for many writers when he responded to an
interviewer's comment "I get the impression that you don't really like
being interviewed" as follows:

> It's not that I mind being interviewed. I think it's really a waste of
> time. Critics would do better to write essays upon the plays and not
> upon the writers. I get a little disturbed by the concentration upon
> the writer rather than what he writes. All the matters we've been
> trying to talk about—what a writer thinks about his own craft—are
> very private, and it's best that most writers don't think about them
> consciously. And there is the awful jeopardy that the interviewer is
> in by having to phrase questions that will make communicable sense
> both to the interviewee and to the audience if the questions are
> answered. It's a mess. Interviews are a mess. (Philip C. Kolin, ed.,
> *Conversations with Edward Albee*, 1988)

Margaret Atwood could hardly agree more. In the interviews which
follow we see her concern that the Margaret Atwood we find there is not
the writer of the fiction and the poems, but the "public" Margaret Atwood
who is forced to contrive responses to satisfy her questioners—responses
which may at best be only partial truths. We see her desire to avoid
"pontificating" about her own work lest she foreclose alternative interpretations. Like other writers she well knows that returning to her own work
after its publication she can offer only *a* reading but not *the* reading
which her questioners may be naively in search of. Also, perhaps more
than other writers, she is concerned that her readers avoid the seemingly
irresistible temptation to interpret her fiction as autobiography. Even
when she tells her audiences that she was never overweight as a child
nor anorexic as a young woman, the power of her fiction will not allow
readers to believe that she is not drawing upon her own experience.

One function of these interviews, then, is to provide Ms. Atwood with
an opportunity to set the record straight. She can tell us that despite the
death of the narrator's parents in *Surfacing*, her own parents are very

much alive, or that unlike the heroine of *Lady Oracle* she is not a closet writer of Harlequin Romances. Reading literature as autobiography is "North American," she thinks, since Americans and Canadians aren't as used to having writers around as, say, the English or French. It happens more often to women than to men, she speculates, with Joyce Carol Oates, in the *New York Times Book Review* interview, "probably because women are viewed as more subjective and less capable of invention." She adds: "Also, we have a somewhat romantic notion on this side of the Atlantic about what an author is. We think of 'writing' not as something you do but as something you are. The writer is seen as 'expressing' herself; therefore, her books must be autobiographical. If the book were seen as something made, like a pot, we probably wouldn't have this difficulty."

The recent appearance of *Cat's Eye* renders the issue of autobiographical and biographical roots for fiction even more problematic. The heroine, Elaine Risley, is a painter (a fairly consistent vehicle for novelists depicting their art) returning to the Toronto of her childhood for a retrospective exhibition of her painting and sculpture. Like Atwood herself Risley is fifty, looking back to a childhood with striking similarities to Margaret Atwood's. Both young girls follow their entomologist-fathers into the North woods and assist in the collection of insects, for example. Both Elaine and Margaret experience a culture shock in returning to middle-class suburban Toronto where they are expected to wear skirts and study to become housewives. Aware of how the novel would be (mis)read Margaret Atwood includes the following "warning label" on its copyright page:

> This is a work of fiction. Although its form is that of an autobiography, it is not one. Space and time have been rearranged to suit the convenience of the book, and, with the exception of public figures, any resemblance to persons living or dead is purely coincidental. The opinions expressed are those of the characters and should not be confused with the author's.

At the same time, as the interviews suggest, the novel contains so much of Margaret Atwood's early experience and her opinions that "coincidence" would be phenomenal. Familiarity with her "biography" simply enhances the postmodernist "play" with her audience here and with conventional notions of the dichotomy between "fiction" and "reality."

In their own more informal manner, these interviews offer us a kind of "biography" of Margaret Atwood—indeed, the only biography she is likely to sanction. It's not so much that she shares what was T. S. Eliot's aversion to authorized biographies; to her, a writer's life is "boring."

When approached by a television producer who considered doing a biographical piece on her life, she was puzzled that anyone would want to. What would it show but a writer sitting with pencil in hand? she wondered. She commented in her conversation with Joyce Carol Oates in *Ontario Review*:

> I am not a very glamorous person. Writers aren't, really. All they do is sit around and write, which I suppose is as commendable as sitting around painting your toenails, but will never make it into the fashion magazines. So when I see myself being glamorized or idealized, it makes me squirm somewhat.

At the same time, few writers deserve a "biography" more than Ms. Atwood. Much as it may make her "squirm" to be reminded of it, her eminence in contemporary literature, Canadian or otherwise, is unquestionable. Reviewing her recent venture into speculative fiction, Lawrence Parrinder in *The London Review of Books* (20 March 1986), a journal not given to extravagant praise, said: "*The Handmaid's Tale* is, quite simply, the work of the most distinguished novelist under fifty currently writing in English." But that kind of "stellification," to use her term, makes her uncomfortable, one suspects, not because of false modesty but because of a true artist's reverence for the whimsy of the muse who might stop appearing to those who have been elevated to the "stars." We need to listen to the Atwood of the interviews not to discover what we already know from reading her work but to acquaint ourselves with the Margaret Atwood who has been too often misunderstood. "Misunderstood" may be putting it mildly for a writer who has been caricatured as an "octopus" with her tentacles around Canadian literature or as a petrifying "Medusa," perhaps the unfortunate consequence, she suggests, of being born with naturally curly hair.

Ms. Atwood distrusts the interview, yet she has submitted to well over fifty of them. Her start as an interviewee was not particularly auspicious, however. In 1967, in one of her first encounters with the form, she was asked by her interviewer who had just returned from Vietnam, "When are you going to say something interesting?" Her willingness to share that anecdote is just one expression of a dominant characteristic of the Margaret Atwood we come to know in the interviews—her sense of humor, especially when the humor is at her own expense. It is a *Canadian* attribute, she feels—and one of which she is particularly proud. In Scotland, speaking to William Findlay, she remarks on her "style" as a Canadian writer: "I find that when I go to other countries, such as France and Germany, in which literature is regarded with a capital 'L,' and I talk about myself and my work and I make jokes, they're really shocked"

(*Cencrastus*, 1979). Since so much of her work seems satirical, these interviews offer the reader a sense of perspective and balance: Ms. Atwood can laugh at herself as well as at others. Beyond that, her sense of art as "play" and her attraction to pastiche clearly put her in the center of Postmodernism.

These interviews also demonstrate one aspect of her personality which may help to explain the dominance of irony and satire in her work. All too frequently in her writing she seems to be looking at humanity with an icy detachment. The most notorious expression of that misapprehension of her personality is "Margaret the Magician" by Linda Rogers (*Canadian Literature*, 1974), a piece Ms. Atwood sees as preoccupied with a study of her cover photographs in which she is not smiling. What her responses in these interviews indicate is a detachment or coolness which has helped her to survive as an artist in a culture which attempted to deny the validity of her vocation. Again and again we see Ms. Atwood's audience—academic or not, feminist or not, Canadian or not—less than willing to accept her commitment to her art above all else. She has spoken out for women's rights and yet she is wary of becoming an ideologue who would "desacralize" men in order to make women "sacred." She has stood in the forefront of Canada's cultural nationalism, on occasion acidly commenting on the struggle to exist as a culture on the doorstep of the American "Empire"; still, she reserves the independence to point up her nation's need to escape not only its "colonial mentality" but its perception of martyrdom. She has risked offending socialists or feminists, with whom she might agree in general, by arguing for cultural nationalism, the impulse not to dominate other nations but merely to shout, "We exist, we exist," when cultural absorption by megacultures seems inevitable. At the same time, she turns her gaze unblinkingly upon the limits of her own culture, finding elements of the "small town" resentments and apprehensions generated by the success of one of its own. The cool detachment so central to her public image is more than anything an expression of her self-conscious struggle to maintain the integrity of her art.

Some of the humor and cool detachment evident in these interviews is the product of their inevitably retrospective nature. Much has changed in the past thirty years of Ms. Atwood's life and her nation's cultural history. She mentions to Joyce Carol Oates that she began writing at five, but between the ages of eight and sixteen she went through what she jokingly termed a "dark period" when she didn't write. When another interviewer, Karla Hammond, asks for clarification of that "dark period," suspecting perhaps some ominous grounds for the darkness, Ms. Atwood responds that during those years she was concerned with how she would

earn a living, never imagining in her wildest fantasies that she could
support herself as a writer. At that time the guidance books recommended five careers for women: airline stewardess, teacher, school nurse,
secretary, and home economist. When at sixteen she decided suddenly
to become a writer, for reasons she cannot herself explain, she determined that she would have to find the means of supporting that extrava-
gance. Since she had read virtually no literature except American and
English before 1900, her role models were, almost to a woman, unmarried, and she concluded that her writing would have to take precedence
over any relationship with men. In her *American Poetry Review* conversation with Karla Hammond, she remarks:

> I chose being a writer, because I was very determined, even though
> it was very painful for me then (the late '50s and early '60s), but
> I'm very glad that I made that decision because the other alternative
> would have been ultimately much more painful: it's more painful
> to renounce your gifts or your direction in life than it is to renounce
> an individual.
>
> People a little bit older than myself wrote in cupboards at night
> because they didn't want anyone to know that they were writing or
> criticize them for taking that time away from their family. They
> tried to fulfill all their roles. When they gained recognition, they
> would immediately have marital difficulties because their husbands
> couldn't deal with their success. So I felt that if I were going to
> marry or form a permanent relationship that that individual had
> to know, from the beginning, who I was and what I was doing. I
> wasn't going to conceal it. Many people thought I was really cold
> and perhaps I am in a very specific way. It's a necessary protective
> device.

As the interviews also indicate, Ms. Atwood came to her maturity as
an artist during the period in which Canadian literature came into its
own internationally, and, perhaps more importantly, in Canada. She
recalls the condition of her nation's literature in the late '50s when she
made the decision to become a writer. There were very few Canadian
literary magazines. Perhaps a handful of novels and twenty or so books
of poetry by Canadians appeared each year. Canadian literature was not
being taught, even in Canada. "'Canadian writer' was a term of derision,
even to Canadian writers," she recalls. In the three decades that have
elapsed, she has seen the growth of indigenous publishing houses and
unions of writers. Her own book *Survival*, an introduction to Canadian
literature aimed at the non-academic reader, has sold 70,000 copies since
it appeared in 1972. Canadian literature has become a recognized disci-

pline and has its own separate entries in the annual bibliography of the PMLA. Canadian studies programs have been established throughout the United States. The changes which have taken place since she began to write in the late '50s have been so dramatic that the past must seem more fantasy than reality to a writer midway through a successful career.

The interviews which follow were selected from a group over double their number. They appear in roughly chronological order by the date of the interview or by the date of publication in those cases in which the date of the interview cannot be identified. This organization allows the reader to explore the range of Ms. Atwood's interests and attitudes over the past two decades to note both the changes and the consistencies.

All of these conversations have already appeared in print. Many have appeared in readily accessible journals such as the *Ontario Review* and *Shenandoah*, or in collections such as Graeme Gibson's *Eleven Canadian Novelists* and Geoff Hancock's *Canadian Writers at Work*. Many, however, have appeared in small-circulation or short-lived magazines such as *Waves* or *Manna*. In the face of occasional difficulties of determining rights to reprint, I have tried to gain permission from the participants in each of these interviews. And Ms. Atwood, of course, exercised editorial control over her responses in these conversations.

The interviews have been edited to achieve consistency in matters of mechanics, such as American spelling, and to remove redundant or unimportant material. Such passages are denoted "//." On occasion repeated passages have been allowed to stand in order to emphasize matters important enough to Ms. Atwood to bear her "repeating" them or to show how she characteristically responds to frequently asked questions. As Ms. Atwood reminds us, the writer interviewed is often—but one hopes not *always*—a fictive self, the writer as interviewee, created for that interview. The reader will find here also a range of responsiveness. The openness of the responses, their tone as well as their length, the repetition of earlier answers—all these indicate significant factors surrounding what the words of the responses themselves denote. In the end we have a series of dialogues meant to be read together as one expression of the artist's life in the past twenty years.

EARL G. INGERSOLL
December 1989

Chronology

1939 Born 18 November, in Ottawa, Ontario; parents, Carl Edmund Atwood and Margaret Killam Atwood. Her brother, Harold, was born in 1937; her sister, Ruth, in 1951.

1946–61 Moves with her family from Ottawa to Toronto, where her father, an entomologist, is a member of the University of Toronto faculty.

1952–57 Attends Leaside High School in Toronto and begins writing at sixteen.

1957–61 A student at Victoria College, University of Toronto. Publishes in *Acta Victoriana*, *The Canadian Forum*, and *The Strand*. Graduates in 1961 with honors in English. Her collection of poems, *Double Persephone* (Hawkshead Press), appears and receives the E. J. Pratt Medal for Poetry.

1961 Receives a Woodrow Wilson Fellowship and begins graduate work at Radcliffe, attracted by the reputation of Jerome Buckley, the Canadian specialist in 19th-century English literature.

1962 Granted a Master of Arts in English and continues work on a Ph.D.

1963 Leaves Harvard to work in market research in Toronto and begins work on the manuscript of a yet-unpublished novel.

1964–65 Moves to Vancouver to teach at the University of British Columbia and works on the manuscript of *The Edible Woman*, between April and August, using U. of British Columbia exam booklets.

1965 Returns to graduate work at Harvard.

1966 *The Circle Game* (Contact Press; Anansi) appears.

1967   Receives the Governor-General's Award for Poetry for *The Circle Game*. *The Animals in That Country* wins first prize in the Centennial Commission Poetry Competition. Marries James Polk, whom she met at Harvard in 1963.

1967–68   Teaches Victorian literature and American literature at Sir George Williams University in Montreal. In 1968 *The Animals in That Country* (Oxford, Atlantic Little-Brown) appears.

1969–70   Teaches at the University of Alberta. In 1969 *The Edible Woman* (McClelland and Stewart, Andre Deutsch; Atlantic Little-Brown, 1970) appears, its publication delayed because the publisher misplaced the manuscript for two years. *Poetry* magazine awards her the Union Poetry Prize. In 1970 *The Journals of Susanna Moodie* (Oxford) and *Procedures for Underground* (Oxford, Atlantic Little-Brown) appear.

1971   *Power Politics* (Anansi; Harper and Row, 1973) appears.

1971–72   Teaches at York University, Toronto.

1972   *Surfacing* (McClelland and Stewart; Andre Deutsch, Simon & Schuster, 1973) and *Survival: A Thematic Guide to Canadian Literature* (Anansi) appear.

1972–73   Writer-in-Residence at the University of Toronto.

1973   James Polk and she get divorced, and she moves to Alliston, Ontario, with Graeme Gibson, whom she met in 1970. Trent University grants her a D. Litt.

1974   *You Are Happy* (Oxford; Harper and Row, 1975) appears. *Poetry* of Chicago awards the Bess Hopkins Prize; Queen's University, the LL.D.

1976   *Selected Poems* (Oxford, Simon & Schuster) and *Lady Oracle* (McClelland and Stewart, Simon & Schuster; Andre Deutsch, 1977) appear. Daughter Eleanor Jess Atwood Gibson is born.

1977   *Dancing Girls* (McClelland and Stewart; Simon & Schuster, Cape, 1981) appears. *Lady Oracle* receives the City of Toronto Book Award and the Canadian Bookseller's Association Award.

1978   *Two-Headed Poems* (Oxford; Simon & Schuster, 1980) and *Up in the Tree* (McClelland and Stewart) appear. Recipient of the St. Lawrence Award for Fiction.

1979   *Life Before Man* (McClelland and Stewart; Simon & Schuster, Cape, 1980) appears.

1980   *Anna's Pet* (James Lorimer & Co.) appears. Moves to Toronto, receives the Radcliffe Graduate Medal and a D. Litt. from Concordia University.

1981   *True Stories* (Oxford; Simon & Schuster, 1982) and *Bodily Harm* (McClelland and Stewart; Simon & Schuster, Cape, 1982) appear. Awarded a Guggenheim Fellowship.

1982   *The Oxford Book of Canadian Verse in English* (Oxford) and *Second Words: Selected Critical Prose* (Anansi; Beacon Press, 1984) appear. Receives an honorary degree from Smith College.

1983   *Murder in the Dark* (Coachhouse Press) and *Bluebeard's Egg* (McClelland and Stewart; Houghton Mifflin, 1986) appear. Receives an honorary degree from the University of Toronto.

1984   *Interlunar* (Oxford) appears.

1985   *The Handmaid's Tale* (McClelland and Stewart; Houghton Mifflin, Cape, 1986) appears. Spends the spring semester at the University of Alabama as holder of the Endowed Chair in Creative Writing and receives honorary degrees from Mount Holyoke, the University of Waterloo, and the University of Guelph.

1986   *Selected Poems II: Poems Selected and New 1976–1986* (Oxford) appears. Holds the Berg Chair at New York University for three months and receives the Governor General's Award.

1987   *Selected Poems II* and *Selected Poems I* (Houghton Mifflin) appear.

1988   *Cat's Eye* (McClelland and Stewart, Bloomsbury; Doubleday, 1989) appears.

MARGARET ATWOOD
Conversations

Dissecting the Way a Writer Works
Graeme Gibson

Graeme Gibson's interview was conducted in 1972, and originally appeared in his collection of interviews *Eleven Canadian Novelists* (Anansi, 1973). Copyright © 1973 by Graeme Gibson. Reprinted by permission.

Gibson: What is it about the novel that is opposed, say, to poetry or the film script that you've done, what is it about the novel you like?

Atwood: I don't know. I don't think it's a positive attraction towards the novel—it's just that there are things you can't do in any other form. Things you can't do in poetry unless you want to be E. J. Pratt and write very long narrative poems. You can't have characters, you can't have very involved plots—it's a whole different thing. Poems are very condensed, and a film script isn't a primary form for a writer—it's a secondary form. It's a primary form for a director.

Gibson: Are novels less personal?

Atwood: No, no, it has very little to do with that. It's more a question of how much room you have. You have a lot more room in a novel to move around, and you can build a much more complex, I won't say "complex" because poems can be very complex, but you can build a larger structure.

Gibson: Perhaps you never think this way, but do you think of yourself differently as a poet than as a novelist, when you're working.

Atwood: I don't think of myself at all when I'm working. I think of the thing I'm doing, and obviously I think of the novel as a different kind of thing than a poem...it's a lot more hard work. It's physical labor in a way that poetry isn't. You can write a poem very quickly, and then it's done, and you've had everything, all possible satisfactions and engagements with the thing, condensed into a short period of time. The equivalent for that with a novel is when you get the idea or when you get a few of the key scenes. But the problem then is sustaining your interest long enough to actually sit down and work it out, and that is difficult for me because I don't like work. I will do anything to avoid it, which means that in order to actually finish a novel I have to isolate myself from all distraction because if it's a question of a choice between the work and the distraction I'll take the distraction every time.

Gibson: What about a collection of poems, like *Susanna Moodie*, where in fact you do have a character?

Atwood: Yes. That assumes that I sat down with the conception of a character and wrote the thing through from chapter one through the middle to the end, but they came as separate poems and I had no idea when I began that I was going to end up with a book of that size. It wasn't planned that way. I wrote twelve at first and stopped and thought, You know, this is just sort of a long short poem, twelve short poems, that's it. And then I started writing more of them but I didn't know where it was going. I don't write books of poetry as books. I don't write them like novels.

Gibson: With a novel presumably you know where you are going when you begin?

Atwood: Not entirely, but I know there is enough of a skeleton so I'll end up with a book of a certain length.

Gibson: How do you write novels? I mean you write quickly, I gather.

Atwood: I write them in longhand which is very bad. I wish I could write on a typewriter—it would save a lot of trouble. I do write very quickly, but under a lot of pressure. I try to work through something like ten pages a day, which of course never happens....

Gibson: Do you write the first draft of a novel pretty well in one spurt?

Atwood: Well, I don't know. I've only written two, actually I've written three, the first one didn't get published, and the first one took a long time because I had a job, I didn't have uninterrupted time and it took me about three months. With *The Edible Woman* I went through the first draft in about a month and a half. And the other one, *Surfacing*—when did I finish it? last summer? there's no sense of time—it got interrupted; I wanted to write it through and I did get something like a first draft.

But then I had to go off and work on the film script, and not until I was into something like the third draft did I have a straight period of time.

Gibson: You do a fair amount of rewriting then?

Atwood: Yes, a lot. I think the pressure is to get the thing down in some form or other so that it's out there and then can be worked with.

Gibson: Do you enjoy writing?

Atwood: Do I enjoy writing? I guess I would have to, wouldn't I, or I wouldn't do it. I don't like the physical thing and I don't like the sort of willpower involved in making sure that your sentences are O.K. and that you haven't repeated the same word about nine times on one page. That sort of busy-work is editing. I enjoy the initial thing. I don't enjoy the tidying up very much because it's like work.

Gibson: What is the writer's role? Do you think he has a role?

Atwood: I don't know. I'm sure he has lots of roles, but I very much object to other people telling me what my role is in any area of life whatsoever. I think people define their own roles, and my "role as a writer" may be entirely different from somebody else's. Somebody else may feel that his role is to write a novel about being saved for Jesus Christ and the novel should convert people, or that what he should be writing is a novel about how to get rid of the Americans. I don't see writing as having that kind of function. I think if you are going to save souls or save the world, you should be a preacher or a politician, so I don't see my role in any one-to-one relationship with society. I think anybody who does is deluding himself. Books don't save the world.

Gibson: Does a writer have any responsibility to society?

Atwood: Does society have any responsibility to the writer? Once society decides it has responsibility to me as a writer, I'll start thinking about my responsibility to it. You know, I think its general attitude towards me when I started to be a writer was that I was crazy or somehow undecorous, and if society regards me like that, I don't see that I have any particular responsibility towards it. I think that's society's attitude towards anybody when he's first starting. But if you become successful, then it's an O.K. thing for you to be doing because, as we all know, this society pays a lot of attention to success. But that is not a respect for writing *per se* as a legitimate activity; that's a respect for success, which is a different thing. It would have the same respect for you if you were a successful used-car salesman.

Gibson: Do you think this is particularly Canadian, our response to writers?

Atwood: No, it's American. It's getting better, but one always sees things in terms of one's struggling youth to a certain extent, and that was certainly the case with mine. I could count on the fingers of one hand people whose attitude towards what I was doing was positive. The rest were either incredulous or negative.

Gibson: Do writers know something special, say, in the way physicists or astronomers or sociologists do?

Atwood: Do they have a body of knowledge that is transmittable? No. They have presumably a skill with words. Apart from that they can be very different from one another. They don't necessarily share any body of knowledge, any viewpoint, any psychological pattern, although sometimes they try to. There's a certain amount of pressure on them to see themselves in terms of society's idea of what the writer should be. You know, you should go to Paris and drink a lot, or you should kill yourself, you should be Lord Byron or T. S. Eliot or something like that. I think they have common problems, but that's different. That may shape you to a certain extent, having problems in common.

Gibson: Do you mean problems professionally or personally?

Atwood: Professionally. I mean what they do entails a certain kind of problem, such as how do you write and make enough money to live? How do you get published? Are publishers fair to writers? How to get your books distributed? How do you deal with your audience, supposing you acquire one?

Gibson: Do you feel kinship with other writers?

Atwood: With some, yes, with others, no. Just because a person is a writer is no guarantee that I'm going to like them or like their work or have anything in common with them at all. I don't think people get a gold star on their forehead for being a writer. There seems to be no connection whatsoever between whether I like someone's work and whether I like them. //

Gibson: What do you like most about your own writing?

Atwood: Doing it. After it's done, you mean? Looking at it as an object? I don't know. I don't tend to like it very much after a certain point, and I think that's maybe a healthy sign; that is, if you get too stuck on your own earlier work it probably means there's nothing else new coming along that you're interested in. I think the book you always like best is the one you're about to write. And what you think about the ones you have written is what you did wrong, or how you would do it if you were going to do it over again, or whether you ever would do it over again.

Gibson: Who do you write for?

Atwood: Once upon a time I thought there was an old man with a gray beard somewhere who knew the truth, and if I was good enough, naturally he would tell me that this was it. That person doesn't exist, but that's who I write for. The great critic in the sky.

Gibson: This feeling you have—it presumes some standards?

Atwood: Oh yes, but I don't always know what they are. I would say that's a personification of some ideal which is unattainable, but various human beings can embody certain parts of that, and they'll come along and, if it's somebody whose opinion you really respect, that's part of it, and you never know where those people are. You may never meet them, but if you don't have the faith that they are out there somewhere, then you'd stop writing.

Gibson: Do you feel part of a tradition?

Atwood: Yes.

Gibson: Now is it particularly a Canadian tradition or ... ?

Atwood: Yes. I can only talk about poetry because the Canadian tradition in novels isn't old enough. It's there, but you have to go searching a lot more for it than for the poetry one. It has partly to do with when I was born and when I started writing. If I had been born in 1920 there wouldn't have been a tradition for me to feel part of, or it would have been one that was hopeless or inaccessible. // But when I did discover Canadian writing it was a tremendously exciting thing because it meant that people in the country were writing and not only that, they were publishing books. And if they could be publishing books, then so could

I. // I was talking with P. K. Page a couple of years ago, and she said that when she was writing there wasn't any Canadian tradition, they were all turned on to people like W. H. Auden; their models, the people they were learning to write from, were all in other countries, and that isn't true of me. I learned to write from people in this country.

Gibson: And that carried over when you came to the novel?

Atwood: People have only started to write novels in the same way, with the same profusion and the same confidence, if you like, in this country during the last seven years, and they weren't doing it when I was learning to write and I always wrote both poetry and prose. It's just that the prose took a while longer to get published, and that says something too, because people weren't publishing novels either at that time. The novel is a much more recent development.

Gibson: Have you any idea why it's happened in the last ten years or seven years?

Atwood: There's always a connection between what people write and what they read; and what they read depends partly on the availability of publishing facilities; that is, if what they are reading are all imported novels about New York or about London, England, nobody in this country is going to feel that they can write a "real" book unless they go to those places, and even then they can't really write a real one because they aren't from those places. So when you don't have a publishing industry in your own country that is publishing fiction about the country, you are automatically defeated because you have no audience, you have no models. You are a kind of amputee and you have to either go away and write as an exile or you can go away and write as a fraud, but you can't stay there and write real books about a real place, because there's no input for it, and there's no outlet for it.

Gibson: There tended to be for the short story, didn't there, during the '20s and the '30s?

Atwood: Yes, there were magazines and the CBC, and a lot of people wrote short stories as a result, but novels were another thing. Very seldom was one published, and very seldom did it acquire an audience. Historical romance is another thing, and books like *Jalna* and *Anne of Green Gables*. Those were different; you could write those if you wanted, but if you had other ambitions you were doomed to paralysis.

Gibson: Perhaps that's why there were so many one-book people writing.

Atwood: Yes. Sure they wrote their book, they put everything into it. They got no feedback, and they gave up, and I would too. The increase in the number of good novels has something to do with the growth of the Canadian publishing industry and places like Oberon and Anansi, if you like, and New Press.

Gibson: We were talking about advantages and disadvantages of being a writer in Canada; are there any advantages?

Atwood: Oh, tremendous. All that I've been saying about this is changing very rapidly, obviously. It's almost reached the stage where there are more publishing companies than there are good writers. Also, as I found when I lived in the States, because there is no longstanding tradition, because there are no huge giants hanging over you in Canada, you're very free. You don't feel you're competing with Herman Melville or William Shakespeare, you know; the thing is wide open. You can do anything, although I think the desirable thing to do is to find what in the tradition is usable and use it. //

There are two things. One is how good the book is and that's got nothing to do with your country or anything else. The other thing is what is in it? You can take any body of material—let's just take the Western as an example—and you can use the tradition and you can make a good one or you can make a bad one, using essentially the same kind of thing. You learn to write really from two directions; one is the formal direction and the other is the social mythology direction. The formal thing you can learn from anyone who happens to plug into your own formal direction. He could be from Mars. It wouldn't matter, if he was doing something you found formally interesting; but if you're trying to use somebody else's social mythology, you're doomed. If you try to write like an American or an Englishman, and you aren't one, you will just produce a piece of plastic. No matter how formally skillful you are.

We've been so cut off from our social mythology that we hardly know what it is; that's one thing that has to be discovered. The other thing you have to learn, and you don't learn it from "Canada" necessarily, is how to be a good writer, how to do the thing you're doing in the best way possible.

Gibson: Because we don't have within our own tradition "giants," for want of a better word, is there a danger that it's too easy for us to make an impact or too easy for us to...

Atwood: You can be as good as everyone else fairly easily, but to be really better, that is harder. //

Gibson: Does writing demand a particular kind of selfishness?

Atwood: Everything demands a particular kind of selfishness. If you're asking is the kind that writing demands different from everybody else's kind, I don't know. There again that assumes that writers have personalities in which you can identify an X factor common to all. And I'm not too sure that is true. Partly my suspicion of questions like that is the wish to avoid romantic stereotypes of the writer. You know, all writers are crazy, or they're all geniuses, or some nonsense like that; and to say that all writers have a peculiar kind of selfishness seems to me to fit in a bit with that. But you sort of have to go into a room and shut the door and say, "Go away everyone, because I'm going to write," and you get very annoyed at people who interrupt you, but I don't know whether that's selfish. It seems to be just a kind of condition. If you were a watchmaker and somebody interrupted you, you would probably be just as aggravated if you dropped your dial or whatever. //

Gibson: What sustained you as a writer?

Atwood: My next book. What keeps me going as a writer? That's a very mysterious area. I don't really want to find out. There are a lot of things that I just would rather not know about writing, because I think that if you get too curious about it and start dissecting the way you work and why you do it, you'd probably stop. Maybe not. Anyway that's one of my superstitions. //

Gibson: Have you encountered any particular problems as a woman writer?

Atwood: Sure. I don't think they are typical. At the time I started writing, since writing was such a freaky thing in itself and since very few men were doing it either, it wasn't that I was a woman who was writing that people found peculiar, it was that anybody at all was writing. For so long writing was regarded as a freak thing to be doing, and in a frontier society what is important is work and building houses and bridges and things like that. And writers are viewed as irrelevant or redundant. Men writers overreact to that and define writing as a really male thing to be doing. And if you're a woman doing it, that really threatens their position, considering they've gone to all this trouble to tell anybody who sort of scorns their activity that what they're doing is really very hairy-chested.

Reviewing is something else; there is no critical tradition that the reviewer or critic can draw on for treating the work of women seriously. It's better in this country than in the States, and looking back through *Letters in Canada*, you don't find much of that garbage about feminine sensibilities; but in your run-of-the-mill review it often comes up, though not so much in connection with my own work because they can't really do that easily. What you get instead is the other side of the coin. If people can't say you have a water-color feminine sensibility, they'll say something like she thinks like a man; they find it very hard, if they want to say something that's good, to say that it's good and also admit that the writer is female. They feel that they have to make you an honorary male if they're going to say you're good. So there's that.

What else? Certainly not with publishers. Publishers are in business to make money, and if your books do well they don't care whether you are male, female, or an elephant. I've seldom had any of that kind of thing from any of my publishers.

Gibson: What about the response of other women; do they try to categorize you or . . .

Atwood: Well, of course, now that Women's Lib has come along, it's very curious. Back in the days when you were supposed to pay attention to the diapers and the washing of dishes, I was a threat to other women's life positions. Now I get made into a kind of hero, which is just as unreal. It makes me just as uncomfortable. It's turning me from what I am as a writer into something I'm not.

Gibson: Another general question, hopefully the last one: what do you think are your major preoccupations as a novelist?

Atwood: I don't know. We're talking as though I've written ten novels. I've only written two, and one that didn't get published.

Gibson: That's three and you're going to write another one.

Atwood: They're all so different from each other that I can't really talk about it. It's the sort of thing that critics do, and although I'm willing to talk about somebody else's preoccupations and do critical studies of them, I'm not at all willing to do that on myself. Other people should do that if they're so disposed, but I don't want to make myself the subject of my own criticism.

Gibson: Let's talk about your two novels. There seem to be two kinds of problems, and each novel emphasizes one of them. The first one is the alternatives that are open to people, and specifically women, and that's in *The Edible Woman*; and the second is the destructiveness of society, or in some cases the mere banality of it or the irrelevance of it, but in *Surfacing*, your second book, it's the evil of it. In both novels there's the question of how to survive, given these two problems. Does that seem, generally, a relevant assumption?

Atwood: I guess so. The last thing you said, about how to survive, is certainly true.

Gibson: Marian in *The Edible Woman* is confronted with a frequently silly, irrelevant kind of social situation, like her fiancé is not up to her in any way, her job isn't up to her in any way, and there don't seem to be any alternatives in the lives around her, and what she's got to figure out is how to escape from this trap she finds herself in, survival in that way. The protagonist in the second book has a much more fundamental need to survive.

Atwood: Here we're getting into critical analysis. I can say certain formal things: *The Edible Woman* is an anti-comedy, and *Surfacing* is a ghost story. That sort of determines not only what happens in the book but the style.

Gibson: Let's pause here. What do you mean by an anti-comedy? *The Edible Woman* is an anti-comedy?

Atwood: In your standard 18th-century comedy you have a young couple faced with difficulty in the form of somebody who embodies the restrictive forces of society and they trick or overcome this difficulty and end up getting married. The same thing happens in *The Edible Woman* except the wrong person gets married. And the person who embodies the restrictive forces of society is in fact the person Marian gets engaged to. In a standard comedy, he would be the defiant hero. As it is, he and the restrictive society are blended into one, and the comedy solution would be a tragic solution for Marian.

Gibson: In *The Edible Woman*, it seems to me that society is really unreal or irrelevant. It's the object of Marian's wit and her considerable kind of objective humor, which keeps coming through; but in *Surfacing*, it has become evil, society has become an evil force.

Atwood: Yes.

Gibson: The protagonist of *Surfacing*, who in a sense has gone through all of Marian's experiences, but has lived them out, the marriage...

Atwood: Oh no. The marriage isn't real. She made it up.

Gibson: But she's lived through it in her head, the implications of it, in a way that Marian hasn't. And there's another thing which I found in *Surfacing* which intrigues me and that's guilt. That protagonist of *Surfacing* says at one point when she's talking about the dead heron: "The trouble some people have being German I have being human"; and she also, a bit later, talks about the cruelty of children, the cruelty that she partakes of...

Atwood: It all comes back to original sin, doesn't it? This is too complicated to talk about. // It depends on whether you define yourself as intrinsically innocent, and if you do, then you have a lot of problems, because in fact you aren't. She wishes to be not human, because being human inevitably involves being guilty, and if you define yourself as innocent, you can't accept that.

Gibson: Why does she define herself as innocent, or how does she define herself as innocent? Is it need because of...

Atwood: Ever since we all left the Roman Catholic Church we've defined ourselves as innocent in some way or another. But what I'm really into in that book is the great Canadian victim complex. If you define yourself as innocent then nothing is ever your fault—it is always somebody else doing it to you, and until you stop defining yourself as a victim that will always be true. It will always be somebody else's fault, and you will always be the object of that rather than somebody who has any choice or takes responsibility for their life. And that is not only the Canadian stance towards the world, but the usual female one. "Look what a mess I am and it's all their fault." And Canadians do that too. "Look at poor innocent us, we are morally better than they. We do not burn people in Vietnam, and those bastards are coming in and taking away our country." Well, the real truth of the matter is that Canadians are selling it.

Gibson: You seem to imply in the book that there are two kinds of people. There are the Americans, not based on nationality, but based upon a kind of approach—like hunters, because the people which they mistake for Americans turn out to be Canadians and they're the ones that killed the heron. Is there a distinction? Are there the two types?

Atwood: Are you asking me or are you asking the book?

Gibson: I'm asking you about the book.

Atwood: In both of the books you have a choice of thinking the central character is crazy or thinking she is right. Or possibly thinking she is crazy and right. To a large extent the characters are creating the world which they inhabit, and I think we all do that to a certain extent, or we certainly do a lot of rearranging. There is an objective world out there, I'm far from being a solipsist. There are a lot of things out there, but towards any object in the world you can take a positive or a negative attitude or, let us say, you can turn it into a positive or a negative symbol, and that goes for everything. You can see a tree as the embodiment of natural beauty or you can see it as something menacing that's going to get you, and that depends partly on your realistic position towards it; what you were doing with the tree, admiring it or cutting it down; but it's also a matter of your symbolic orientation towards everything. Now I'm not denying the reality, the existence of evil; some things are very hard to see in a positive light. Evil obviously exists in the world, right? But you have a choice of how you can see yourself in relation to that. And if you define yourself always as a harmless victim, there's nothing you can ever do about it. You can simply suffer.

Gibson: And the protagonist of *Surfacing*, does she do more than identify herself as a victim?

Atwood: At the end she does. She refuses to identify herself as a victim, that's step one. Only if you stop identifying yourself as a victim, you know, fated by powers that be, can you act.

Gibson: Right. Then she says at one point too: "If I had turned out like the others with power, I would have been evil."

Atwood: Yes, but you have to think of where in the book she says that.

Gibson: Yes, it was at the beginning, yes.

Atwood: Yes. That's a refusal too. The other thing you do, if you are defining yourself as innocent, you refuse to accept power. You refuse to admit that you have it, then you refuse to exercise it, because the exercise of power is defined as evil, and that's like people who refuse to get involved in politics because it's dirty.

Gibson: So at the end when she says that she must be a survivor—is that her phrase? something to the effect that she mustn't be a victim?—is she accepting then the responsibility of some power?

Atwood: Of action.

Gibson: Of action, which is a kind of power.

Atwood: Sure. Every time you act you're exercising power in some form, and you cannot predict the consequences of your actions entirely. You may hurt someone, but the alternative is closing yourself up in a burrow somewhere and not doing anything ever at all.

Gibson: Which is what at one point she tries to do. Now is Marian's revolt against the situation she has found herself acquiescing to comparable? Is she asserting herself in the baking of the cake and offering it to Peter?

Atwood: I don't know, nobody's ever been able to figure that out. When writing the filmscript we had long conversations on just exactly what that means. Obviously she's acting, she's doing an action. Up until that point she has been evading, avoiding, running away, retreating, withdrawing.

Gibson: Hiding under the bed.

Atwood: Yes, to begin with; secondly in refusing to eat; and she commits an action, a preposterous one in a way, as all pieces of symbolism in a realistic context are, but what she is obviously making is a substitute for herself.

Gibson: Again in *Surfacing* the protagonist says: "but I was not prepared for the average, its needless cruelties and lies. My brother saw the danger early, to immerse oneself, join in the war or be destroyed. There ought to be other choices." Are there any other choices?

Atwood: We'll put it this way. You're standing on the edge of the lake, right, and you can do three things. You can stay standing on the edge of the lake, you can jump in and if you don't know how to swim you'll drown, or you can learn to swim, supposing you want to have anything to do with the lake at all. The other thing would be to just walk away, but we will suppose that this is the entire universe.

Gibson: One of the things that happens to both of them, but more clearly to the woman in the second book, in the popular phrase, is alienation or isolation, the deadening of sensibilities. I think it's towards the end of *Surfacing*, she says: "Language divides us into fragments: I wanted to be whole." Is this her attempt to be inhuman or to be nonhuman or to be like an animal or a plant?

Atwood: The ideal thing would be a whole human being. Now if your goal is to be whole, and you don't see the possibility of doing that and also being human, then you can try being something else...there are great advantages in being a vegetable, you know, except you lose certain other things, such as the ability to talk. Life is very much simplified. If you think you're a watermelon, you don't have to do anything, you can just sit around. The ideal, though, would be to integrate yourself as a human being, supposedly. And if you try that and fail, then you can try being something else for a while, which she does.

Gibson: By the end of both books, the women seem to have come a long way towards being human beings.

Atwood: Does anyone ever achieve it? If you define human beings as necessarily flawed, then anybody can be one. But if you define them as something which is potentially better, then it's always something that is just out of reach.

Gibson: In *Surfacing* there are the surveyors, the hunters, the // people who kill. One of the assumed definitions is that the Americans, not a nationality, but a state of mind, are the killers. And there are other people who aren't.

Atwood: O.K., let's think of it this way. If the only two kinds of people are killers and victims, then although it may be morally preferable to be a victim, it is obviously preferable from the point of view of survival to be a killer. However, either alternative seems pretty hopeless; you can define yourself as innocent and get killed, or you can define yourself as a killer and kill others. The ideal would be somebody who would neither be a killer or a victim, who could achieve some kind of harmony with the world, which is a productive or creative harmony, rather than a destructive relationship towards the world. Now in neither book is that actualized, but in both it's seen as a possibility finally, whereas initially it is not.

Gibson: O.K., just one more question, regarding the unacceptable roles open to your characters in both books. There aren't many things in society which give anybody enough, and in many cases they're filling in time. They're just doing things. It's a kind of busy-work living, and the men tend to be either pompous, like Peter, a kind of meticulous pomposity, or they're like Joe in the second book who is an observer. Then if you scratch them, beneath the surface you find a sense of failure and a sense of being threatened.

Atwood: Yes. I don't think that's very unrealistic. Let's say that I think of society in two ways; one is simply the kind of thing that Western Industrialism has done to people, and the other is the Canadian thing, where men particularly have been amputated. Women haven't been amputated as much relatively, because absolutely they've been amputated a lot more, but they didn't have as far down to go and Western Industrialism hasn't changed their lives that much. They still have some kind of connection with their own bodies, and the celebrated woman's role, although many people may find it aggravating, still is something to do. If you can't think of what you are supposed to do you can always have a baby, and that will keep you busy enough. But some guy who is doing nothing but punching little holes in cards all day, he has no connection with himself at all, and guys who sit around on their asses in an office all day have no contact with their own bodies, and they are really deprived, they're functions, functions of a machine.

Gibson: And they tend to feel themselves as failures, at least the characters in your books, well, particularly Joe. And David.

Atwood: In a way. They tend to blame that on other people.

Gibson: And they feel put down by women.

Atwood: Yes, sure. It's all true. That doesn't seem any great insight on my part. It just seems a state that is fairly widely acknowledged. And all the things that you've been talking about are really just the jam on the sandwich, because the interesting thing in that book is the ghost, and that's what I like. And the other stuff is there, it's quite true, but it is a condition; it isn't what the book is about.

Gibson: Your protagonist has returned looking for her father, and at one point she says that one of the things about her father was his quite remarkable ability to give the illusion of peace. She grew up during the war, not knowing about the war, and her mother and father had been able to give this illusion of peace. And her return, and the whole ghost thing, seems tied in to that. Peace and being in touch with the land.

Atwood: That's all true, but it's much easier for me to talk about the formal problems involved in writing a ghost story, which I've always been fascinated by. You want to talk about ghost stories?

Gibson: She sees her own ghost, doesn't she?

Atwood: There are various kinds of ghosts you can see. You could have just a simple straightforward ghost story in which somebody sees a ghost which has no relation to them whatsoever. You could have a sort of primitive myth in which dead people are as alive as living people and they're just accepted. Nobody is too surprised by it because it happens all the time. Or you can have the Henry James kind, in which the ghost that one sees is in fact a fragment of one's own self which has split off, and that to me is the most interesting kind and that is obviously the tradition I'm working in. But I wanted to write a ghost story for the same reason that I'd like to make a good horror film. It's an interesting area which is too often done just as pulp.

Gibson: I'd like to relate the ghost, the fragment of self that is split off, to the society that is overwhelming her and isolating her, the victim thing. Because in some sense the father, the ghosts that she perceived, were not victims.

Atwood: That's true. And they aren't evil ghosts.

Gibson: And having perceived them, she is somehow stronger.

Atwood: I haven't worked this out. Again, it's like the cake in *The Edible Woman*; I just can't be that analytical about my own work. I could give you all kinds of theories as to what I think they're doing in there, but my guess is really as good as anybody else's. I know by the logic of the book what they are doing, but I don't have a whole lot of theories about it. They exist. You can make of it what you will.

Gibson: She's accused at one point of disliking men, this is in *Surfacing*, and for an instant she wonders, but then she says: "Then I realized it wasn't men I hated, it was the Americans, the human beings, men and women both. They'd had their chance, but they turned against their gods."

Atwood: Everybody has gods or a god, and it's what you pay attention to or what you worship. And they can be imported ones or they can be intrinsic ones, indigenous ones, and what we have done in this country is to use imported gods like imported everything else. And if you import a god from somewhere else, it's fake; it's like importing your culture from somewhere else. The only good, authentic thing is something that comes out of the place where you are, or the reality of your life. // Christianity in this country is imported religion. The assumption of the book, if there is one, is that there are gods that do exist here, but nobody knows about them. Anyway this gets us into metaphysical realms. The other thing that the imported gods will always tell you to do is to destroy what is there, to destroy what is in the place and to make a replica of the god's place, so that what you do is you cut down all the trees and you build a Gothic church, or imitation thereof. The authentic religion has been destroyed; you have to discover it in some other way. How that fits in with the book I don't know, but I'm sure it has something to do with it.

Gibson: We were talking about the irrelevance of society to the people living in it. In some sense, we're pushing it, but in some sense they're godless...

Atwood: They have gods. A kind of futile adjustment is probably the god. It used to be success. It used to be the individualist thing where you stomped on everyone and made a million dollars, but that isn't even the god anymore. The god is probably fitting into the machine.

Gibson: Somebody else's machine.

Atwood: Yes, somebody else's machine. People see two alternatives. You can be part of the machine or you can be something that gets run over by it. And I think there has to be a third thing.

Magical Forms in Poetry
Christopher Levenson

Christopher Levenson's interview was conducted on April 4, 1972, at Carleton University in Ottawa, and originally appeared in *Manna* 2 (1972). Copyright © 1972 by Christopher Levenson. Reprinted by permission.

Levenson: You've been very prolific, five or six books in as many years. Looking back over this relatively short time do you notice any change in your poetry?

Atwood: First of all it's not so crowded as it appears. I started writing when I was sixteen, I'm now thirty-two, that's sixteen years. It's true that it looks as if all that writing was crowded in, but for instance I wrote *The Circle Game* in roughly 1963-4-5. That's three years for one book. It was published in 1966. The next one didn't appear till '68—again two years. Then there's a fairly rapid period. Has there been a change? Yes, enormous. If you go back to the first poetry I was writing, it read like Edgar Allan Poe because that's all I was reading at that time.

Levenson: You're not talking about *The Circle Game* then?

Atwood: No. I think everybody when they write, unless they are flaming geniuses, write through a lot of influences for a while, and their poetry changes very rapidly at that time.

Levenson: Who do you feel have been the people who have influenced you?

Atwood: Different people at different times. Edgar Allan Poe for one. I was very keen on Lord Byron around that time too. That was in high school. Then I started to read Canadian poetry, and I guess there's a difference between people who influence you and people you like. I was excited by people I was reading then. People like Jay Macpherson, James Reaney, P. K. Page, and A. M. Klein. Later on I read Al Purdy and

Doug Jones. I was conscious of Irving Layton, though I don't think he's been much of an influence.

Levenson: Are you aware of other influences, maybe non-Canadian?

Atwood: I read a lot of poetry written in French by people living in Quebec. For instance, Anne Hebert I was very fond of in 1960. In some terms that may be a non-Canadian source. And Marie-Claire Blais when her stuff first came out was very exciting. It's not that I wasn't reading, it's that there are springboards you take off from, and there's no way that I'm going to take off from something in New York. It isn't my place.

Levenson: You find that this sense of locality...

Atwood: Poetry is local. It may be appreciated internationally, but one sure doesn't write it internationally. No poet ever has. When people say "international" what they are talking about is *their* way, their nationality rendered international. That is very true of England, by the way. //

Levenson: You're going to wince at this, but what do you feel about the work of Sylvia Plath, Anne Sexton, and the Robert Lowell of *Life Studies*? Do you see any resemblance between your work and what is called confessional?

Atwood: No. I don't think Sylvia Plath is a confessional poet. A lot of her poems are, in fact, very formal.

Levenson: I would say that the so-called confessional poets are successful largely because they are formal.

Atwood: You mean they are bad when they are confessional and good when they have sublimated their confessionality to some kind of formal thing?

Levenson: I don't think it's a sublimation. It's getting something into order. Every adolescent poet who just writes for a couple of years is confessional.

Atwood: If you read a lot of adolescent poetry you know they aren't being confessional. In fact, they are being stereotypical. That is, they haven't reached through to the level of language at which they can really be confessional and individual. If you put a whole group of them together they're almost all the same. That is just a level of writing. It has nothing to do with being confessional or non-confessional.

Levenson: I ask because I am interested in the formal aspects, and in many of your poems you are primarily distancing or removing yourself from situations or making separations between things, between people.

Atwood: Well, I don't know about that. I don't think poetry expresses emotion. It evokes emotion from the reader, and that is a very different thing. As someone once said, "If you want to express emotion, scream." If you want to evoke emotion it's more complicated. Listening to someone scream doesn't necessarily make you want to scream. It makes you want to shut the window or say, "Stop it!"

Levenson: In *The Edible Woman* there is a keen sense of tactics and strategies in personal relations. One of the ways in which you are able to make very direct statements, which I find particularly attractive about your poetry, is by setting up a context in which you can say something very straightforward and direct. Is this due to a concern with strategies?

Atwood: That's really a complicated question. One would think that a great concern with tactics and strategies would render one Machiavellian and incapable of making any direct statement whatsoever for purposes of manipulation, which is certainly not my ideal of the good life. One's concern with tactics and strategies comes from the society we live in, which is largely one of tactics and strategies, but when you're writing a novel about that society or when you're acting as a lens focusing on that society, that element has to come into it. That doesn't make it desirable; as a matter of fact most of one's negative structures are there for the same reasons Hell is in *Paradise Lost*: they are examples of what you don't want—of the bad thing. Unless you know what the bad thing is you sure aren't going to be able to escape or avoid it. You have to identify what is bad, acknowledge that it is bad and that it is indispensable.

Levenson: So the poems are acting in a way like a magic charm?

Atwood: There's always that element in it. There are always concealed magical forms in poetry. By "magic" I mean a verbal attempt to accomplish something desirable. You can take every poem and trace it back to a source in either prayer, curse, charm, or incantation—an attempt to make something happen. Do you know anything about autistic children? One of their symptoms is mistaking the word for the thing. If they see the word "clock" on the paper they pick it up to see if it ticks.

If you write "door" they try to open it. That sort of thing is inherent in language in some funny way and poetry is connected with that at some level.

Levenson: You mentioned the word "incantation." I noticed recently that someone reviewing an anthology which contains some of your poems criticized your use of line breaks. Your poetry reads very well aloud and it has a strong sense of rhythm or verse movement, though one that I find rather difficult to locate. Do you write fairly consciously to be read aloud?

Atwood: I *am* conscious of rhythm. Any poet is. No, I don't write consciously with the idea of being read aloud, but I always read poetry orally. // I could never do that. I read with my vocal cords. I hear it as a voice, but that's not the same as saying I mean it to be read aloud. I would like the reader to be hearing it as a voice also.

Levenson: I notice your own reading is as neutral as possible.

Atwood: That gets into the difference between actors and poets. The actor feels he has to dramatize the thing, and I feel this is wrong. The way to read poetry is to transmit it to the reader and let him do his own connections with it rather than taking the reader for some sort of fool for whom you have to *emphasize* each *word*.

Levenson: Which volume do you feel the most satisfied with? Though I suppose the answer is "the next one."

Atwood: Right. I don't know anything about the next one. I'm still writing poetry but I have no compulsion to do a book. The trouble is around this time publishers ask hopefully, "What's next?" As far as books go I'm into prose. I have a novel coming out in the fall and I want to start another this summer. I continue to write poems, but it seems to be right now something I'm doing for myself. I'm not even sending them out much.

Levenson: You spoke just now almost as if you conceived the earlier poems, apart from *Susanna Moodie*, which obviously hangs together, in terms of being complete books rather than accumulations of poems.

Atwood: I didn't conceive *Susanna Moodie* ... well even then, I've never conceived a book as a book. With *Susanna Moodie* I wrote twelve poems, then stopped. It was a little suite. Then I started writing more of them.

It wasn't until I'd written about fifty or fifty-five that I decided I'd make them into a book. So again it was separate poems. Then you get to a point where you feel you've finished with the thing. Then you say, "There's a book there."

Levenson: You don't follow Yeats's practice of keeping some poems over because they may fit better into the mood of a subsequent work?

Atwood: Not consciously. I throw a lot out.

Levenson: You say you are moving into prose? Is that partly because you feel there are some kinds of moods or attitudes you've been unable to capture adequately in poetry?

Atwood: It's two entirely different things for me. You can do all kinds of things in prose you can never do in poetry and vice versa. You deal with characters rather than with words and rhythms. You're also dealing with words and rhythms, but in another way. I always wrote both, you see, but seldom in my early life was the prose published. As a matter of fact I have a lovely early novel dating back to 1963, which no one ever published. I wrote *The Edible Woman* in 1965 so it's an old piece for me. The publisher lost the manuscript for two years, which is why it only appeared in 1969.

Levenson: You were teaching a course at York University on Canadian women writers. Do you see any significance in the fact that so many of the more interesting Canadian poets of the last two or three decades have been women?

Atwood: First of all when people say "so many" they sure don't mean half, do they?

Levenson: But it's a much higher proportion than is the case in America or England.

Atwood: Your whole question assumes that if it's more than about two it's a remarkable freakish situation. // If the social situation were normalized fifty-four percent of the more interesting poets ought to be women because fifty-four percent of the population are women. Fifty-four percent of everything ought to be women. Someone proposed that in an oppressed cultural minority, such as the blacks in the States, usually the women emerge as strong people and upholders of the family. Could it be that Canada is an oppressed cultural minority? This would explain the unnatural upsurge of good female writers.

Levenson: Your poetry seems to evoke or create nightmare or dream situations. Does this actually come from dreams and nightmares?

Atwood: Some of it, yes. As a matter of fact almost every time when it's a dream I will identify it as such in the piece of writing.

Levenson: This suggests that you regard poetry really as a form of exploration—what I oppose to self-expression.

Atwood: Partly it certainly is that.

Levenson: Do you find your poems come from images and lines rather than from ideas?

Atwood: Yes, I start with images. People are often outraged by this because they want you to have an idea or a feeling that you are trying to express.

Levenson: I'm always quoting Mallarmé: poetry is made with words.

Atwood: It is made with words, and you can take that a lot further. It is impossible to have a meaningless word. All words are evocative and also have an intellectual side to them. They are combinations of these things.

Levenson: One of the techniques I've noticed in your poetry is the use of parentheses. Why do you do that?

Atwood: I did that much more at one point than I do now.

Levenson: Certainly in the first volume.

Atwood: Yes, I'd just discovered the parentheses.

Levenson: It wasn't consciously being used as some sort of distancing device?

Atwood: It's a sort of hesitation device, like an "um" or a "maybe" or a "perhaps." Sometimes it's a device to set one thought off from another.

It means a thought is intruding and breaking up the main line of the thing. And sometimes you can have two things going on at once. One in parentheses and one not in parentheses. I'm quite capable of following two thoughts at once. I do it all the time.

Levenson: One notices a large influence of Canadian landscapes and locale in your poetry. Is there any other sense in which you feel particularly Canadian, or is this not a possible question?

Atwood: Oh sure, it's a very possible question, but it would take me nine hours to answer it. I'm about to write a book on the subject. I'll send you a copy.

Preserving Mythologies
Margaret Kaminski

Margaret Kaminski's interview was conducted in 1975, and originally appeared in *Waves* 4 (1975). Copyright © 1975 by *Waves*. Reprinted by permission.

Kaminski: Do you consider *The Edible Woman* a feminist novel?

Atwood: I wrote it in 1965, but it didn't appear till 1969 in Canada and 1970 in the States. In 1965, if you'll recall, there wasn't a feminist movement. There had been, but there wasn't at that time, and it didn't really get going, I think, till '68 or '69 in the States and in Canada later than that. So, at the time I wrote it, I did not consider it a feminist novel because that terminology was not in use.

Kaminski: Well, aside from the terminology, there are things in it that remind me of feminist themes, such as women not being able to get good jobs although they have college educations, and "the men upstairs" having the good jobs.

Atwood: I don't consider it feminism; I just consider it social realism. That part of it is simply social reporting. It was written in 1965 and that's what things were like in 1965.

Kaminski: Still are in some cases. The occupation of the book's main character, Marian, was a market researcher and this, as well as the title of the book, suggests to me consumerism, and that women, and Marian herself in the novel, are viewed as commodities. Is this the intent of the novel? And would you say that it is truer today or when you originally wrote the novel?

Atwood: Yes. It's a metaphor in the novel. I have to keep saying I'm a fiction writer, you know, I'm not a propagandist. The central image in *The Edible Woman* is the cake in the shape of a woman. In fact, they become interchangeable, because Marian does come to view herself as a kind of cake. This image radiates out into the rest of the novel, and to my way of thinking you can't use these metaphors and make them work unless there's some truth in them. It has to do with the nature of the society that you're working within. I live in the society; I also put the society inside my books so that you get a box within a box effect. Marian's difficulty is that she comes to identify with the objects the society is consuming, especially food. And because she's making that identification and seeing herself as the consumed rather than the consumer, she stops eating.

Kaminski: I think it might be, too, the locale of the book. I gather it took place in Toronto. But, anyway, it is a Canadian city. What would be the glaring differences, say, if it took place in New York or Detroit?

Atwood: For that particular novel, I don't think there would be that many glaring differences. It's a novel about a city, a small-to-medium city. It could possibly have taken place in Detroit, probably not New York, which is a world unto itself. As we all know, people in New York think that if they walk to the edge of New York, they're going to fall off, because there's nothing else. But it wasn't consciously a novel about Toronto; it just happens to be set there . . . it could have been set in any Northeast, commercial, technological city.

Kaminski: The marketing research and the commercials and ads which are invading the character's milieu remind me of Detroiter E. M. Broner's new novel, *Her Mothers.* Broner calls the instructions inside the boxes of women's hair dye and the printed matter explaining other women's products "documents." Do the ads in *The Edible Woman* fulfill a similar function?

Atwood: I think they're images rather than documents—I don't know what the difference is. I always read the backs of packages myself, and I'm fascinated with the instructions on the insides of boxes. But the ads in the novel are obviously chosen for the fact that the words that they contain resonate with other words in the book. As I recall, one of the ads is for the Red Cross, and it's a nurse holding a bottle of blood, saying, "Give the gift of life." And other ads are used for similar purposes. But I don't have very many theories about why I do what I do in books; I just do it.

Kaminski: In some cases, I think, the ads that you wrote for the beer commercial . . .

Atwood: I have a really terrible story to tell about that. I thought that I was making up that product, which is called Moose beer, and I made up this ad, and when I went to New Brunswick, everybody was just overjoyed to see me. There is a beer there called Moose Head beer, and it has a moose on the label, and they got one of these labels and presented it to me. So truth and fiction are not always that different.

Kaminski: I saw it as an amazingly funny parody; I was laughing out loud throughout the book. I was telling you about this and you told me some women told you that they were crying or almost crying. How do you feel about that?

Atwood: They must have had some kind of awful event in their lives which was similar to the awful events that the central character has. In fact, this is true; some people think that I'm the central character and that all these things happened to me, so they say, "Oh, I had an experience just like yours. I went off eating and I was throwing up on the bus and I went down to ninety-two pounds and they had to put me in the hospital." And then I have to tell them the sort of crushing news that, in fact, this never has happened to me, and I'm not a vegetarian. Then they feel betrayed. But you end up saying, "This is a book of fiction and it says 'A Novel' on it."

Kaminski: In the novel, Marian literally interiorizes her problems by being unable to eat or to "swallow" them, and you wrote, "The subconscious has its own logic." Is this, to use the school term, the theme of the novel?

Atwood: I don't know what the theme of the novel is!

Kaminski: O.K., so much for themes of novels.

Atwood: I'm sure there is one, but the difficulty with the book is that I did write it in 1965 and it's now 1975, and so I'm much more obsessed with the novel that I'm writing at the moment than I am with that one. I'm not obsessed with that one at all.

Kaminski: Why don't you tell us about what you're writing now?

Atwood: I can't, because I can't talk about things before they're published. But I did write a second novel which is called *Surfacing*.

Kaminski: Well, then we'll go to poetry. You are also the author of many books of poetry, and I can see some of the poetic images filtering into your fiction. Do you consider yourself a poet first?

Atwood: No, I wasn't a novelist first either. When I was five, I did write a book of poetry. First I did the cover and the title; then I assembled the pages and inserted them in the book, and then I wrote the poems. So you could say that I'm a bookmaker first. And that's a reasonable thing to call a writer, somebody who makes books.

Kaminski: Your latest book of poetry, *You Are Happy*, received a good review in *The New York Times*, I heard. I've often wondered, do poets feel encouraged by good reviews or discouraged by bad ones?

Atwood: I used to feel encouraged by good reviews and discouraged by bad ones, but I'm old now, you know. I'm thirty-six, and by the time you get to this age, which really feels like about ninety-two, you don't have the energy to be too upset or even too overjoyed by anything that appears in a newspaper because so much print and ink has gone under the bridge that you realize that not everything you read in a newspaper is true, and that basically it doesn't matter. So, you know, I'm happy when I get a good review; I'm sometimes somewhat pissed off when I get a bad one. I've got an absolutely stunning one here with me today which is the worst review you've ever read in your life, but I carry it around with me to read a certain poem out of the book, and then I read the portion of the review that refers to the poem.

Kaminski: The review has no similarity to or connection with the poem, is that what you mean?

Atwood: This is correct. In fact, it misinterprets the poem to such an extent that anybody can see that there is a large discrepancy, and that the person writing the review can't read!

Kaminski: I read in a book by a television personality that it was mainly the misinterpretation and wrong information that irritated him, not well-founded criticism.

Atwood: No, well-founded criticism is always welcome because that's somebody who's intelligently looked at what you've done and is making thought-out, considered comments based on some kind of overview, whatever it may be. They may disagree with you, they may think you're a bad writer, but at least they have given some thought to the matter and actually read what is on the page. Whereas people who look at something and just leap to their own conclusions, which have nothing to do with the words—it's just pathetic.

Kaminski: One of your poetry books, *Power Politics*, is being taught in a women-oriented literature course. You write: "Your heartful of medals / made of wood..." and "you long to be bandaged / before you have been cut." Are you suggesting that the masculine image is counterfeit?

Atwood: Certainly it's a counterfeit. But then you have to say, "Counterfeit of what?" Maybe "counterfeit" isn't the word you're looking for. I would say "fraud," or "mask," or "a costume." Probably "costume," because there is something about a costume and it does mean something. It just isn't the same as what is underneath it. It's an ornament or a decoration or a disguise.

Kaminski: I was expecting *Power Politics*, from its title, to be more radically political, yet most of its poems deal with relationships. Does this mean that you see man-woman relationships as more political than other aspects of the Women's Liberation Movement, such as, say, women in unions or something else?

Atwood: Women dealing with unions is an objectified, external encounter. The place where all the little Nazis come out of the woodwork is more likely to be personal relationships. If you have a labor union situation, there's the union, there's management, and there are rules for playing that bargaining game. Society regards it as legitimate. It can be very acrimonious, but it's easier to handle in the same way that fighting in a war is easier for men to handle than family disputes between fathers and sons, because all that range of emotions is not involved. There's you, and there's the enemy, and you do what your commanding officer tells you and you go bang bang, and all those things, but it's not your childhood fears.

Kaminski: You mentioned before costumes, and this is a political image, I think, the war costumes. What is the relationship between this and androgyny? Are you interested in androgyny?

Atwood: You mean people changing their sex back and forth?

Kaminski: Yes, or just the masculine in women and the feminine in men?

Atwood: Yes, it certainly exists. I think I'm more interested in mirror-images. A friend of mine who studies Gothics and romantic novels and image patterns dating back to the Renaissance has a theory that deals with counterparts and complements. Your counterpart is someone who is the mirror reflection of yourself, and your complement is someone who supplies those elements that are lacking in you. What you're talking about is more a counterpart. I'm interested in complements, image structures in which other people are perceived not as necessarily you, you inside, or hidden you, but as something quite other.

Kaminski: Does this mean that you think men and women can live together?

Atwood: Well, they *do* live together. I don't know whether it means that they *can* or not. But my own personal life is fairly simple right now. My novels tend to be, therefore, somewhat complicated. There are areas, there are certain battle lines that have been staked out now that were always there but not acknowledged. The Women's Movement hasn't invented new things or new areas of conflict; those areas of conflict were always there. It has made it possible for people to acknowledge that they *are* there, and this makes it therefore easier for them to be resolved. If you know what the thing is and you don't feel that you have to repress it and say, "No, dear, it doesn't really bother me that you do this and you do that," then it's—O.K., some kind of a deal can be made. It's only when you feel that everything you're experiencing cannot be talked about, that things get explosive.

Kaminski: As a last question, would you like to say anything about *You Are Happy*?

Atwood: What can I say? You know, it's a book of poems. It's got one secret. I heard from some women who did a theological conference out on the West Coast using *Surfacing*, which is my second novel: one woman did a paper on it extracting from it a female religious viewpoint. So I referred her also to the third section of *You Are Happy*, which is a piece of mythology. I'm very interested in mythologies of various kinds, because I think most people have unconscious mythologies. Again, I think it's a question of making them conscious, getting them out in the place where they can be viewed. And I don't believe that people should divest themselves of all their mythologies because I think, in a way, everybody needs one. It's just a question of getting one that is livable and not destructive to you. A lot of the interest in that book, for me, is mythological, as it is in *Power Politics*.

Thinking About the Technique of Skiing
When You're Halfway Down the Hill
Mary Ellis Gibson

Gibson: At your reading here the other night you commented that given the present situation of Canadian writing you would not have found it necessary to write *Survival*, your book of criticism on Canadian literature. How have the conditions in Canada changed since 1972?

Atwood: I don't know whether there was any cause and effect, but after *Survival* came out, several other people wrote books of criticism. Before *Survival* there was no readily accessible book of criticism on Canadian literature for the general reader. You might say that I was writing it for the person that I was in 1960, when I was trying to find out about this literature and was having little success because it wasn't taught in high school, it wasn't taught in university. In order to find out about it you really had to do a lot of detective work. It wasn't visible at all. Reviews of Canadian books did not appear with any great regularity in Canadian newspapers. Nobody was paying any attention to them. That began to change around 1965 or 1966 for some reason. It might have started a bit earlier with a couple of poets, namely Irving Layton and Leonard Cohen. But there was an invisible literature, a literature that the people of the country had no access to.

Gibson: That must have been stifling to the literature as well?

Atwood: It certainly was for many years. There was more activity in the '20s, but then the Depression came along and wiped out a lot of indigenous publishing houses. And then the war came along and by the time you got to the '50s you had very few Canadian publishers, a large number of imported books coming in from England and the States, most people reading those books because those were the ones that got reviewed, and the indigenous publishers very unwilling to take risks on things like new novels. This all changed with the growth of new publishers in the '60s. You might say the book *Survival* came out of that whole movement. But it doesn't, you know, have any footnotes. It's not an academic book. It is a book meant for the reader who says, "Where do I begin?" It gives you a way into the literature from which you can go on and explore further.

Gibson: Is Canadian literature now being taught in the schools of Canada?

Atwood: Much more than it was. To take you back in history, this same battle was fought in the United States in the 1920s, that battle to establish departments of American literature. It went on in Quebec a little bit earlier than in English Canada, the push to get Quebec literature taught in universities. It's really typical of colonies, and even though it had its revolution America was a cultural colony for some time. Literatures of colonies are disregarded both by the people outside and inside the colony because part of the colonial state of mind is to think that the mother country or the dominant culture has the real goodies and that anything that you yourself might produce is either an inferior imitation or out of the question. //

Gibson: You made an interesting remark at the reading about Canadian audiences versus American audiences. In your readings in the United States what sort of differences do you find?

Atwood: Well, the people who turn out to a reading in the States are more likely to be people who have a specific interest in literature. That is, they will be students. They will be working on literary magazines. They will be reviewers; they will be in the field. They're much less likely to be members of the general public, your local shoestore operator or whatever. America is more divided into little segments. Here there are people who read books and people who watch television, and the two don't have too much to do with each other, though I'm sure that the people who read books also watch television. There seems to be a kind of literary subculture here which is a thing unto itself. People who read *The New York Review of Books* and, what's the other one, *The New York Times Book Review*, and who are really up on all of it. I think in Canada that your local shoestore operator is more likely to read books, shall we put it that way? And also it's a small country. The population is a tenth that of the United States. I can walk into the supermarket or into a store and buy something, and if they see my name on a check it is possible that they will recognize it, even though there are not a lot of extensively watched talk shows on the arts. The population at large seems a bit more plugged into books. Let me give you an idea. I would say that the sales figures of a book of my poetry in Canada and the United States are likely to be equal. That is, I will sell as many books in Canada, possibly more, as I will sell in the States even though the population is a tenth the size. The ratio of readers to non-readers seems to be larger, especially readers of poetry.

The other difference is that in the States there are so many writers and so many poets that it is impossible for anybody to keep up with them. Until very recently there were so few in Canada that you really could keep up with all of them without that much difficulty. Back in 1960 every book that was published in Canada was reviewed every year in one issue of the *University of Toronto Quarterly*. That includes little chapbooks and very small publications. So at that time there was not much publishing going on. There's an awful lot more now. It's almost getting to the point where you can't keep up with it. In fact, it's probably gone a bit beyond that, but still there are not the multitudes of writers in Canada that there are here. //

Gibson: Getting finally to your own writing, I was reading your novel *Surfacing* at the same time I was reading *Survival* and it seemed the two came together. You have the same sense of the American, of something coming up over the border, which isn't necessarily a good something.

Atwood: That's not a flight of fancy on my part. It's a very widespread feeling in the country itself. Gallup Poll asked the question, would you like to see Canadian businesses nationalized even if it would mean a drop in your standard of living, and I think something like fifty-seven percent of the people said yes. This is not something I cooked up all on my own. In my novel, of course, it's used in a very symbolic way, and it has other implications, and in the literary criticism it's impossible to talk about Canadian literature without also talking about the fact that Canada's an economic and cultural colony. This is simply a fact of life, but for many years it was disguised. Nobody ever talked about it, and now people are talking about it.

Gibson: The word "survival" was echoing through what I've been reading of yours, in the sense of survival first in the Canadian environment and the really exciting role nature plays in your poetry and in the distinctions you make about the way Canadians look at animals, natural objects, or natural powers in general. I was particularly taken with the poems you read from *You Are Happy*, the transformation poems which seem to be a culmination of various animals in your earlier poems. Is this something you developed consciously as material or looked back and found?

Atwood: Well, the transformation poems in *You Are Happy* are really not sort of true-blue-Canadian in the tradition because a true-blue in-the-tradition animal poem would have to be much more from the point of view of a non-humanized animal, whereas the poems in *You Are Happy* deal with animals which once were human beings. They're much more mythological, if you like. Let's see now, how did that whole concept come into being? A friend who had to judge a literary contest some time ago said that the typical kind of story that she was looking at would be a story about somebody involved in the death of an animal and experiencing nausea and feeling terrible about it. I can think of a couple of stories that get into anthologies that are exactly this. And then I remember Leslie Fiedler making a remark in *Love and Death in the American Novel* that in American literature killing an animal is an initiation into adult life. You somehow come of age by indulging in this ritual of killing the bear. And it seemed to me that there was a different, an almost opposite way of approaching the death of the animal. In American literature you killed the animal and achieved something by doing it; in the Canadian one, you killed the animal and it was a negative achievement. You didn't get good things from doing it. You got the horrible realization that you had killed your brother, your relative.

Gibson: I got a sense of this relationship to animal nature and to nature in general in your poem "The Trappers."

Atwood: Oh yes, that much predates any of this critical work. That goes way back to 1967. But if there is an operative tradition, then presumably that tradition will inform work, even though the tradition has not been articulated.

Gibson: At the end of "The Trappers" you write, "I understand / the guilt they feel because they are not animals / the guilt they feel because they are." The trappers feeling this sort of doubleness, of unity and disunity with the natural world, seems to come back again at the end of *The Journals of Susanna Moodie*.

Atwood: Yes, it's certainly in some of those poems, but you can find it very strongly in the short stories of Ernest Thompson Seton and Sir

Charles G. D. Roberts written in the nineteenth and early twentieth century. This is the kind of thing that one would be given as a child to read, these stories about animals, *Kings in Exile, Wild Animals I Have Known*. You've probably never heard of any of them, but a lot of Canadians were brought up on this. Certainly the stories are told very much from the point of view of the animal. People when they appear in these stories at all are usually seen as bad, or they are seen trying to kill or capture some animal and coming to a point where they can't do it.

Gibson: The interesting thing to me about *The Journals of Susanna Moodie*, too, is an effort there to take a simultaneous look at Canadian history through her eyes and at the problems of the settlers and her understanding of what it was to be almost an exile.

Atwood: Oh, she was very definitely an exile. Of course, there was a real woman of this name and she did write books which are interesting in themselves. I don't know; it's kind of hard for me to talk about all this because I wrote it such a long time ago.

Gibson: Perhaps we can move on to what you're working on now. Particularly, I'm interested in finding out when you are planning to complete the novel you're at work on.

Atwood: The novel is almost finished. It just has a few little details to be altered, and it's coming out in the fall with Simon & Schuster, and the title is *Lady Oracle*.

Gibson: Perhaps you could comment on the differences or the similarities to *Surfacing* and *The Edible Woman*. Do you see it taking a new direction?

Atwood: Yes, it's very different from *Surfacing*. It's probably quite a lot different from *The Edible Woman* too. It's bigger—there are more people in it and it covers a much longer span of the central character's life. It's very hard to describe, of course. I would say that it has some funny parts, although it's not funny all the way through. //

Gibson: On the biographical side, I gathered from your comments and some of your poems that you live on a farm in Alliston, Ontario?

Atwood: I now live on a farm near Alliston, yes. It's about twelve or fifteen miles away from it, but my post office box is in Alliston. That means I only have to collect my mail once a week. My working set-up there is very convenient. I have a room with two doors that close and I can't hear the telephone with both of the doors closed. My cats and dogs can't get in and that's good. Also it means that anyone who wants to phone me has to phone long distance which means I get fewer trivial phone calls than I did when I was living in the city. You concentrate things like shopping into certain periods, you have to plan for them. So you take, in fact, less time doing it. It's better for writing.

Gibson: Speaking of the contrast with urban living, I was curious, at the end of the *The Journals of Susanna Moodie*, about her return to the city years later as the "woman in the bus across from you," because the whole business, the men with bulldozers who feel they can plow her under, seems to me in some ways analogous to the American threat at the end of *Surfacing* and also to the general threat of urbanization. Is that as deeply felt in Canada as it is by many people here?

Atwood: We're less far along the road, of course. In fact, we've got to the point now when we can look down and say, "Well, let's not do that. Look how badly it's worked out..."

Gibson: Down there?

Atwood: Right, in fact we were going headlong in that direction, but some American urban planners moved up and said, "No, don't do it. Don't build an expressway in the middle of the city," and so people have organized into citizens' groups and stopped, for example, what they call the Spadina Expressway, which was supposed to come into the middle of Toronto discharging all these thousands of cars into little narrow streets that weren't big enough for them. Canada is a conservative country; it's more interested in conserving what is there. It's not that some people in the States aren't interested, a lot of them are. But they don't seem to have enough access to power.

Gibson: Do Canadian writers feel this whole issue strongly? I think of Gary Snyder and other poets of the West Coast particularly who are very much involved in the whole idea of preservation.

Atwood: Yes, about the most popular writer in Canada is Farley Mowat. He doesn't write fiction and he doesn't write poetry. He writes nonfiction prose books about the Arctic and things like that. And he certainly is very much of this mind. There's a lot of naturalist writing in Canada that's very much like this. It's not that things exist in Canada that don't exist in the States—it's a matter of proportion.

Gibson: Are you planning after *Lady Oracle* to take a rest or a writing rest?

Atwood: I guess I'm not taking a rest. I just took one. I was in Mexico for six weeks, and that was pretty much of a rest. But the thing about writing, of course, is that it's enjoyable, and taking a rest from it is often not too restful. It's more restful to do writing than it is to do a whole lot of other things I can think of, as long as you're not at a really frustrating point in the writing. It is exhausting in its own way, but it's not exhausting in bad ways. //

Gibson: I've probably skipped many things you would really prefer talking about, so if there's anything particular I've left out?

Atwood: It's been really more a conversation on Canada, but I feel in a way that's easier to talk about than writing...writing is very difficult to talk about. In fact, it's almost impossible to talk about because the decisions that are made about writing are made on the page; they're made when you're actually working with something. About the only real way you can talk about writing is to take an individual poem and all your back drafts of it and say, "Well, this is what I changed." Nothing else really makes a whole lot of sense. //

Gibson: But writing about your own writing?

Atwood: I'll let other people do it. I'm always interested to see what they have to say, mind you, and sometimes it's revealing—that is, they come up with things I hadn't thought of. So that's fun. But if you start doing that too much with your own work, it's like thinking about the technique of skiing when you're halfway down a hill.

Gibson: And then you fall?

Atwood: That's right, that's exactly right. I think the French are about the only people who do the theory first, and then write the works that will prove it's *true*.

A Question of Metamorphosis
Linda Sandler

Linda Sandler's interview was conducted at Margaret Atwood's farm outside Alliston, Ontario, during March and April 1976 and originally appeared in the special issue of *Malahat Review* 41 (1977), devoted to Margaret Atwood. Copyright © 1977 by *Malahat Review*. Reprinted by permission.

Sandler: Why do people believe you have to compromise your integrity to be successful? George Jonas believes that a writer who finds common ground with a large audience deserves all the glory she gets. But others are less generous.

Atwood: In the States, of course, you're *supposed* to be successful. Failure is in bad taste. In Canada, success is somehow considered vulgar ... although Canadians go both ways. Say you write a good novel and it's not well received: there is a small cult who will say, "She's a real writer, the others are selling out." But others are contemptuous. They will say, "She's a failure, her book isn't selling."

I suppose I'm a successful writer. I don't know why, I don't know what the "common ground" is. But I do know that there are all kinds of people who read books, who aren't members of cliques, who don't care what Joe down the street says in his review. Someone in Lethbridge will write to me and say, "I read your book, it meant a lot to me, I wanted to tell you."

Sandler: How do you respond to the media images of yourself? In the *Survival* era you were portrayed as an inspired national prophet; more recently, the press favors the Circe image.

Atwood: You should know that a political image is invented by other people for their own convenience. They need a figurehead or they need a straw person to shoot down. It's that simple. I don't know about the Circe image. Alan Pearson believes I'm a Medusa, but that has more to do with the kind of hair I have than my writing.

What success means is that you become a cult figure for a whole lot of strangers. And since they don't know you personally, they're dealing with two-dimensional images, courtesy of the media. Eventually you become a target and you are attacked. This is the pattern.

But bad reviews in Toronto don't kill a book. Far from it. No matter how much people bitch about Toronto, the fact is the literary world in Canada is far less centralized than in the States. There are umpteen papers around the country and they all have a local audience. In the States, the success of a book depends on the author's status in New York. And that is such a small world, a small number of influential people writing for a couple of "organs" which have undisputed authority.

Sandler: You've had a powerful impact on the cultural scene. I remember Frank Davey saying that writers with a different aesthetic are in danger of being driven underground.

Atwood: I am always amazed to find what powers and motives these people ascribe to me. Davey's remark reminds me of that caricature of me in *The Canadian Forum*: Here is this enormously powerful and malevolent female, and she is gonna getcha! It's an infantile projection.

What people fail to understand about poetry and novels and criticism is that they are hypothetical, and they are *patterns* of words and ideas. You can write just as convincing an opposite number, as Davey has tried to do. The fact that I prefer one pattern to another probably means that I'm better at that kind. If I wanted to propagate my vision of Canada, I'd be a philosopher. And if I wanted to impose it on everyone, I'd be a politician or a minister.

Sandler: Has it made any difference to you, getting the kind of recognition you have?

Atwood: Some people love this kind of attention, they revel in it. I don't. And I don't particularly like being a public figure. It's not something I set out to do; it's something I found happening to me. I was quite unprepared, and rather horrified by some of the results. I couldn't understand why people I had never met would go in for malicious personal attacks. Now I'm prepared for just about anything. What else can one do but laugh at it? //

Sandler: What about the scale of your audience? I think your writing has become more dramatic, less introverted than it was.

Atwood: Whether something is dramatic or not is a question of style, rather than anything else. *Susanna Moodie* is quite contemplative. *Power*

Politics is epigrammatic, so it sounds more "intimate," and I think that people found it shocking for this reason. But I haven't really altered my approach to writing; I've always written all kinds of things. When I was in high school and college I was writing borderline literary material that people don't usually associate with me—musical comedies, commercial jingles, various things under pseudonyms. I even wrote an opera about synthetic fabrics for my Home Economics class. It was about that time I realized I didn't want to be a home economist; I wanted to be a writer. That was a great change, because I was supposed to be practical and sensible; that was my "image."

Sandler: *The Servant Girl* was one of the best TV plays the CBC has done. Are there more to come, aside from your screenplays?

Atwood: I do that kind of thing to support my other writing; it's what I do instead of teaching. If I do a television play I like to do it well, but the possibilities are limited. What you're really constructing is the skeleton of a play which the actors and directors will either foul up or flesh out. I can't take all the credit for *The Servant Girl*, because television is a group activity and the writer has least control over the final product.

Sandler: How do you see the relation of your art to popular art? Serious writers in Canada don't usually relate to it at all.

Atwood: "Popular" art is a collection of rigid patterns; "sophisticated" art varies the patterns. But popular art is material for serious art in the way that dreams are. In *Power Politics* I was using myths such as Bluebeard, Dracula, and horror comic material, to project certain images of men and women, and to examine them.

You could say that popular art is the dream of society; it does not examine itself. Fairy tales do not examine themselves. They just *are*, they *exist*. They are stories that people want to hear. Some of them sell hope; others sell disaster, which seems to be equally appealing. You can ask all sorts of questions about *why* people wish to hear these particular stories, but popular art itself does not ask these questions. It merely repeats the stories.

Sandler: You seem to pick up the right signals, because *The Edible Woman* pre-dates feminism, *Surfacing* is about the wilderness, *Lady Oracle* is about a cult figure, and these are all stories people want to hear.

Atwood: I don't have any special clairvoyant gifts. As "prophecies," reading my books is rather like going to the fortune teller. She peers into her crystal and she says, "Babble, babble, babble." You forget most of it, but then you meet a dark stranger and you say, "Gee, what clairvoyance!"

Plugging into the popular sensibility, though, is not peculiar to me. A lot of women are writing sophisticated soap operas, for instance. I'm not putting them down, I'm saying that their material, although they deal with it in complex ways, is soap opera material. I use it myself. Iris Murdoch, after all, writes psychological Gothics—so did Henry James— and *Surfacing* has elements of the mystery story and the ghost story.

I once had a letter from a woman in the States, complaining that her book club was advertising *Surfacing* as a novel of suspense, and not only were there all these dirty words in it, but she couldn't tell who did the murder. Her response wasn't entirely dumb—at least she saw that it was a mystery story.

Sandler: What about the controversial ending of *Surfacing*? The bloodhounds say that according to the logic of the story the heroine should have killed herself.

Atwood: They could be trying to say that I should kill *myself*. Dead authors are easier to deal with than living ones. But *Surfacing* is a ghost story which follows a certain formula. The heroine should no more have killed herself than the protagonist in Henry James's story "The Jolly Corner" should have. She is obsessed with finding the ghosts, but once she's found them she is released from that obsession. The point is, my character can see the ghosts but they can't see her. This means that she can't enter the world of the dead, and she realizes, O.K., I've learned something. Now I have to make my own life.

I was going through my papers recently and I came across an old paper on ghost stories that I'd written in university. I'd forgotten all about it, but it contains the "recipe" for the ghost story in *Surfacing*.

Sandler: What about the theory that you gave the novel a positive ending for ideological reasons?

Atwood: From the people who think I wrote *Surfacing* to illustrate *Survival*? They should get their dates straight. It's nice that she doesn't want to be a victim, but if you examine her situation and her society in the cold light of reason, how is she going to avoid it? I'd say the ending is ambiguous. People say to me, "What is she going to do? Will she marry Joe?" I don't know what she's going to do. I fill in what I know, and after that anybody's guess is as good as mine.

Ideas in fiction are closer to algebra than you might think. What the heroine does at the end of *Surfacing* results from taking a hypothesis and pushing it as far as it goes: what happens when you identify with the animals? And she concludes that she can't stay on the island, because that will mean death...which isn't necessarily so. There are ways of dealing with the wilderness.

Sandler: In his essay on you in *Open Letter*, Frank Davey suggests that you endorse the ideas and perceptions of your heroine. Is he wrong?

Atwood: You would think a literary critic would distinguish between an author and a character, especially when he doesn't know the author. You have to regard everything my heroine says as the utterance of a fictional character. The reader who endorses the character suddenly finds out that she's been telling horrible lies. The reader ought to be more cautious.

We like to trust the person telling the story, especially when the novel is written in the first person. There's one of Agatha Christie's, *The Murder of Roger Ackroyd*, where you go along with the narrator only to find out that he is the murderer. You've been lied to, all the way through.

Sandler: Were you trying to create a positive heroine, the way George Eliot did in *Middlemarch*?

Atwood: Is Dorothea so positive? Look where she ends up. What you have in *Middlemarch* is an idealistic young woman living in a society which will not permit her to be so. Saint Theresa achieved sainthood, but what happens to somebody in the nineteenth century who has similar impulses? So Dorothea ends up marrying this rather simpy young man.

The question is, why did George Eliot not write about a successful female writer? Why did she kill off Maggie Tulliver and marry off Dorothea? Perhaps Eliot was attempting to portray the fate of the *average* woman in her society—the average intelligent woman with no options. You could ask the same question of me. Why am I not writing about a successful female writer? Which is what I am. Why is the woman in *Surfacing* not a writer? Why isn't she a poet? Instead she's a rather mediocre illustrator of children's books. What point is that making about my society?

Sandler: You could say that the woman in *Surfacing* performs a typical act of Canadian heroism. She works out her connection with the wilderness and with her past, and she *survives*.

Atwood: We would have to say what we mean by a hero, but most of the characters in twentieth-century fiction are not heroes in the traditional sense, and I would not use the term in connection with the woman in *Surfacing*. She was not a savior, actually or potentially.

Who are the Canadian heroes? We have figures like Norman Bethune and Louis Riel, who have an organic connection with some society and are killed in the process of trying to save it. You could ask, In what sense is Bethune a Canadian hero? Well, he was a Canadian hero who found it impossible to be heroic in Canada, so he died for somebody else's society. And Riel? Are the Métis any better off because of his actions? This is always the question: has the hero lived and died in vain? //

Sandler: Don't victims have the same function as romantic heroes—to make negative statements about society? Isn't that why you call *The Edible Woman* an anti-comedy?

Atwood: That's stretching the point, but the book does make a negative statement about society. In traditional comedy, boy meets girl, there are complications, the complications are resolved and the couple is united. In my book the couple is not united and the wrong couple gets married. The complications are resolved, but not in a way that reaffirms the social order. The tone of *The Edible Woman* is lighthearted, but in the end it's more pessimistic than *Surfacing*. The difference between them is that *The Edible Woman* is a circle and *Surfacing* is a spiral . . . the heroine of *Surfacing* does not end where she began.

Sandler: How did *Lady Oracle* start? She's the least doomed of all your heroines.

Atwood: I probably started with the Gothic romances, but that was a long time ago and my books tend to evolve into something quite unrelated to the original idea. *Lady Oracle* was more tragic to begin with—it was going to start with a fake suicide and end with a real one. As you know, it turned out differently . . . it's a question of metamorphosis. I started with one voice and one character, and she changed during the writing, she became a different person. There's no accounting for how that happens.

Sandler: You have some futuristic poems like that, "Eventual Proteus" and "At first I was given centuries," where the speaker goes through a series of evolutionary changes.

Atwood: It's been a constant interest of mine: change from one state into another, change from one thing into another.

Sandler: How come?

Atwood: Who knows? But my father is an entomologist and he used to bring home these "things" in one form; they would go through some mysterious process and emerge as something else. So metamorphosis was familiar to me from an early age. Later on I studied chemistry and botany and zoology, and if I hadn't been a writer I'd have gone on with that. The U.S. publisher of *The Animals in That Country* found it very significant that I'd grown up in a family of biologists. You might link it up with that, I don't know how credible that would be. Ovid's father wasn't an entomologist.

You could also link it with my childhood reading; most fairy tales and religious stories involve miraculous changes of shape. Grimm's tales, Greek and Celtic legends have them. North American Indian legends have people who are animals in one incarnation, or who can take on the shape of a bird at will. I would say that *Grimm's Fairy Tales* was the most influential book I ever read.

Sandler: Reversals and metamorphoses seem to be the key principles of your work, and they come together in "Speeches for Dr. Frankenstein." That's a mirror poem, isn't it?

Atwood: Yes. The monster is the narrator's other self, and the process of writing that poem involved separating the two selves.

Have you read Mary Shelley's *Frankenstein*? It's a creation parable, where God forsakes Adam: instead of taking care of the monster, Dr. Frankenstein deserts him because he can't face the grotesque creature that he's produced. But the monster's not *evil*—as the movie would have it—that's just Hollywood hokum. He's totally innocent, and he can't understand why people find him so horrible.

There's a marvelous "chase scene" in the original version, when Dr. Frankenstein decides to hunt him down. The monster leads him on a merry chase, and when they get to this Arctic setting Dr. Frankenstein collapses and dies. There's a peculiar finale where the monster comes back for his body and carries him off across the ice floes.

My setting comes from the original novel, but in my poem it's the monster who deserts his maker—not the other way around. Although I tend to be more interested in plots than in allegorical meanings.

Sandler: The plot of *Lady Oracle* is your most intricate, what with various time zones and the interlocking of real action with Gothic plot.

Atwood: *Lady Oracle* is the most rewritten of my books and it took about two years to write. *Surfacing* and *The Edible Woman* each took six months, approximately, although I'd been thinking about them for a long time before I started writing. With *Lady Oracle* the conception and the writing were much closer together.

Sandler: The heroine says that writing Gothics is like moving through a maze, and *Lady Oracle*'s plot is something like that.

Atwood: Mazes are interesting. Apparently they were originally built for two reasons, religious initiation or defense. Edinburgh Castle is constructed that way and it was never taken—except once, by treachery.

In Gothic tales the maze is just a scare device. You have an old mansion with winding passages and a monster at the center. But the maze I use is a descent into the underworld. There's a passage in Virgil's *Aeneid* which I found very useful, where Aeneas goes to the underworld to learn about his future. He's guided by the Sibyl and he learns what he has to from his dead father, and then he returns home. It's a very ambiguous passage and scholars have spent a lot of energy analyzing it.

Sandler: Are people going to assume that *Lady Oracle* is just another version of your life?

Atwood: Undoubtedly. People are always asking me if I'm vegetarian and when my parents died. And they are astonished when I tell them that I am carnivorous and my parents are very much alive.

With *Lady Oracle* I was determined to make the character physically unidentifiable with myself, so I made her very fat and I gave her red hair—I had a friend with marvelous red hair that I always envied, so I took her hair and stuck it onto this character. What happens when I read these chapters to an audience? Someone immediately sticks up a hand and says, "How did you manage to lose all that weight?"

This probably wouldn't happen in England, where readers are more sophisticated. But even in Canada, where fiction is a fairly recent phenomenon, writers of escape literature are exempt—nobody would suggest that because Agatha Christie wrote eighty thousand murder mysteries she must have murdered at least *one* person, to find out how. But if you write a "serious" book, everybody wants it to be autobiographical. You can protest till you're blue in the face, it doesn't make any difference...as my fat lady story illustrates.

Shakespeare is in an enviable position. Nobody knows a thing about him, and they can speculate all they like, but what they have to deal with is his poems and his plays. And that's what counts. You don't need biographical information unless the work is unintelligible without it. It's most unfortunate that Dorothy Wordsworth kept a diary. I don't care whether William Wordsworth *ever* saw a field of golden daffodils and I certainly don't care to know that he saw them on the seventeenth of March, or whenever it was.

Sandler: That's fair enough. But you must be interested in the way a poem or a novel is written, because there's a running parody of the creative process in *Lady Oracle*. Her writing is more or less automatic, dreams and nightmares.

Atwood: Parody, well ... I'm reading the galleys now, and you don't really know what you've done until a couple of years later. But there's certainly some parody going on.

The trouble with dreams is that they're fragments and they're incoherent, most of them. And the unfortunate thing about the creative process is that you can have a wonderfully inspiring experience and still turn out a *rotten* poem. You soon find that out if you have anything to do with creative writing classes.

In my experience, writing is not like having dreams. It's not that unconscious. It's much more deliberate. You can add or subtract anything, and you can shape your material into a coherent pattern. When I write a poem or a novel I'm not interested in transcribing my dreams or "expressing myself." If I want to express myself I can go out in the back field and scream. It takes a lot less time.

Sandler: Susanna Moodie appeared to you in a dream, didn't she?

Atwood: Yes. I hadn't read her books, but I remembered quite vividly a winter scene with a house burning down; eventually I tracked it down in a Grade Five reader, I think it was. But I also remembered a scene with a child shrouded in a primitive oxygen tent. I thought it was Moodie, but in fact it had nothing to do with her.

I read her two books, *Roughing It in the Bush* and *Life in the Clearings*, after dreaming I had written an opera about her. They were very disappointing, but *she* interested me. I wrote poems about her, and I thought that was that. But six months later the other poems started happening. These things are always unpredictable.

After the radio broadcast of *Susanna Moodie* the CBC came to me and said, Could you do one about Sir John A. Macdonald now? They thought it would be nice for me to write a poem cycle about a really famous

Canadian, and I had to explain that I didn't work that way; I didn't pick a likely candidate and then make up suitable poems.

Sandler: The business of dreams is interesting, because the dreamer is an *involuntary* poet who lies there and watches the show. But there's also the idea of the poet as an inspired dreamer.

Atwood: It's worth looking at poets in different ages to see where they think the inspiration is coming from. There's Milton saying, Descend, O Dove! and right up to the eighteenth century, poets were looking "up there" for inspiration. Then it got reversed. With Blake it's definitely coming from below, and this sterile, controlling figure sits upstairs. Shelley has lots of caves, he's invoking dark powers. Keats has an early poem where the narrator goes under the sea and there he finds Proteus, the shape-changer.

One of the few poems I've written about the creative process is "Procedures for Underground," and I do see it as a descent to the underworld. But—I repeat—having that inspired feeling doesn't guarantee that you'll write a good poem.

Sandler: What's your opinion of the West Coast people's view of your poetry? George Bowering, reviewing *Power Politics*, said you'd arranged your material like a bowl of fruit, and there were things he wanted to know that you didn't tell him.

Atwood: You could say that about your next door neighbor! There are things I want to know that George would *never* tell me!

Is "spontaneous" versus "arranged" a real issue? Everybody thinks of Jay Macpherson's poems as "finely crafted," but she hardly ever revises them; and in fact, it's much easier to write *spontaneously* if you're firmly grounded in metrics and rhyme.

My poems in *Double Persephone* are metrically formal, but there's no way of knowing whether I "crafted" them. If you look at my worksheets you'll see that some poems write themselves and some, like Circe's poem about the suicides, are quite hard to write. And I suspect it's like that for every poet. The finished version of "Tricks with Mirrors" is basically what I scribbled on this sheet of paper. The same with "Threes." I wrote it down and that was it. It's the poem that counts. I don't care how it was written, and I distrust people who give out prizes according to extra-poetic factors. If you wanted to join the club you'd have to include or exclude poems in your canon according to their "spontaneity." Or you could *arrange* them that way, because once the style is established it's easy to imitate. Lots of white spaces, shrugs and asides and awkward spots, no punctuation. What does that prove? Some of them are very good. Others are very bad.

Sandler: Do you remember the origin of the Circe sequence in *You Are Happy*?

Atwood: Nobody really knows where poems come from, and it's not something I want to know. I would probably be disappointed if I knew where I got my ideas. I do know that I could never write anything like *Geneve*, where George Bowering turned up a Tarot card every day and wrote a poem about it. I would find that too formal, too deliberate.

What happened with "Circe" was that fragments started appearing before I had any idea that I was writing a connected sequence. This is generally the case; you accumulate a couple of poems and that acts as a priming agent, and you write more. You could stretch a point and say that it's the same process as writing a novel or a short story; incidents accumulate, details and phrases accumulate.

Sandler: Is it possible to talk about the difference between conceiving a poem and conceiving a novel?

Atwood: You can talk about it, but not very successfully. A poem is something you hear, and the primary focus of interest is words. A novel is something you see, and the primary focus of interest is people. But that's a huge generalization, it probably means nothing.

It's hard to talk about this process, because you can't observe it. It's not *ultramysterious*. The brain just works in a certain way, and if you're a poet you turn out poems rather than recipes for apple pie. But if you started observing it while it was happening, you would kill it. And I'm not too interested in observing it after the fact. It's too much like picking pieces of apple out of your teeth. I will say this: you can't write poetry unless you're willing to immerse yourself in language—not just in words, but in words of a certain potency. It's like learning a foreign language.

There was a time when I couldn't understand any poetry beyond simple narrative verse. I remember reading modern poems and being completely baffled by them, not knowing what they meant or how they worked. You try and try and all of a sudden you know how they work. It's like learning to ride a bicycle. How can you explain it? What is a sense of balance?

Sandler: The foreign language analogy might explain why people reacted so oddly to your presentation of sexual politics in *Power Politics*.

Atwood: Well, it's a question of what people find acceptable. Poems by men about the wicked behavior of women are part of a venerable tradition going back at least as far as the Elizabethans' Cruel Mistress, and few people bother to analyze conventional modes. We don't bat an eyelid when we read about bitch goddesses or when we see portraits of women with big tits and no heads. But women aren't supposed to say nasty things about men. It's not nice, and it's not *conventional*.

Sandler: When *Power Politics* was published, people started thinking of you as an Ice Maiden. What do you think of Susan Sontag's idea that coolness and distance usually conceal a passionate intensity?

Atwood: It's partly a matter of style, because every culture sets its own distances. Think of your reactions when you meet people. If a stranger taps you on the ass and says, "How's the little lady today!" you will probably cringe. But if he's an American, he's only being friendly. If you're sitting next to him on a plane trip he will take out the family photos, and within five minutes he'll be telling you the story of his life. In Nova Scotia, you can have endless conversations with people about genealogy, which is not regarded as "personal," but they will not get around to asking you what you do for a living or whether you're married. Canadians are like the English, in this respect.

Sandler: If Canadians tend to be distant, *Power Politics* shouldn't have bothered them. But I don't know anyone who finds the hook-and-eye epigram amusing.

Atwood: There are people who won't laugh unless you flash an orange neon sign that says LAUGH NOW. You have to accept that. And the usual response to that epigram is horror—as I found out when I started reading those poems in public. The shock value is what gets across. Here again it's a question of what is and is not acceptable. Irving Layton could read his extremely nasty poems about women, and his audience would find them hilarious. My poems about men are not received that way, although *I've* never written a poem about a male academic who has pimples on his bum. I don't go in for explicit personal attacks like that. I don't know why. Maybe I have a lingering feeling that ladies should be polite.

Sandler: How much of the impact of *Power Politics* has to do with its cut-off lines and rhythms? I remember Robert Weaver saying that the poems are like sharp pieces of glass.

Atwood: I don't think there's anything formally distinguishing about my writing as a whole. Much of *Power Politics* is epigrammatic, and the line is just about as short as you can get without disappearing altogether. In *You Are Happy* the line gets longer again, and it will probably go on changing. What you're doing is finding out how to write the poem while you're actually writing it. Once you know how to do that poem or that kind of poem, that's the moment when you should stop and go on to something else. Otherwise you become an imitator of yourself.

Sandler: A permanent self-parody, like Mary Tyler Moore? Do people expect continuity?

Atwood: Not usually. I think, though, that critics are always reviewing the book before last. They've assimilated your previous books and they have an idea about the kind of poet you are, and if you do something different it takes them a while to see what is happening in the new book. A lot of people were so obsessed with *Power Politics* that when *You Are Happy* appeared they went on reviewing *Power Politics*.

Sandler: There's another reviewer's heresy surrounding your guide to Canadian literature: people have said that *Survival* is an extension of *Surfacing*—of your interest in victims and your view of nature.

Atwood: It's unfortunate that the two books were published around the same time, because people make that connection. But in fact, *Surfacing* was finished and at the publisher by the time I started working on *Survival*. Some time before that I had begun to notice certain common themes in my own writing and in other peoples, and I thought, Isn't it funny that such and such happens in all these books? Some people think that I deliberately *invented* these themes in order to write a book about them, but that's not the way it happened. The themes were there; I noticed them.

Survival was a hard book to write. It was too close to home. I'd much rather write about somebody else's culture. That's why I enjoy teaching Victorian literature. That's not my country, that's not my time. I'm not involved and I can have nice aesthetic reactions. The literature of one's own country is not escape literature. It tells truths, some of them hard. //

I tend to be shy of theories because I know their limits, but theories are useful for teaching. You can draw diagrams on the blackboard, and they will provide partial illumination; they are easy to react to, and to react against. And *Survival* is basically a diagram of Canadian literature.

Sandler: What's striking about *Survival* is the coherence of vision under-lying it. It's a writer's book and it has a point of view.

Atwood: I'm not an academic, so I don't have to worry about my col-leagues saying, "Tut tut, this will not do. Why don't you qualify all your statements and hedge all your bets?" I can write what I believe to be true, and I don't have to be plausible to professors; they're not hiring me. Eli Mandel, of course, feels that all works of criticism are novels, and in a way he's right. They *are* imaginative constructs.

Sandler: I guess it's also the only literary survey around that has political overtones.

Atwood: For me, it's axiomatic that art has its roots in social realities; when you see an Aztec statue you don't doubt that it had an essential social function. People believed in that god and made sacrifices to it. I don't know why literature should be any different.

Sandler: You mean that literature is an index of popular faith? I wonder.

Atwood: Not exactly...but it does influence belief. Take nineteenth-century America, which is handy for these purposes. You get Fenimore Cooper writing about huge primeval forests and noble redmen, giving them mythical and even moral dimensions. People accepted these myths; the myths multiplied and became "truths."
  Sinclair Ross didn't invent the Depression, but what could have been more useful to him than the Depression? And once it was over, you could read *As For Me and My House* to find out about it. The Depression became part of the social mythology.

Sandler: Is that the function of art? To be folk history?

Atwood: Must art have a specific "function"? Human societies have al-ways produced art. Almost as far back as we know, people have been painting pictures; we assume they have also been singing songs and telling stories. Therefore, art must be an essential human activity. People create art for ostensibly different reasons from age to age. You can say that originally the impulse was magical, or religious, as with the Aztec statue. But what does that mean? It could mean that art is a way of explaining or controlling the environment.

Sandler: Does that mean your art could be an agent of change—as you said in your notes on *Power Politics*?

Atwood: As I said before, I'm not a politician, and it's wrong to suppose that the artist is a vanguard revolutionary. A literary work may have some political content, but it's not a book of political theory. It isn't a book of metaphysics, it's not a book on economics. It can include these ideas because they exist in the real world, because they are filtered through people's minds; they come up in conversation and they influence people's behavior.

Sandler: It's kind of ironic that feminists saw you as a leading proponent of their cause.

Atwood: A few years ago Women's Lib was looking for any woman writer who seemed to be dealing with "feminist" issues. The writings of Margaret Laurence, Marian Engel, Alice Munro were all enlisted as supporting evidence. A lot of women, though, have been writing about "special" women's problems: she's trapped in the home, three small kids, where is her identity, etcetera. In those terms, *Surfacing* fails as a feminist novel because it doesn't say whether you can marry Joe and still have a career. My characters are not role models. I don't try to resolve the problems of living, deal out the answers, and I'm not dealing with my female characters as members of a separate species. However, I probably am a feminist, in the broad sense of the term.

Sandler: I wanted to ask you about the satiric side of your work.

Atwood: A lot of things that may seem to be satiric are quotations from real life. Americans say to me, "What about this horrible anti-Americanism that David expresses in *Surfacing*? Does that mean you hate Americans?" And I have to say, "Number One, I'm not David. Number Two, if you think I invented him, why don't you go spend a weekend in Canada?"

Sandler: But once David is in your book, you've put a frame around him; he can't have a neutral value. Likewise Arthur in *Lady Oracle*, plotting to blow up the Peace Bridge.

Atwood: The principle of selection is important, of course, and I try to select characters who are outgrowths of their society. But my writing is closer to caricature than to satire—distortion rather than scathing attack—and as I say, it's largely realism. The market research scenes in *The Edible Woman* are an example of realism verging on caricature, they are very slightly exaggerated. Arthur is probably some facet of myself, distorted and carried to an extreme.

Sandler: Wyndham Lewis insisted that satire *is* realism, a kind of mirror.

Atwood: Literature *can* be a mirror, and people *can* recognize themselves in it, and this may lead to change. But in order to write satire in the traditional sense, you must have certain axioms in common with your audience. When something happens in the book that outrages common sense, your audience must agree that it is in fact outrageous. That's the problem with the century we live in. There's almost nothing you can write about which has not been outdone in absurdity or ghastliness by real events. People see so many horrible and grotesque things that they become deadened. They *have* to deaden themselves; otherwise, they'd be in a constant state of psychic disturbance. In theory, satire is impossible, but in fact, satire is being·written. Canadian satire tends to be quite vicious, particularly in the earlier poetry. The *Harvard Lampoon*, you know, is run largely by Canadians, and its edge is much sharper than *Mad* magazine's. And Robertson Davies's early novels are all quite cutting.

Sandler: But as you said in your essay on Canadian humor, contempt for the uncultivated locals is the usual source of satire in novels.

Atwood: Possibly, but you have to try to visualize what it was like for Davies or Mordecai Richler, living in a society which was so hostile to art. People tend to forget what it was like. But using all one's imagination and charity, one has to say that Mordecai Richler *had* to leave the country when he did. There was no place for him here.

Sandler: Did you go to Harvard for similar reasons? One theory is that you went there because America was generally regarded as the country of light.

Atwood: Not at all. Not at all. I'm of a later generation, remember. // My cultural roots are in Nova Scotia, and if you want to see cultural nationalism, that's the place to go. It's not nationalism—it's regionalism. But I certainly didn't grow up regarding America as the land of light. Even Ontario was *deeply* suspect. I remember that in the '50s *everybody else* regarded America as the land of light, and *Saturday Night* was publishing articles extolling the glories of baseball and the American Dream.

I didn't have an image of Canada to counter that, but *that* was never my view.

Sandler: Tell me about your association with the House of Anansi. Did you see the press as Dennis Lee did, as the source of a literary renaissance?

Atwood: Anansi was certainly part of a literary renaissance, but I wasn't involved in it. I was in Montreal in 1967 when Dennis published *Kingdom of Absence* and then in Edmonton and then in Europe. I wasn't back in Toronto until 1971, and by that time the Anansi revolution had already happened. Dave Godfrey had left, Dennis was on the verge of leaving, and the press was embroiled in internal warfare. I was called in to infuse some new blood into its veins. I got a letter when I was in Italy, asking if I would sit on the Board of Directors, and I'd been making all these noises about an indigenous literature so I thought I should put my money where my mouth was. I didn't envisage becoming an editor for two years. I thought I was going to be an unpaid and marginal participant, mainly lending my name. I was wrong. It was a whirlpool. Lots of people got sucked *in* and *down*. But now it's on its feet again.

Sandler: You've been less active politically since the *Survival* days. Does activism get in the way of your writing?

Atwood: Activism isn't very good for the writer, and I'm not very good at it. I believe in saying what I think, and that's no way to be a politician. But I still think my analysis of the country was essentially correct. And despite the literary renaissance, and despite the level of national consciousness, things seem to be getting worse economically. It's a process of erosion.

Sandler: What are your politics?

Atwood: I don't have party loyalties as such. What's important to me is how human beings ought to live and behave. I doubt, for instance, that I would have gone along with Stalin, no matter how faithful he was to Karl Marx's theories. If people end up behaving in anti-human ways, their ideology will not redeem them.

All you can do is opt for the society that seems most humane. People don't seem to function well in very large groups, and that's why I prefer Canada to the States. It's more intimate, and people can still involve themselves in the political process. If you get enough people together, you *can* stop the Spadina Expressway from cutting through Toronto.

You *can* stop the politicians from building an airport in Pickering ... by the skin of your teeth.

In the States they have Citizens' Action groups too, but the machinery of government is out of control. It's too big, it doesn't respond. You can throw your body in front of it and it runs right over you. America is a tragic country because it has great democratic ideals and rigid social machinery. // But Canada is not tragic, in the classical sense, because it doesn't have a utopian vision. Our constitution promises "peace, order and good government"—and that's quite different from "life, liberty and the pursuit of happiness." It doesn't suggest that you will be *happy* if you have peace, order and good government—nor does it say that you will be *free*. It just says that the government will take care of everything. //

Playing Around
J. R. (Tim) Struthers

J. R. (Tim) Struthers's interview was conducted in October 1976, and originally appeared in *Essays on Canadian Writing* 6 (1977). Copyright © 1976 by J. R. (Tim) Struthers. Reprinted by permission.

Struthers: It seems to me that your *Selected Poems* is much more of a unit, much more of a whole than other volumes of that type.

Atwood: That's probably because I used to be an editor, and I selected them myself. I think if you had done a *Collected*, it would probably have looked less like that—probably a bit spottier. And if you had taken everything I've written as opposed to everything I've published, not only would you have a much bigger bulk, but it would also look quite a lot spottier. //

Struthers: It seems to me that your poetry has always been objective in the sense that it has opposed certain social myths and any simple romantic view of reality. In a different sense, though, it seems to me that *The Journals of Susanna Moodie*, the "Songs of the Transformed" from *You Are Happy*, and the large ironic gap between yourself and the narrator of *Lady Oracle* suggest that your writing is becoming increasingly dramatic. I'm thinking here about the notion that your *Selected Poems* represents the reaching of a plateau. I also have in mind Stephen Dedalus's comment about writers, in Joyce's *A Portrait of the Artist as a Young Man*, that they begin with the lyrical, move into the epical, and then reach into the dramatic.

Atwood: Mm. I don't think I've gone through the epical yet.

Struthers: What about *Susanna Moodie*?

Atwood: Still lyrical. It's not subjective lyrical. I would drag in Yeats at this point and say anti-mask, etc. etc. But it's still a lyric form. It's short, discrete units which are put together to form a whole, like Shakespeare's sonnets, or whatever, but the things themselves are still lyrics.

Struthers: Would you ever write a dramatic historical novel like Rudy Wiebe's *The Temptations of Big Bear*?

Atwood: I don't know that. It probably wouldn't be very historical, simply because I'm too lazy. You have to do a lot of research on that kind of novel. // It's very hard to predict your own future. But it's also very dangerous to start saying what you're going to do because what if you do something else?

Struthers: In your fiction you've shown an interest in different popular forms: the ghost story with *Surfacing*, and the anti-romance to a degree . . .

Atwood: Anti-Gothic.

Struthers: . . . anti-Gothic romance with *Lady Oracle*, which functions on all kinds of levels, as I see it.

Atwood: Yes. *The Edible Woman*, by the way, is an anti-comedy. It's not my own theory, but as we all know, all "literature" comes out of "popular literature" on whatever level.

Struthers: Do you think there are any indigenous Canadian forms?

Atwood: I'd have to think about that one.

Struthers: The journal, for example.

Atwood: Lots of cultures write journals. Canadians developed the journal to a certain eminence. Let us say there's a difference in ratio among Canadian forms. The journal is more important in Canada than it has been in other literatures. The documentary is more important in Canada. It's not that other people haven't done them. It's just that if you look at the whole literature, *that* is something that Canadians do a lot of. Canadians invented the animal story from the point of view of the animal. Nobody else was writing them before Thompson Seton and Roberts started doing them. After they started, other people picked it up and wrote them, however. But you can't say that just Canadians do certain things. You can say that Canadians have a tendency to do certain things. Canadians have a tendency to do a certain kind of satire which I don't find a lot of elsewhere. I'm thinking of the four radio shows that we have at present. They do a lot of political satire. I'm thinking of the *Spring Thaw* of the olden days where this kind of thing started. It's a revue format. Something like *Monty Python* does it, but it's a lot sillier than the Canadian ones. The Canadian ones are very pointed political and social satire. Do you listen to any of them? *The Royal Canadian Air Farce, Dr. Bondolo's Pandemonium, Eclectic Circus*, from Vancouver, *Inside from the Outside*. They're all CBC shows and they're very, very funny and very good. You find that kind of thing in the Canadian international... *National Lampoon* is run by Canadians.

Struthers: In terms of the popular forms—the ghost story, the Gothic romance—are there any other popular forms that excite you?

Atwood: We've gotten off Canadian now, I take it, and on to popular forms in general. I started out as a reader of fairy tales. //

Struthers: I greatly enjoyed your illustrations to *The Journals of Susanna Moodie*, and I regretted that they weren't included in the *Selected Poems*.

Atwood: Couldn't do it. Technical problems.

Struthers: It seemed to me that they were an integral part of the work. // They captured a lot of the spirit of the poems.

Atwood: My ambitions, in order, and I mean in order not now but as I was growing up, were: first, I wanted to be a writer, then I wanted to be a painter. I abandoned writing and took up painting for a while at the age of eight or nine. Then, becoming more practical, I wanted to become a dress designer, and, becoming more practical yet, I thought that I would probably go into Home Economics. And then when I found out how boring that was, I went back to writing. So I had a period there of being very visually oriented, and I still am.

Struthers: Let's talk a little bit about the Canadian tradition. Has your sense of the Canadian tradition in fiction changed over the very last few years?

Atwood: Yes. One change is that four or five years ago you wouldn't have been asking me that. Instead, you would have been asking me, "Is there a Canadian tradition?" or saying, "I don't think there is a Canadian tradition." But now your question simply assumes that there is one and we go on from that. And that's a big change. It means that people don't have to scramble around trying to make a Canadian tradition. There already is one and you can work out of it. You don't have to be so self-conscious all the time. You can take off in different directions. It allows you more freedom. Instead of being at that stage that we were at for so long of having to *name* everything and *justify* everything—and if you're writing about London, Ontario, you had to say, "In the beginning London, Ontario, was a city situated at... with X number of population" —and *describe* everything. You can just take it for granted that it's perfectly O.K. for you to be writing about London, Ontario, without having to make a big thing about it. //

Struthers: Does the Canadian tradition in fiction stand behind your fiction?

Atwood: Does it stand behind it? You mean, do I draw on it? Of course. Of course. I even play with it. Why in *Lady Oracle* is the con-create artist's form squashed animals? It's a direct reference to my own book of criticism, *Survival*, as well as the whole tradition of Canadian animal stories. In Italy the animals come in rococo poses. They're all a lot of stuffed animals, but they're all very Italian expressionist things. I saw a donkey there that was stuffed and mounted standing on its hind legs and braying. This is Italian. But for Canada they have to be squashed and frozen.

Struthers: But perhaps the poetry tradition influenced you earlier.

Atwood: Oh sure. A lot earlier.

Struthers: Pratt? Reaney?

Atwood: Reaney. Sometimes Pratt, although I've never tried what Pratt was doing. But there's a Canadian form for you. When Pratt was writing those long narrative poems, nobody else working in English literature was even attempting to do that. They all deemed it was passé, had gone out with Milton. They were all subscribing to Poe's theory that you had to have lyric poems or nothing. This was the only person, and then various other people went on to write them, such as Birney and so on. But this is not a form invented by Canadians but one that has been used by Canadians more than it has elsewhere. Anyway, that's a digression. What were you saying? Oh yes, was I influenced? Yes. I was lucky enough to be living in a house when I was twenty that had a library of current Canadian poets in it. I started off in 1957 with A. J. M. Smith's *The Book of Canadian Poetry*. That had a lot of early stuff which I, at that age, wasn't very interested in. But then it also had moderns, and moderns at that time were Reaney and P. K. Page and A. M. Klein, Pratt a bit before that, Frank Scott, Layton, Macpherson. Avison I was very smitten with at that time and still am.

Struthers: Northrop Frye was doing review articles on Canadian poetry in the *University of Toronto Quarterly* at that time. Did you study with him at one point or did you read him?

Atwood: I was in a class that he taught. That's not the same as saying you've studied with Frye. I was never a graduate student at U of T. I didn't know him personally or any of those things. People just hear "Victoria College" and they say, "Ah-hah, influence of Frye." But we were sitting in a class with fifty people in it. You're watching him do his thing up at the front. It wasn't this heavy-handed influence. He recommended at some point that I not run away to England and become a waitress. It's just *that* influence.

Struthers: Do you think that Canadian writers want to be part of a Canadian tradition and are therefore purposely working with their ancestors?

Atwood: A lot of them are, but not in that desperate way that people felt compelled to do for a while. // I grew up in the '50s, but I remember what it was like. A desert, really. All those jokes about Toronto were true then. I mean really true. There was nothing to do on Sunday. There was only one theater. That was the Crest Theatre. There wasn't anything. It wasn't there. It was somewhere else. That's why everybody moved. It wasn't snobbish on their part to say all those things at that time that they said. They were simply telling the truth. That essay by E. K. Brown on the difficulty of writing in Canada was true. Ask James Reaney. He remembers it all quite clearly. He'll tell you. It's not like that anymore. It's a place where you can actually live and write at the same time. You don't become a hermit or bitter, and it doesn't seem that you're completely cut off from your culture. It is possible to be published. You can sell books. None of these things used to be true. Everybody takes them all for granted now. If I had been ten years older, I would have had to emigrate if I wanted to be a writer. If you meet writers from the West Indies and talk to them, it's the same story there. If you're a writer, you have to leave because there's nobody publishing down there and you can't publish a book there. So you go to London, England; you write about the West Indies; and you become a well-known West Indian writer in London; and people in the very place that you're writing about don't know who you are.

Struthers: To return to *Lady Oracle*, what is your response to Brigid Brophy's so-called review?

Atwood: I hate to tell you, but I haven't read it. I was out of town. I simply had all these people come up to me and say, "Wasn't that a terrible review?" and "This person obviously didn't understand the book." All I can say is that once upon a time *The Globe and Mail* and I had a dispute. The dispute was as follows. A fellow there, an editorial writer, wrote an editorial attacking me for optioning film rights to *Surfacing* to Americans. He based it on some erroneous information from the National Film Board. He phoned me to check and I said, "No, this information is erroneous and I have the letters to prove it." He said that he had written "Hold" on the editorial, but they ran it anyway. *The Globe* was then forced to print an apology. They had to do it because otherwise it would have been fairly libelous. So they did, grudgingly. But this fellow apparently took exception to this and ever since then *The Globe* and I haven't been on very good terms. I think that by mistake they happened to review the book well the first time around.

Struthers: Dennis Duffy is a good critic, although I thought he was a little baffled by your book.

Atwood: He did better than a lot of other people, but not as well as some. In fact, there's one sentence in his review that I've been quite baffled by. What is Canadian about hair? "Margaret Atwood has dealt with all these Canadian themes such as animals and hair." What hair? What's from hair?

Struthers: Perhaps he meant fur.

Atwood: He might have. I must ask him sometime. So they did one good review of the book, much against their better judgment I'm sure, because of my two previous books *You Are Happy* went to Alan Pearson—you don't know who he is—well, he's the one who misunderstood one of the poems in it so much that I use it as a one-liner when I give poetry readings. I read the poem; then I read what he said about it, and everybody laughs. And then the *Selected Poems* they gave to John Colombo, who is a great fellow in his own way but not noted for accuracy. In fact, he made about ten mistakes. He should have known better. I've known him for fifteen years. My father isn't a doctor, and you can go on from there. Anyway, I guess that *The Globe* felt that they hadn't come out with the right result from Dennis Duffy, so they gave *Lady Oracle* to somebody who was well-known for writing bad reviews of everything but Ronald Firbank.

Struthers: I'd like to raise a couple of criticisms that have been made of your writing, though I think there are answers to them. First of all, what is your response to the view that many of your fictional characters are two-dimensional?

Atwood: It depends on which characters. If it's a book written from the point of view of a central character, which mine all have been, what you're getting is a view of what is going on within the mind of that character. That's one thing you can say. The other thing you can say is that it's not untoward in literature for some of the characters to be two-dimensional.

Struthers: Especially in romance or satire.

Atwood: Well, this is it. I think in an anti-Gothic what you're doing is examining the perils of Gothic thinking, as it were. And one of the perils of Gothic thinking is that Gothic thinking means that you have a scenario in your head which involves certain roles—the dark, experienced man, who is possibly evil and possibly good, the rescuer, the mad wife, and so on—and that as you go to real life, you tend to cast real people in these roles as Joan does. Then when you find out that the real people don't fit these two-dimensional roles, you can either discard the roles and try to deal with the real person or discard the real person.

Struthers: Your poem "Comic Books vs. History" suggests that there are dangers not just to the Gothic but to comic books, to the fabulous generally.

Atwood: Of course. But people think that way. That's just the thing. We all have our scenarios. That does go on inside.

Struthers: Fantasy is realistic.

Atwood: It's realistic to describe people as having fantasies because everybody does, and they all involve two-dimensional roles. It's only when you get so completely wrapped up in your fantasies that you cannot untangle your fantasy projections from the real person. But we all do this to a certain extent. You know yourself when you meet somebody for the first time that you often get quite a different idea about them than what they turn out to actually be. Or you take an immediate like or an immediate dislike to them on the basis of very little evidence because they're fitting in with your scenario. You know, you like people like *that*. You expect them to be a certain way. People's attitudes towards me changed remarkably in many cases once I became A MOTHER. You wouldn't believe it. It's not that I'm a different person. I'm exactly the same as I always was, pretty well, give or take a little evolutionary change along the way. But it's not as though becoming a mother suddenly renders you this warm, cozy, cookie-handing-out individual, if you weren't before. I always have handed out cookies, as a matter of fact.

Struthers: How do you reconcile the ultimate insistence upon actuality in a poem like "Comic Books vs. History" with the satisfactions that writing Gothic poems or writing anti-Gothics may give you?

Atwood: The thing about writers that people don't realize is that a lot of what they do is play. You know, playing around with. That doesn't mean that it isn't serious or that it doesn't have a serious meaning or a serious intention. In our society children are a little squashed at school; you know, play is bad and work is good, and therefore we develop this idea about literature that if it's good it's got to be absolutely dead serious. It's hard work, you know, *hard* for you, not fun, something that you *take* to improve yourself.

Struthers: I only realized the seriousness of the way you were using the popular forms, for example, the implications of that, and the seriousness of all this humor, after a while, after I started thinking about the book.

Atwood: Yes. The other thing about the heroine which is quite true about real people, if you've met any like this—often women (often men, too, as far as that goes) who feel awkward and not "the thing," which is most of us in this society who have been brought up with toothpaste ads, and nobody really feels up to being a toothpaste ad...anyway, some people's way out of it is to accentuate that, to play up their awkward side, to tell funny stories about themselves all the time, to make themselves in these stories appear even more awkward and out of place and doing the wrong thing and so on than they really are. It's playing clown, and it's a defense. You know, "Look out, you may think I'm awkward but let me tell you one. Listen to this."

Struthers: What works of fiction would you say are in the tradition that *Lady Oracle* belongs to?

Atwood: *Northanger Abbey*, for sure. Part of Max Beerbohm's *A Christmas Garland*—the Gothic parts of the book are parodies of Gothic style. Further back, the popular Gothic descended—it's a corrupt form descending—from *Wuthering Heights*, on the one hand, along with *Jane Eyre* and *Pride and Prejudice*, I would say, on the other hand. I pick *Pride and Prejudice* out of Jane Austen's other novels because it has Mr. Darcy in it who is the prototypical Gothic hero, except he doesn't have sinister qualities—but he has the sort of romantic, Byronesque thing about him, you know, aloof.

Struthers: I want to ask you about Joan at the end of *Lady Oracle*. Does she remain in her muddle? Or does she develop as much in understanding as, say, the protagonist in *Surfacing*?

Atwood: I think that people have overestimated the amount to which the protagonist in *Surfacing* really has developed in understanding.

Struthers: Well, it's an inch, a scrupulously earned inch.

Atwood: Yes. An inch, O.K., I would say Joan, three-quarters of an inch.

Struthers: What is the importance of Joan's return to Toronto?

Atwood: She is taking the parts of her life which she has kept very separate. They will finally be together and she will be able to say, "O.K., that's really who I am." // Before, she said: "I will hide who I am because nobody will like who I am. They will not accept me. They will think I'm ridiculous. If I can conceal myself, then I will be safe." So she's gotten as far as saying, "I am who I am—take it or leave it," and the reason that she feels better with the fellow she has hit over the head with the bottle than with anybody else is that at least she knows, at least the new relationship will be on some kind of honest basis, if there is one. I must also say that I felt at the time I was writing this book that a number of the things I was putting in it were really quite absurd. But then after it was published, all these people come up and sort of confirm your invention by saying "Such-and-such happened to me" and "How did you know exactly what it was like?" and "I know a fellow exactly like that." I made up that whole thing about the Royal Porcupine, you know, that whole scenario. I used a friend of mine's warehouse and a few other settings. Then a friend of a friend got very angry at my friend because she had a friend who actually lived in a freezer.

Struthers: There was that sculptor in Toronto a couple of years ago.

Atwood: Mark Prent, who did parts of bodies. Yes, I had him in mind, as a matter of fact. And there was another fellow who covers everything in fur. I can't call his name to mind, but this is a real person as well, a real artist who does it. So there's a lot in mind. But the whole thing was just the costumes and everything—that's all it had to do with it. So many people come up to me and they seem to think they know who it is. But this person doesn't exist. And they know who it is.

Struthers: I have a question about the problem of irony. Some critics have cited the lack of an authorial voice in your fiction as a flaw. How can you avoid confusion on the part of readers and possible misinterpretation without overtly tipping the balance, putting your hand in, which D. H. Lawrence called the real immorality in art?

Atwood: Well, I don't like to put my hand in, in that way, when I'm writing that kind of book. There are obviously various ways of approaching the novel, and in nineteenth-century writing the author can emerge from the wings every so often, make a speech at the footlights to the audience: "Oh Dear Reader, you see what a dreadful mistake Dorothea has made in marrying Mr. Casaubon." I love George Eliot, and *Middlemarch* is one of my favorite books, but that does go on so much in the book.

Struthers: How do you account for the fact that the majority of the best of contemporary Canadian literature is indeed being written by women?

Atwood: First of all, I would have to say that's a question like "Are you still beating your wife?" I don't think it has yet been proven that that is so.

Struthers: Well, when I reach for Canadian books, I reach for Alice Munro and Margaret Laurence and Margaret Atwood.

Atwood: And Robertson Davies and Mordecai Richler and James Reaney. I don't know. It used to be that people would say to me, "Why are there so many good Canadian women writers?" and I would say, "How many do you mean by so many?" Then they would say, "Uh, well..." and it would turn out that they didn't mean so many—they meant some. And it was really a question that was saying, "How come women can write?" If it was ninety percent, then I would say you had a phenomenal situation. If it was fifty percent, I would say that you had something that represented the way it should be. But I think if you count up, you'll find it's about a third in anthologies—short story anthologies, poetry anthologies. So I would say to you, "This isn't so many; it is some."

It's more, maybe, than you would find in similar anthologies in the States, and I think it is true that women cannot be ignored in Canadian literature. They're too central for that. There were women writers in the States who simply got left out. There were so many possible male ones that got put in. Emily Dickinson would always get in, but nobody else. Edith Wharton got completely overshadowed by James, etc. etc. I would say that from the beginning the pioneer women tended to do the writing. You could start it there. You could say, "O.K., well, what do we have?" We have Susanna Moodie and we have Anna Jameson, etc. etc. We also have some men as well. Journals of trappers, explorers, etc. Hudson's Bay Company. But women tended to do the writing because that was supposed to be their role—to write home, to do the letters home, do the journals, do the diaries. The diary is supposed to be a female form. I don't know why. Pepys wrote one. Maybe it's because Canada really got populated in the nineteenth century, I mean English Canada, and by that time women could write. Whereas if it had been populated in the seventeenth century, they would all have been illiterate. Once you teach them to write, you can't stop them. They just keep on writing and writing and writing. Then you have to put them on your course.

Struthers: A last question. Do you feel that you are being treated too seriously, like right now for example?

Atwood: By many people. By that I mean that, first of all, I'm only thirty-six; second, I'm not dead yet; third, whenever we're treating any-body at all, we have to remember that we should always invoke, we should always bow to, the ghosts of people like William Shakespeare and other people who wrote quite well. I lent Henry James's *The Portrait of a Lady* to a student who was working for me this summer and who had never read it before—she wasn't in literature. She started reading it. "You know, this is really quite good," she said. "I'm glad to hear you say that," I answered. Let me put it this way. I think a lot of the furor is extra-literary; that is, it doesn't have that much to do with my actual work. It has to do with the phenomenon of somebody my age, of my sex, and, as Marian Engel said, who looks like me, doing all these different kinds of books, and also making fairly strong statements, and what you have is a conflict of roles. If I were male and sixty-two, nobody would bat an eyelash about a lot of this, I'm sure.

My Mother Would Rather Skate
Than Scrub Floors
Joyce Carol Oates

Joyce Carol Oates's interview was conducted by mail and telephone in February 1978 and originally appeared in the *New York Times Book Review*, May 21, 1978. Copyright © 1978 by Joyce Carol Oates. Reprinted by permission.

Oates: Are you interested primarily in a poetry of "music" or a poetry of "statement"?

Atwood: I don't think of poetry as a "rational" activity but as an aural one. My poems usually begin with words or phrases which appeal more because of their sound than their meaning, and the movement and phrasing of a poem are very important to me. But like many modern poets I tend to conceal rhymes by placing them in the middle of lines, and to avoid immediate alliteration and assonance in favor of echoes placed later in the poems. For me, every poem has a texture of sound which is at least as important to me as the "argument." This is not to minimize "statement." But it does annoy me when students, prompted by the approach of their teacher, ask, "What is the poet trying to say?" It implies that the poet is some kind of verbal cripple who can't quite "say" what he "means" and has to resort to a lot of round-the-mulberry-bush, thereby putting the student to a great deal of trouble extracting his "meaning," like a prize out of a box of Cracker Jack.

Oates: After the spare, rather sardonic exploration of the relationship between the sexes in *Power Politics, You Are Happy*, your recent book of poems, seems to have marked a radical transformation of vision. Could you comment? And what are you working on at the present time?

Atwood: At the moment, and in my most recent poems, I seem to be less concerned about the relationships between men and women than I am about those among women (grandmother-mother-daughter, sisters) and those between cultures. I am in the process of editing a new volume of poems to be called *Two-Headed Poems and Others*, and I'm working on some stories which I hope to include in the American edition of *Dancing Girls*. I have two novels in my head, and I hope to start one this summer.

Oates: What is your background? Did your family encourage your writing?

Atwood: I was born in the Ottawa General Hospital right after the Gray Cup Football Game in 1939. Six months later I was backpacked into the Quebec bush. I grew up in and out of the bush, in and out of Ottawa, Sault Ste. Marie, and Toronto. I did not attend a full year of school until I was in grade eight. This was a definite advantage. My parents are both from Nova Scotia, and my "extended family" lives there. I have one brother who became a neurophysiologist and lives in Toronto and one sister who was born when I was eleven.

I began writing at the age of five, but there was a dark period between the ages of eight and sixteen when I didn't write. I started again at sixteen and have no idea why, but it was suddenly the only thing I wanted to do. My parents were great readers. They didn't encourage me to become a writer, exactly, but they gave me a more important kind of support; that is, they expected me to make use of my intelligence and abilities, and they did not pressure me into getting married. My mother is rather exceptional in this respect, from what I can tell from the experiences of other women my own age. Remember that all this was taking place in the '50s, when marriage was seen as the only desirable goal. My mother is a very lively person who would rather skate than scrub floors; she was a tomboy in youth and still is one. My father is a scientist who reads a great deal of history and has a mind like Leopold Bloom's. But as far as I know, the only poems he ever composes are long doggerel verses, filled with puns, which he writes when he has the flu.

Oates: Have fairy tales, Gothic romances, and other fantasies played a significant part in your reading background?

Atwood: The Gothic, the supernatural fantasy, and related forms have interested me for some time; in fact, my uncompleted Ph.D. thesis is called "The English Metaphysical Romance." This may or may not have something to do with the fact that in childhood—I think I was about six—we were given the complete *Grimm's Fairy Tales*, unexpurgated. My sister was terrified of it, but I loved it. These are, of course, not "children's stories"; they were originally told by adults to anyone who happened to be there, and there is quite a lot of material that we wouldn't consider suitable for children today. It was not the gore—being rolled downhill in barrels full of spikes and so forth—that caught my attention, but the transformations. "The Juniper Tree" was and remains my favorite, followed closely by a story called "Fitcher's Bird." The other interesting thing about these stories is that, unlike the heroines of the more conventional and re-done stories, such as "Cinderella" and "Little Red Riding Hood," the heroines of these stories show considerable wit and resourcefulness and usually win, not just by being pretty virtuous, but by using their brains. And there are wicked wizards as well as wicked witches. I would like to write about this sometime. I have an article on this exact subject in a book which was just published by Harvard University Press. The book is called *The Canadian Imagination*, and the article is called "Canadian Monsters: Some Aspects of the Supernatural in Canadian Fiction."

Oates: You work with a number of different "voices" in your poetry and prose. Have you ever felt that the discipline of prose evokes a somewhat different "personality" (or consciousness) than the discipline of poetry?

Atwood: Not just a "somewhat different" personality, an almost totally different one. Though readers and critics, of course, make connections because the same name appears on these different forms. I'd make a bet that I could invent a pseudonym for a reviewer and that no one would guess it was me.

If you think of writing as expressing "itself" rather than "the writer," this makes total sense. For me, reviewing and criticism are the most difficult forms, because of the duty they involve, a duty to the book being talked about as well as to the reader. Poetry is the most joyful form, and prose fiction—the personality I feel there is a curious, often bemused, sometimes disheartened observer of society. The "public speaking"— there again it depends on whether I'm reading poetry, reading prose, or merely speaking. Making speeches is not something I like to do. I suppose, like many fiction and poetry writers, I don't like being in the position of pontificating about the truth. When I taught in universities I was a great diagram-on-the-board person, partly because you could draw arrows to indicate more than one thing at a time.

Oates: I am often astonished, and at times rather dismayed, by the habit that presumably intelligent readers have of assuming that most writing, especially that in the first person, is autobiographical. And I know that you have been frequently misread as well. How do you account for the extraordinary naiveté of so many readers?

Atwood: As far as I know, this is a North American problem. It doesn't happen much in England, I think, because England with its long literary tradition, is quite used to having writers around. And it doesn't happen as much (in my experience) in the United States as it does in Canada. And it doesn't happen as much to men as it does to women, probably because women are viewed as more subjective and less capable of invention.

I think it's the result of several factors. First, it may be a tribute to the writing. The book convinces the reader, therefore it must be "true," and who is it more likely to be "true" about than the author? Readers sometimes feel cheated when I tell them that a book is not "autobiographical," that is, the events as described did not happen to me. (Of course, every book is "autobiographical" in that the images and characters have passed through the author's head and in that he or she has selected them.) These readers want it all to be true.

Also, we have a somewhat romantic notion on this side of the Atlantic about what an author is. We think of "writing" not as something you do but as something you are. The writer is seen as "expressing" herself; therefore, her books must be autobiographical. If the book were seen as something made, like a pot, we probably wouldn't have this difficulty. But the idea is remarkably tenacious. I was talking about this at a reading one time. I explained that my work was not autobiographical, that the central character was not "me," and so on. Then I read a chapter from *Lady Oracle*, the chapter in which the fat little girl attends dancing school. The first question after the reading was over was, "How did you manage to lose so much weight?"

After saying all that, though, I'll have to add that I find it necessary, in order to write about a place, to have actually been there. I can invent characters, but I am absolutely dependent on the details of the material world to make a space for my characters to move around in.

Oates: In recent years Americans have become aware, at times to their chagrin, that Canadian nationalists are extremely anti-American and very much resent American "influence" in Canada as well as American economic exploitation. Apart from your nonfiction writing, your novel *Surfacing* deals with this feeling most explicitly. When some particularly brutal hunters in the novel turn out to be, not Americans, as the heroine believes, but Canadian, the heroine nevertheless thinks: "It doesn't matter what country they're from, they're still Americans, they're what's in store for us." Could you comment on this statement?

Atwood: It's dangerous to lift a statement out of context and take it as "the view" of the character and especially of the author. Cultural attitudes in novels are not usually invented by the novelist; they are reflections of something the novelist sees in the society around her.

But if you're saying that Canadians have no reason to resent the foreign and trade policies of the United States, I'd have to disagree. No one likes being dominated to this extent, whether it's women, blacks, Quebecois, or Canadians. But each group—including Canadians—should have a good look at their past and present behavior to see to what extent they have contributed to their plight. In the case of Canada, I'd say the extent is considerable.

Oates: Finally, Yeats once said that the solitary imagination "makes and unmakes mankind, and even the world itself, for does not the 'eye alter all'?" What is your feeling about the function of poetry? Why, in effect, do you write?

Atwood: I'm not sure what the function of poetry is. That is, I know what it does for me, but I don't know what it does for other people. Probably many things, since each reader is different. We talk a great deal about the subjectivity of the reader. I sometimes say that poetry acts like a lens, or like a thread dipped in a supersaturated solution, causing a crystalization, but I'm not sure that's it either. Perhaps because of my earlier scientific background, I like things that can't ever be quite pinned down. But I know we're in trouble when we start talking about what poetry "ought" to do, about the supposedly good social effects of it.

I don't feel that all art is a consequence of neurosis. I tend to see it as the opposite. Not that some artists aren't neurotic—but that art, the making or creating, is done in spite of the neurosis, is a triumph over it. Anne Sexton, for instance, was obviously "neurotic," whatever that is—unhappy and self-limiting, let's say. But even when she's writing about that the impulse to write at all seems to me a positive one. A defiance, if you like. If all art were pearls secreted by the miseries of the oysters, the totally healthy human being would be the one without a creative or joyful bone in her body. Can this be true? (Sorry to use words like "creative," but they're hard to avoid.)

Why do I write? I guess I've never felt the necessity of thinking up a really convincing answer to that one, although I get asked it a lot. I suppose I think it's a redundant question, like "Why does the sun shine?" As you say, it's a human activity. I think the real question is, "Why doesn't everyone?" But when you ask a roomful of people whether there's anyone who, at some time or other, hasn't written something, very few hands go up.

Dancing on the Edge of the Precipice
Joyce Carol Oates

Joyce Carol Oates's interview was conducted by mail and
telephone in February 1978 and originally appeared in *The
Ontario Review* 9 (Fall-Winter 1978-9). Copyright © 1978 by
The Ontario Review. Reprinted by permission.

Oates: Your books of poetry—*The Circle Game* (which was awarded the
Governor-General's Award in 1966), *The Animals in That Country, The
Journals of Susanna Moodie, Procedures for Underground, Power Politics,* and
You Are Happy—differ a great deal in content, yet there is a remarkable
similarity of tone, of rhythm, of "texture." Your earlier poems, for instance "Journey to the Interior" and "The Circle Game" itself, show a
mastery of craftsmanship that is rather unusual in first books. From
whom did you learn, consciously or unconsciously?

Atwood: When I first started writing I was sixteen and in high school,
in Toronto, in the '50s, and I knew nothing about either modern poetry
or Canadian poetry. So my first influences were Poe and Shelley! When
I got to university, I began discovering modern and Canadian poetry,
chiefly the latter. I read my way through the library of a faculty member
who, being a poet herself, had an extensive collection. I might mention
such names as P. K. Page, Margaret Avison, whose *Winter Sun* I reviewed
when I was in university, James Reaney, D. G. Jones, and certain poems
of Douglas Le Pan. These poets were important to me not only as poets
but as examples of the fact that you *could* get a book published. You
would have to have known the situation in Canada at the time to realize
how important this was to me.

It's kind of you to say that you found my first book accomplished,
but by the time it came out, I'd been writing for ten years. Also, *The
Circle Game* isn't my real "first book"; there was another one, seven poems
long, which appeared in 1961, for which I set the type and designed
and printed the cover. I doubt that you would find it quite so unusual!

Oates: Do you enjoy reading your poetry, in general?

Atwood: A good poetry reading is a delightful and exhilarating experience. A bad one is awful. It depends on the audience, on your mood at the time, on whether you and the audience "like" each other. I guess we've all run into the resident madman and the faculty member who thinks he can put a notch in his gun by being gratuitously rude to you at the little luncheon or whatever thrown in your honor. Mostly I just get colds.

Oates: Your sense of the absurd—and of the essential playfulness of the absurd—is one of the elements in your writing that I particularly admire. What inspired your novel *The Edible Woman*—especially that surreal scene—and *Lady Oracle*?

Atwood: *The Edible Woman* was written in 1965, before the Women's Liberation Movement had begun. It was still very much the model pattern, in Canada anyway, to take a crummy job and then marry to get away from it. I was writing about an object of consumption (namely, my bright but otherwise ordinary girl) in a consumer society. Appropriately, she works for a market research company. Even in 1969, when the book was finally published, some critics saw the view as essentially "young" or "neurotic." I would mature, they felt, and things (i.e. marriage and kids) would fall into place.

About the cake in the shape of a woman—all I can tell you is that I used to be a very good cake decorator and was often asked to reproduce various objects in pastry and icing. Also, in my walks past pastry stores, I always wondered why people made replicas of things—brides and grooms, for instance, or Mickey Mice—and then ate them. It seems a mysterious thing to do. But for my heroine to make a false image of herself and then consume it was entirely appropriate, given the story—don't you think?

Lady Oracle was written much later—almost ten years later. Again, I'm not sure where it began, but the central character is a writer of Gothic romances partly because I've always wondered what it was about these books that appealed—do so many women think of themselves as menaced on all sides, and of their husbands as potential murderers? And what about that "Mad Wife" left over from *Jane Eyre*? Are these our secret plots?

The hypothesis of the book, insofar as there is one, is: what happens to someone who lives in the "real" world but does it as though this "other" world is the real one? This may be the plight of many more of us than we care to admit.

Oates: Your novel *Surfacing* has been related to James Dickey's *Deliverance*. I see only a superficial, rather misleading relationship. Could you comment?

Atwood: There is a relationship of sorts, but for me it's one of opposites. For the central figure in Dickey's book, as I recall, nature is something wild, untamed, feminine, dangerous and mysterious, that he must struggle with, confront, conquer, overcome. Doing this involves killing. For me, the works cognate with Dickey's are Mailer's *Why We Are in Vietnam*, Faulkner's *Bear*, Hemingway's "Short Happy Life of Francis Macomber," and, if you like, *Moby Dick*, though Ahab was not seen by Melville as having chosen the right path. The books cognate with mine are Canadian and probably unknown in the United States; Howard O'Hagan's *Tay John* is one of them.

Oates: "The Man From Mars," which appeared in *Ontario Review*, is a delightful story, and drew a great deal of favorable comments from our readers. Were your hapless heroine and indefatigable suitor based on "real" people? And is there any political significance to the title?

Atwood: I've found over the years that I can never explain or account for any reader response to my work. It constantly amazes me—and this isn't false modesty—that my work sells as well as it does. I consider it rather quirky and eccentric.

Real people? In a way. The situation was real, the characters are fictional.

The title... I'm not sure whether the significance is "political" or not; what it means to me is that we all have a way of dehumanizing anything which is strange or exotic to us. In our arrogance, we take ourselves to be the norm, and measure everyone else against it. The man, of course, is not from Mars; he is from Earth, like everyone else. But there's no way of accounting for the atrocities that people perform on other people except by the "Martian" factor, the failure to see one's victims as fully human.

Oates: I believe you're one of the few Canadian writers who is not associated with any university, and I assume this is deliberate.

Atwood: Yes, I enjoyed students when I taught in 1967-68, but I could not handle faculty meetings and departmental politics. I don't understand it. I'm not good in those situations. The reason I don't teach is the same reason I don't wait on tables, which I also used to do: right now I don't have to. If I have to do either again, I will. If it's a choice, I'd take teaching, which is less physically exhausting and doesn't put you off your food so much.

Oates: You have drawn upon your student days at Harvard quite infrequently in your writing. Did you enjoy your stay there?

Atwood: Well... Harvard is sort of like anchovies. An acquired taste. But in my case, one that I could never truly acquire, because at that time—early and mid-'60s—they wouldn't let women into Lamont Library, and that was where they kept all the modern poetry and records. So I always felt a little like a wart or wen on the great male academic skin. I felt as if I was there on sufferance. Harvard, you know, didn't hire women to teach in it, so the male professors were all very nice. We ladies were no threat. There was a joke among the woman students that the best way to pass your orals was to stuff a pillow up your dress, because they would all be so terrified of having parturition take place on the Persian rug that they would just ask you your name and give you a pass. One of my female colleagues was almost expelled for dressing like a woman of loose virtue. Actually she was a Latvian Shakespearian scholar with somewhat different ideas of dress than the rest of us tweedy, buttoned types.

So I enjoyed it, yes, in a nervous sort of way. There were some fine lecturers, and Widener Library is wonderful. And little madnesses go on there which seem unlike those of any other place. I often wondered what happened to the man who was rumored to have broken into Houghton Library (Rare Books) in order to expose himself to the Gutenberg Bible. I do have two "Harvard" stories, which are in *Dancing Girls*.

The most important things about the experience for me were: it was the place where I first learned urban fear. (Before I went there, I always walked around at night, didn't bother about locked doors, etc. If you behaved that way in Cambridge you were dead.) And, for various reasons, it was the place where I started thinking seriously about Canada as having a shape and a culture of its own. Partly because I was studying the literature of the American Puritans, which was not notable for its purely literary values—if one can study this in a university, I thought, why not Canadian literature? (you must understand that at that time Canadian literature was simply not taught in high schools and universities in Canada)—and partly because Boston was, in certain ways, so similar, in climate and landscape, to parts of Canada. One began to look for differences.

Oates: Did you discover any odd or upsetting attitudes toward Canada while living at Cambridge?

Atwood: It's not that anyone in Boston—few in the Graduate School were *from* that area in any case; they came from all over the U.S. and from non-North American countries as well—it's not that the Americans I met had any odd or "upsetting" attitudes towards Canada. They simply didn't have any attitudes at all. They had a vague idea that such a place existed—it was that blank area north of the map where the bad weather came from—but if they thought about it at all they found it boring. They seemed to want to believe that my father was a Mounted Policeman and that we lived in igloos all year round, and I must admit that after a while I took a certain pleasure in encouraging these beliefs. (Recall that this was before the Vietnam crisis, during which many Americans came to regard Canada as the Great Good Place or game refuge to which they might escape.) I met a number of Southerners and got to know some of them; they seemed to resent "the North" in some of the same ways as did the handful of Canadians there, though for different reasons.

Oates: Why had you gone to Harvard in the first place?

Atwood: Because—to trace it back—Canada had not hired one Jerome H. Buckley back in the Depression when he was looking for work. He had gone to the States and had become a leading Victorianist. The Victorian period was "my period," and I had won a Woodrow Wilson Fellowship, so I went to Harvard to study with Dr. Buckley. There is, you know, a kind of Canadian Mafia at Harvard and elsewhere in the States. Quite a few of the well-known professors at Harvard were closet Canadians. However, they kept their identities secret, for the most part, except when talking with other Canadians. They'd learned by experience that Americans found a revelation of one's Canadian-ness, dropped, for instance, into the middle of a sherry party, about as interesting as the announcement that one had had mashed potatoes for lunch. The beginning of Canadian cultural nationalism was not "Am I really that oppressed?" but "Am I really that boring?" You see, we had never been taught much about our own history or culture—but that's another whole story.

Oates: Is there a very distinctive difference between American "literary" responses and Canadian?

Atwood: I feel that American literary responses are, quite simply, more literary—at least in the groups of people with whom I'm likely to come in contact. I think the difference is that in the States there is a "literary" culture and a largely non-literary one, whereas in Canada these overlap a great deal more. I'm saying this only on the basis of who is likely to turn up at a poetry reading. But my experience isn't really wide enough to justify such general statements.

I always enjoy going to the States; it's an escape for me, from my own demanding culture. People there are polite to me, as they would be to a visiting foreigner (which I am), and, though interested, disinterested. Americans have such enthusiasms. It's a change from the gloom here, the suspicion. But of course, Canada is where I really live. That's why I can enjoy the States so much for brief periods of time.

Oates: What sort of working habits have you?

Atwood: My working habits have changed over the years, according to the circumstances of my life. I started writing seriously—though this may seem ludicrous—when I was sixteen and in fourth-year high school. At that time I wrote in the evenings when I was supposed to be doing homework, on weekends and occasionally during school hours. After that, I was in university for four years and wrote between classes, after hours, etc.—a haphazard pattern. I didn't have very regular habits as a student, either; I was a procrastinator and still am, so it helps me to set myself deadlines. (This applies only to prose, of course. Poetry does not get written, by me at least, as a matter of will.) During my years as a graduate student, odd-job-holder, university lecturer of the lowest order—up till the age of about twenty-seven or so—I almost had to write at night, and would stay up quite late. I'm not sure how I wrote at all the first year I spent as a "real" university teacher (1967-68, in Montreal). I was very busy and exhausted, and lost a lot of weight. But I seem to have been writing some then, too. I can't remember when I did it.

I became an afternoon writer when I had afternoons. When I was able to write full time, I used to spend the morning procrastinating and worrying, then plunge into the manuscript in a frenzy of anxiety around 3:00 when it looked as though I might not get anything done. Since the birth of my daughter, I've had to cut down on the procrastination. I still try to spend the afternoons writing, though the preliminary period of anxiety is somewhat shorter. I suppose this is a more efficient use of time. The fact is that blank pages inspire me with terror. What will I put on them? Will it be good enough? Will I have to throw it out? And so forth. I suspect most writers are like this.

Oates: Do you work on more than one project at a time?

Atwood: One project at a time, ideally. I am by nature lazy, sluggish, and of low energy. It constantly amazes me that I do anything at all.

Oates: How long, approximately, did it take you to write each of your three novels?

Atwood: I wrote *The Edible Woman* in unused University of British Columbia exam books from April to August of 1965. I revised in the fall. For reasons I won't go into, the publisher lost the manuscript, and I was so naive about the process that I thought it normal for them to take two years to tell me anything about it. The book was finally published in 1969. I had written another unpublished novel before this, and wrote another unpublished, unfinished one after it. Then I wrote *Surfacing*, from about December 1969 to August 1970. There were only minor revisions and some retyping, though the handwritten version was extensively revised. *Lady Oracle* took much longer, partly because I was living a life filled with more interruptions, partly because it changed a lot while I was writing it. It took about two and one-half years, off and on.

Oates: I've enjoyed the cartoons of yours I've seen. Is drawing another of your talents...?

Atwood: I paint a little and draw, for my own amusement. I've been drawing a political cartoon strip for a Canadian magazine—*This Magazine* —for some years, under the pseudonym of "Bart Gerrard" (it's nice to get hate mail when they don't even know it's *you*) and I have a children's book coming out in Canada, in March, for the smallest age group, written, hand-lettered and illustrated by myself. I hesitate to call this a "talent," since I know I'm not very good; that is, I have to rub out a lot in order to get the heads the same size and I have difficulty drawing owls flying sideways.

Oates: You must be disturbed by literary journalists' efforts to categorize you—to package you as "The Reigning Queen of Canadian Literature," or a national prophetess, or even a Medusa. What have your reactions been?

Atwood: I dislike the kinds of titles you mention; I find "Reigning Queen" a particularly offensive one, implying as it does that literature, as practiced by women anyway, is either a monarchy or a beehive. In any case, there's only room for one "reigning queen," who will presumably be stung to death later on when she can't lay any more eggs. Such titles are insulting to the many fine women writers in this country (Marian Engel, Alice Munro, Margaret Laurence, to name three) and threatening to me. Anyone who takes language seriously would never use such a metaphor without being aware of its sinister range of meanings.

I suppose Canada is hungry for a few visible "stars," having been without any for so long. The danger to the writer is early stellification—one may become a vaporous ball of gas. But only if captivated by one's image. Luckily, my image here, as reflected in the press, has not been very captivating, at least to me. I can do without "Medusa." (It's one of the hazards of naturally curly hair.)

Oates: Do you think that reviewers and critics have, on the whole, been "fair" to you? Has there been any sort of backlash, as an inevitable consequence of your "rise to fame"?

Atwood: Of course, there has been a "backlash"; there always is, but vicious attacks in Canada tend to be much more open and personal than in the United States, partly because of the Celtic, blackly satiric literary tradition and partly because it's much more like a small town. We live in each others' pockets here, and the dust and gloom is therefore more intense. There are mixed feelings about small-town boys and girls making good, as you know. On the one hand, we're proud of them because they're ours; on the other hand, we don't like them getting too big for their boots, so we cut them down whenever possible; on the other hand (Canada, like Kali, has more than two hands), we can't quite believe that one of ours can *really* be any good—surely it's all some kind of hype or fraud; and on yet another hand, the success of one of our members is a reproach to us. If he could do it, why can't we?

There's that; but also, there have been a number of fair-minded, objectively critical pieces which have dealt genuinely with the shape and characteristics of my work and its strengths and weaknesses. Canadian critics are always more close-mouthed than American ones; they seldom go overboard, and they look with great suspicion upon cult figures, especially their own. This has definite advantages. I think American writers are often made dizzy by a sudden rocket-like stellification, then confused when they are just as enthusiastically banished to outer darkness. Canadian writers are (to put it mildly) seldom permitted to get swelled heads.

Oates: An entire issue of *The Malahat Review* was devoted to you in Winter 1977. I remember being rather surprised by a photographic essay called "Anima," and wonder what your reactions to it, and to the volume as a whole, were.

Atwood: I also was rather surprised. But then, my capacity to be surprised by other people's reactions to me is, I have discovered, infinite. I don't really see myself as a sort of buttock coming out of an egg (or was it the other way around?), and as I recall there were quite a few naked ladies with large breasts. But I think the collage sequence was supposed to have been inspired by my work rather than by my finite personal being, which in this climate is usually swathed in wool. Even so???

The truth is that I am not a very glamorous person. Writers aren't, really. All they do is sit around and write, which I suppose is as commendable as sitting around painting your toenails, but will never make it into the fashion magazines. So when I see myself being glamorized or idealized, it makes me squirm somewhat. Of course, I'm as vain as most people. I'd rather see a picture of myself looking good than one of myself looking awful. But I've seen so many of both by now, some taken minutes apart. . . . A photo is only a view.

Oates: You are a very active member of the Writers' Union of Canada, and along with a delegation of some twelve other writers recently went to Ottawa to protest the importation of American editions of Canadian books. Could you explain the situation? Is it a very serious one? What consequences will follow if the Copyright Act is not modified?

Atwood: There are many writers who are more active than I am at the moment. I was active earlier and hope to be more active later, but having a small child tends to reduce my mobility. However, I do get rolled out like a sort of cannon when heavy guns are required. The Remainders Issue has been one of these occasions.

Briefly, the situation is this. Most English-speaking countries, including the United States, have laws that protect both their writers and their printing and publishing industries against pirated editions and foreign competition. In the U.S., if I understand the law correctly, it is illegal to import any more than a nominal number of books by an American author printed outside the country. That is, a Canadian edition of Allen Ginsberg would be dumped into the Detroit River at the border. (This example is based on an actual case.)

The Canadian law was intended to produce the same result. However, the sloppy wording of the article in question has produced a legal loophole, which was discovered by a Canadian retailer some five years ago. Needless to say, he took immediate advantage of it. He went to the States and bought up remaindered copies of books by Canadian authors originally published by U.S. publishers, imported them into Canada, and sold them at rock-bottom prices, thereby depriving the Canadian publisher of sales and the Canadian author of potential royalties from those sales.

This would not matter much if the book market were not so different in the two countries. The "shelf-life" of a hardback book in the States is ordinarily four to six months. In Canada, it's a year to two years. That is, the book might still be selling briskly in Canada when it's remainder time in the States. The other factor is that—not surprisingly—Canadian authors are more popular in Canada as a rule than they are in the States. In other words, the importer knows he has a market. What we are afraid of is that these importers or jobbers will go to the U.S. publishers and encourage them to overprint by agreeing in advance to buy up any surplus.

Oates: Is there any protection for the Canadian author?

Atwood: The only surefire protection for the Canadian author is to write a contract only with a U.S. publisher, giving him North American rights. If enough authors do this to protect their own royalties, it means the death of the publishing industry in Canada. Partial protection can be obtained by publishing in the States six months later than in Canada. But, of course, the U.S. publisher would rather publish simultaneously. Note that it is not the U.S. publisher who is doing the "illegal" importing. It's jobbers and Canadian retailers. The U.S. publisher has no control over where remaindered books go once they are out of his hands, so clauses in the contract prohibiting this practice are worthless. I'm told they're also illegal.

A simple change in the wording of one clause of the Copyright Act would solve our immediate problem. However, we're being told by the Government that the law is all right as it stands—in the face of much evidence to the contrary. We've also been asked what's the matter with us—why do we want to deny cheap books to the Canadian consumer?

Oates: Do you think there are any problems inherent in the fact that so many of the arts are state-supported in Canada? As an American I am impressed with the generosity of the Canadian government, but as a reader and critic I am frequently disturbed by the kinds of publications funded by the Canada Council and the various arts councils. Small presses do not seem to offer much editing advice, with the consequence that books tumble from presses, are "distributed" minimally, and allowed to go out of print almost at once. Without wanting to discourage young writers, I must say that the sheer quantity of hurried and slovenly writing published in Canada is rather demoralizing. (Of course, the same thing is rapidly becoming true in the States.) There seems to be no tradition any longer of apprenticeship; student writers are being "published"—or at least printed—and in the long run premature publication will have a deleterious effect on their craft. What is your opinion?—or is this too dangerous an enquiry?

Atwood: This is not at all a dangerous enquiry. There are several different questions here, though, and I will try to deal with them one at a time.

The Canadian literary scene has been likened (by myself, in fact) to a group of figures dancing with considerable vigor and some grace on the edge of a precipice. The precipice was always there, though it's become more visible recently. I'm referring, of course, to the Quebec situation and the potential splitting-up of Canada. But the group of figures was not always there—not so long ago there were only a few solitary writers who, in the field of fiction anyway, didn't know each other—and they did not always dance, with or without grace and vigor.

When I began writing, in the late '50s and early '60s, there were five or so literary magazines in the entire country. The number of books of poetry that came out in a year—including small press books and privately printed ones—was under twenty. The new Canadian novels published in a year could usually be counted on the fingers of one hand. Canadian literature was not recognized as a legitimate field of study. Canadian books were not taught in schools. The epithet "Canadian writer" was a term of derision, even to Canadian writers. Almost every writer's ambition was to get out of the country to some place "real" in a literary sense, or at least some place where he could get his books published. Canadian writers were not known in their own country, and even when published were rarely bought or reviewed. (Mordecai Richler's first novel sold three copies in Canada. The press run of even a respectable book of poetry was considered good at 200. The publishers of *The Circle Game* initially printed 450, and were worried that they had done too many. Even now, Canadian paperbacks account for maybe three percent of total paperback sales in Canada, and that includes Harlequin Romances.)

We can't take the publishing industry for granted, as one can in the States. It is *always* tottering on the brink of collapse. We can't take our own existence as writers for granted. True, there has been about a 1,000 percent growth in the publishing industry in the last twenty years, but remember that started from near zero. So what is viewed by an American as "generosity" is seen by us simply as necessity. If the government support that publishers currently receive were to be withdrawn, the industry, by and large, would collapse. The "Canadian Renaissance" in the arts was made possible, in large part, by the Canada Council. None of us like this situation. But none of us want to be back in 1961, either.

Now...editing in small presses. As an ex-editor for a small press, Anansi, I have to protest. Editorial time by the bucketful was poured into our books. Our chief editor at that time was Dennis Lee, who is renowned here as an absolutely devoted editor. So it isn't universal. I'd say you get about the same mix as you might in the States: some presses serious about the writing, some existing only to get their members and friends into print. I think you see the bad writing here because more of it makes its way across your desk. You couldn't possibly even *read* all of it that comes out in the States; the sheer volume is so high.

But to me, small presses, good or bad, are a necessity. They're like all those Elizabethan melodramas. Without them, Shakespeare would have had no milieu. They were a place where a writer could, as it were, "try out." Same with "little" magazines. I guess I have a certain belief in the reader, the intelligent reader. I think books will eventually find their own level. This may be overly optimistic.

Oates: I am often annoyed by critics' attempts to reduce complex works of art to simple "thematic" statements. Why are Canadian critics in particular so obsessed with statement and theme at the expense of a thoughtful consideration of technique?

Atwood: I'm probably one of those critics who has annoyed you, since my only critical work, *Survival: A Thematic Guide to Canadian Literature*, is concerned almost exclusively to demonstrate that there are such things as Canadian themes, which differ either in substance or in emphasis from their counterparts in English and American literature. Would it help if I told you that, even after I had written this book—which caused rather a furor here, almost as if I'd said that the Emperor was naked— many critics resolutely continued to deny that there was any such thing as a "Canadian" literature?

We've tried very hard over the past few decades to demonstrate our own existence, our own right to exist. Usually we ourselves—the writers, that is—don't doubt it; the voices of denial come from elsewhere. But this may explain, a little anyway, the concern with "theme." One can only afford "a thoughtful consideration of technique" when the question of mere existence is no longer a question.

Where Were You When I
Really Needed You
Jim Davidson

Jim Davidson's interview was conducted March 6, 1978, in Melbourne, Australia, and originally appeared in *Meanjin* 37 (1978).

Davidson: Let's start with *Survival*, your somewhat polemical account of Canadian literature. What prompted you to write it?

Atwood: Several things. I was doing a lot of readings around Canada, and after them people would ask me about Canadian Literature. These were Canadians, you must understand, asking these questions: first of all, was it true that there wasn't any? They had been told by their high school teachers that the only Canadian writer was Stephen Leacock. Or, if there was some, was it not true that it was in fact second rate and an inferior imitation of English literature and American literature? And why should they have to read, say, W. O. Mitchell instead of Mark Twain? Well, there's no *instead of*, really: you don't have to read something instead of something else. But this seemed to be their thinking. Thirdly, if there was a Canadian literature, and it wasn't inferior, where was it? Because nobody had ever told them. And it became quite clear to me that most of the people that I was talking to were in the same position that I myself had been in back in 1960. That is, if I wanted to find out about the literature of my own country, there was virtually nothing that could point the way: a couple of academic books, but that was all. The message that got through to me was that Canadians were interested in their own literature and culture, but nobody was paying any attention to the fact that they were interested. So I wrote the book for a general audience, not an academic audience.

Davidson: Would you link some of contemporary Canada's problems to the fact that perhaps there hasn't been enough sense of the common culture?

Atwood: I would link it directly to that. Specifically the English/French problem; I guess that's what you're referring to. That's one thing. French Canada was usually taught its history, but nobody else's. So it was taught the history of the French in Canada, with the English cast as villains. In fact, when we had a common conference not long ago, they were surprised to learn that in the uprisings of 1837-38 there had even been an uprising in the English sector, and second, that anybody at all had got hanged. They thought that the only people who got hanged in Canada, ever, were French—hanged by English. They are as ignorant of us as we are ignorant of them. When any question arises, the English-speaking sector, instead of knowing why, or responding with understanding, responds with bafflement and hurt feelings. Since they don't know the history of the French in Canada, and since they don't know their own history, they have no tools with which to understand their present situation. //

Davidson: There are a couple of hints in one of the poems, and of course in *Surfacing*, that your background may have been northern Quebec.

Atwood: Well, part of it was.

Davidson: One gets the impression there not of hostility towards the French Canadians—of course, there's nothing remotely like that—but a sense that the Quebecois are very much apart from the rest of the nation, even slightly inscrutable.

Atwood: Well, again, I'm not the only person who feels that. They feel that themselves. I don't know that they think themselves inscrutable so much as misunderstood or not understood—and I think in that view they're possibly right.

Davidson: The other thing I couldn't help wondering about was the fascination the French Canadians clearly have for you. It plainly goes beyond the morbid recurrences in their literature you sketch so well in *Survival*. Is it perhaps their inner sense of having been in Canada longer—to the point where they are, in a way, proto-Canadians? Or is it because of their cultural oppression within Canada?

Atwood: I feel that they are the essence of the paradigm I'm dealing with, because they've got a double dose of it. And to me Quebec literature is very different from French literature, and I think they would probably say this themselves. It's not even just North American literature written in French; it is Quebec literature, and it has its own patterns, and styles and nuances and paradigms, and mythology, if you like. A lot of them would say that they've been through the phase of having to feel that they had to destroy the past and burn down the house in order to get anywhere, and that they're now living in a state of liberation ever since they elected Levesque. But I don't think they're out of the woods yet.

Davidson: As you say, they're the essence of the Canadian problem. You've almost set up, in *Survival*, a kind of domino theory: America is to English Canada as English Canada has been both to the Indians and the Quebecois.

Atwood: I think of it as a box within a box, within a box, within a box.

Davidson: Right. Well, let's talk about the American problem. Presumably you'd be greatly distressed if Quebec were to leave Canada, because it would make Canada vulnerable to American penetration.

Atwood: It's vulnerable already. And as I have said repeatedly, it's very hard for somebody like myself to say to Quebec, stay with us, because we'll do better by you than the Americans will if you separate and isolate yourselves. Quite simply, the government and the culture has not done that well even by the artists of the English Canadian sector. We're still lobbying our own government to get them to plug a hole in the badly drafted copyright law: it allows foreign remaindered editions of books by Canadians to be brought into Canada and sold at prices that undercut the Canadian publishers—and for which the Canadian author gets no royalties. They keep saying, "Yes, yes . . . but we've been pushing at this for five years." Meanwhile the books are still coming in, and the upshot will be that it will not be economical for Canadian writers to publish with Canadian publishers any more. They'll have to sell North American rights; that will destroy the Canadian publishing industry. So, if our own government's doing that to us, how can we say to Quebec we'll protect your culture? They've amply demonstrated that their thinking is Continentalist. They'd like to have Quebec cultural nationalism done away with. When the Quebec problem first came up, they tried to drum up "national unity." But nobody wants national unity in the sense of national homogeneity, because there are strong regional identities, regional variants of just about everything I deal with in *Survival*.

Davidson: In talking about English Canada more generally, though, there's a fascinating meeting in *Surfacing* between two batches of canoeists, in which *both* batches mistake each other for Americans! That intrigued me, in that Canadians *in Canada* had a problem recognizing each other. How much further can cultural penetration go? Which itself prompts the reverse question: why do you view the increase in American influence with such alarm?

Atwood: Well, if you take the position that Coca-Cola is good for the world, and that Australia ought to be populated by nothing but Kentucky Fried Chicken stands and people who sell Ford motor cars and show U.S. films in all the movie theaters—doing away with the Australian film industry—then there's nothing wrong with it whatsoever. However, if you happen to believe, as I do, that populations are best represented by people who live among them, and that you ought to have a vote which will help to determine what happens to you, and that there should be . . . No Taxation Without Representation, then the situation is appalling. As it is in Australia.

Davidson: So you've been struck by how far American influence has penetrated here, too?

Atwood: I've been struck by the fact that it's penetrating here and nobody much seems to be concerned about it. You seem to say, "There's this great big ocean between and we're quite secure here, thank you very much." And, "We can handle it." We, on the other hand, have seen what happens at the end of that line of thinking.

And a lot of us are in Canada because we made the choice back in 1776, to go there at the time of the American Revolution. We have been threatened with invasion several times since. We have won a war against the Americans—that was the War of 1812. We have been continually sold out and betrayed by Britain, number one, by our own politicians, number two, because they found it more convenient to make deals. Oregon State was once part of Canada, and a lot of bits and pieces along the border were once Canadian. All these tradings went on.

We feel that our position as an alternative North American society has been fairly hard-won. A lot of people gave up perfectly prosperous homes and farms in New England and went to Canada to start all over again because of politics.

Davidson: There's one thing that worries me slightly about the Canadian nationalist position. In London in 1970 I first encountered some fairly young Canadian nationalists, some of whom were joyously speaking of jamming American broadcasts. Surely there's a problem here in that America, with 220 million to Canada's 20 million is, in one sense at least, a greater society, and isn't there the possibility that in presenting an implacable, hostile front to a larger culture, you could run the risk—as the Afrikaners have done—of cutting yourself off from a lot of contemporary currents?

Atwood: I'm afraid that we aren't quite in the same position. Because what you have in South Africa is a society that's able to isolate itself. You have nothing like that in Canada. I think if it ever got to that point, and I felt I were being boxed in by Canadian nationalism, I'd probably take another tack. The writer, as you know, is always on the side of the underdog.

Right now, Canadian nationalism is the underdog position. Let me give you a few figures. Less than three percent of the paperback books bought in Canada are published by Canadian companies. (That includes Harlequin Romances, one of *the* most successful paperback publishing ventures in the world.) The educational textbook industry is heavily dominated by American companies, which means that Canadians are getting their history biased and slanted to an American viewpoint. Now whose interest does this serve? It seems to me wrong that schoolchildren grow up in Canada thinking that Abraham Lincoln was a Prime Minister of Canada and that Ernest Hemingway was a Canadian writer. Does something not seem to you peculiar about this?

I think the reason for wanting to have a Canada is that you do not agree with some of the political choices that have been made by America and that you want to do it a different way. One that's fairer to the environment, not as hostile to Nature, has a more egalitarian view of citizenship, a more co-operative view towards how the economy should be run—instead of ruthless individualism, every man for himself, the kind of thing you get in the States. And that has been the Canadian way: we've been forced into having co-operatives, we've been forced into a number of things because we're poorer.

But if you want an involved citizenry, it seems to me wrong to give them a view of history which is determined by people in another country.

Davidson: I would agree with that entirely. It seems to me that one of the leitmotifs in your work—and why I'll read more of it—is the concern crystallized in those lines from *The Journals of Susanna Moodie*:

> Whether the wilderness is
> real or not
> depends on who lives there.

You are very much concerned with changing ways of seeing.

Atwood: So that the seeing becomes authentic. And it doesn't seem to me that you can see your own situation in any way that renders it authentic if you believe that primary reality resides elsewhere. And this is probably what Canada and Australia have in common—that they have had a physical environment which has been out of sync with their cultural environment, because their cultural environment has come from elsewhere. And it seems to me that the job in a colony for writers, not imposed by anybody else but simply one they come to recognize, is to somehow get these two things together. The perception of their physical environment and the cultural rendering of it somehow have to be welded in a way that the artist in other kinds of countries doesn't have to face.

I studied American literature quite intensively when I lived in the United States, and American writers went through this, both before the Revolution and after it. Herman Melville—to give you one example—was destroyed by the cultural politics of his time. There were two groups in America in the '40s. One was Young America—it believed in a sort of barbaric yawp and kept expecting the American genius to appear who would be quite different from any that came out of England. The other was the Anglophiles, such as Washington Irving: their terms were, become successful in the way that the English were successful. Fenimore Cooper is an example. He was writing Walter Scott novels with "Red Indians" in them. And he was enormously popular for this reason: the form was quite acceptable and the content was American. But Melville came along and wrote *Moby Dick*. And he'd been taken up earlier by Young America, who felt that he might be it. When the book was published the Anglophiles—who were at loggerheads with Young America— immediately dismissed it. But Young America found it not American enough, so they trashed it too. So Melville was vilified and dismissed by the only two groups of people who were writing anything at all about books in the country, and he sank like a stone. *Moby Dick* was not rediscovered in America until the 1920s. The neglect ruined Herman Melville's life. So that's what this kind of thing can do, and I'm well aware of the dangers.

Davidson: It seems to me that one of the things that's going on in *Surfacing* is this whole change in perception by the major character—in her rediscovery, as it were, of the Canadian Shield. There's a plumbing of its metaphysical meaning, beyond Nature, and beyond the Indian rock paintings she's looking for—they, in fact, become secondary, mere knots thrown up by deeper currents. So the fact that she doesn't actually find them isn't really important.

Atwood: That's right. The other concern in the book is, of course, a very Canadian concern at the moment. It's a concern with language. And one of her problems is that none of the languages with which she has been provided seems to be adequate or accessible. And I think the push is towards a third language, if you like, or another language. And, of course, this is one of our difficulties: both in Canada and in Australia we write in English. And the French write in French. And that means that the literary tradition that history has provided us with was created in another country.

Davidson: And when you say language, it's obviously more than just a question of exotic words being brought in. It's a question of actual syntax and modes of feeling, being....

Atwood: Well, let me put it this way. There are a number of Indian languages which are very interesting; in one of them there are no nouns. What we would call a noun is a variation of a verb. So that you don't say, "A deer is running across a field." You say something like, "fielding" ...or "something which is being a field is manifesting something which is being a deer." That is, the whole language is composed of verbs. The mode of linguistic expression militates against seeing objects as distinct from their backgrounds. You see the whole field as doing a certain thing: the whole area of your perception is behaving in a certain way. There is not a flower sitting on a table; the table is flowering, as it were. It is behaving like a flower in that area of space.

It seems to me that English, on the other hand, and to some extent all European languages, see nouns as hard, separate, distinct, contained things. They are separate from verbs. You know, a rock falls off a cliff. There's another way of seeing that happening. And having seen the Australian bush, I would say that you need another language too. Because the Australian bush is not something in which you see distinct objects; it's quite hard to see distinct objects. You see a space behaving in a certain way.

I think the other thing that happened, both in Canada and Australia, was that certain shapes were picked up and plonked down. So that you have the shape of a church, you know, picked up and transported and then set down in a landscape that did not give rise to it. You can see it at once if you go to England; there a lot of the buildings really came out of the earth, in a way that they don't if you merely imitate them. That is, what was available dictated what was built. But in Canada you have a landscape in which the human artifacts somehow don't grow out of a base. They're like little toy towns. They're perched on top of the land. And therefore transient: you feel they could just slide off, vanish. //

The weird thing about India—weird to cultures such as ours, which are so new and treasure anything old—is the way the whole place is filled with old temples that nobody's paying any attention to. // If you asked anybody about them, people would say, "They've always been there." In Canada and Australia, though, we're very conscious of time, because we can remember a time when none of those things were there. There's nothing lost in the mists of history, because history, as we know it, is not misty.

Davidson: Actually you seem to be very concerned, not only with shapes, but with their transformation; and I was interested—given the kind of change the main character undergoes in *Surfacing*—in your constant inversion of certain propositions in *Survival*. (For example, why look for a hero? It may be, in a sense, not anti-Canadian but un-Canadian or inappropriate to look for an individual hero, so why not, you argue, consider the possibility of collective heroism?) It's also apparent in the poetry, most obviously in the Circe poems. Perhaps there's a sense in which Canada too is a Circe, requiring changes, if not actual physical ones, then at least changes in the psyche of the people living there if they're to become more attuned to it. And then I gather in this latest novel, *Lady Oracle*, you're again concerned with shapes. You seem to me, more than any other writer I've read, interested in the dramatic and sometimes traumatic implications of the changes which are required of people in certain situations. And these are often physical, or so basic in terms of people's psyche that they cannot but have physical implications.

Atwood: That's interesting. I've had people say that to me before. And some people have connected it with the fact that my family background was not literary, but scientific, and that my father is an entomologist. And, of course, the life-cycles of insects have always been something that I knew about—that is, one of the life forms that goes through the most dramatic changes.

The other thing, of course, is that Canada is a land of violent seasonal change. You have an extreme contrast between summer and winter. It struck me, flying over Australia and looking at the coast and what I could see of the interior, that the opposite of green in Australia is not white, it's gray. Or possibly brown. But when you say green in Canada, you immediately imply white. That is the opposite: that's what things turn to. // We only have it at certain times of the year, and when it does appear it's a rebirth. It's part of having gotten through one more winter.

Davidson: Do you think that being a woman, and being a woman writer, you've perhaps been peculiarly favorably placed by fate, as it were, to work through some of the implications of being a Canadian artist?

Atwood: Yes, I feel that quite strongly, for two reasons. The first one is again historical; it is not possible to consider Canadian literature and ignore women writers.

Davidson: It isn't here, either. With Christina Stead, and Katharine Susannah Prichard and Henry Richardson, anyone would have to concede that at least three of our half-dozen best novelists were women.

Atwood: That's interesting. It backs me up, as I'll go on to explain further. It is not possible to study English literature of the nineteenth century and leave out the women. And since I grew up on English literature of the nineteenth century, women writers were quite prominent. It was never stated as a premise that you couldn't write and be a woman. Second, it is not at all possible to ignore the women writers in Canada, because they were the first writers and they continue to be, in fiction anyway, pre-eminent. If you had to name the ten novelists who were most well-known—I'm not making any judgment about literary quality, which seems to me another thing—five of them, anyway, would be women, at this present moment.

Davidson: So you're really conscious of writing within that tradition, within the broader Canadian tradition?

Atwood: Yes, I don't feel I'm going to be trampled and spat upon by my confreres because I'm a woman. I may get some pretty mixed metaphors applied to me because I'm a woman, and that certainly has happened. But it doesn't affect sales, to put it crudely.

Davidson: Where do you see yourself within what is loosely termed the feminist movement in the '70s? *Survival* appeared six years ago, but there's no particularly strong feminist consciousness present there.

Atwood: Well, that's not the subject of the book—although if it had been written by a man there probably would not have been a chapter on women. The other thing is that, of course, women as well as Canadians have been colonized or have been the victims of cultural imperialism, if you like, so that a lot of feminists in the United States have taken up *Survival* not because of its nationalism, but because of the kinds of models it employs—of victimization and the response to it. They take it as a book about women, even though it isn't "about women." They take it as a paradigm of how to get yourself out of certain cultural binds. //

Davidson: What seems to me to be interesting is that though most things in the book apply equally well to Australia as to Canada, the central image of the survivor does not quite work here. If one can draw a comparable characteristic figure from Australian literature, it would more likely be a battler, a loner, or a failed hero.

Atwood: Yes. Some people say to me, "Well, isn't what you're talking about just really a sort of post-war French existentialism, and, you know, gloomy trends and suicides and things?" And I say, "No, it's not." It seems to me that there's a great difference between jumping off a bridge and clinging onto it and trying to get back on. Which is what survivalism involves. There are very few suicides in Canadian literature: it happens more often to be trees falling on you, or...

Davidson: There may very well be more of those in Australian literature. Because there is an element of craggy individualism, and of half-expecting defeat...

Atwood: Do they kill themselves? Do they give up?

Davidson: They don't often kill themselves. But they do give up...settle for less.

Atwood: But in Canada there's that long winter. You can't escape it, not even on the West Coast. So that there's a constant climatic crisis. And the politics are the same: it goes from one crisis to the next, each one of which threatens to destroy the country. I guess we have them instead of typhoons. So that survivalism partly comes from this. It's not just a literary metaphor: politicians are using it all the time.

But here it seems different: you can go on and on. I've read poetry in which things sort of merge and meld, in a way. I think it would be very interesting to be an Australian poet now. It seems to me that you are getting to the point where it's all suddenly going to happen. But, of course, I know Australia, like Canada, is always talking in terms of the future when it's all suddenly going to come together and explode. Colonies tend to be future-oriented!

Davidson: To return to feminism again: have you found that your own position as a Canadian woman writer has been helped to some degree by the rise of feminist consciousness?

Atwood: It certainly has increased my audience. There's no doubt about that. And I think it has increased the perception with which some of my books have been read.

Davidson: What about its effects on your own perceptions?

Atwood: I came to my perceptions some time earlier, because I had to. I mean, if you were a woman and you decided to follow a career in the late '50s, you were automatically politicized. But in an individual way: that is, you didn't feel that there was anybody else who agreed with you. If you had to be regarded as crazy, peculiar, eccentric, queer, and brainy, etc., that was the choice you were making. And a number of people did that. But they weren't a movement. It was the people who got married early and had babies because that's what the culture told them they had to do (not because it was what they wanted to do) who became bitter and disillusioned and gave the real strength to the feminist movement. If no movement had arisen I would have continued to be a writer. And there are a lot of people like myself—Margaret Laurence, Alice Munro, Marian Engel—they're all older than I am. We did it despite the culture.

When the movement came along, I think the feeling was, well, it won't be as hard for some people now as it was for us. It's too late for us to be part of that. Because we've already gone through that in our own quirky ways. I didn't join a consciousness-raising group because my consciousness had already been raised quite enough. Often, inadvertently, by the same people who were now forming the groups. People who many years ago had queried the fact that I wasn't collecting china. I mean, one does have that kind of ambivalent feeling towards it: where were you when I really needed you? You know, I'm very tough now, but I wasn't always then, and I would have appreciated some of that support, at that time. On the other hand, writers like myself got adopted by the feminist movement because it was looking for models. And if one has to ask me, "Do you think it's a good thing or a bad thing?" or, "Are you a feminist or aren't you a feminist?" you have to say the same thing you would say about any political movement, namely, something that has immeasurably improved the lives of a great number of people has to be a good thing; and, as to whether or not I will give it my support, I have given it my support by having chosen to live the kind of life that I've chosen to live. And I don't have to make ideological statements. It seems to me that the freedom to do what you want to do is what the feminist movement is aiming towards. And I've done what I wanted to do. //

Davidson: What kind of problems do you set about answering, or formulating, in the poetry as distinct from the novels?

Atwood: That's the kind of thing that critics have to do. I can do that quite well when I'm reading other people's work, but I can't do it when I'm reading my own. I don't see poetry as an attempt to solve problems, or even to formulate them. I see it as something that takes place at a much less intellectual level. I was at one time a student of philosophy, and I left it, partly because I couldn't see the point of formulating questions or formulating statements such as, A bald man is bald. It seemed to me a misuse of the language. But also because I felt it was developing a part of my mind which was antithetical to the writing of poetry. Antipathetic. You can have a highly developed analytical mind or you can be a poet: the two very seldom go together. //

Davidson: It's a small point, but one immediately apparent to an Australian—since generally more than fifty percent of the population in each State has lived in its capital city—in *Survival* there's very little sense of the city as such. Mind you, our primary national and literary concerns moved away from the land only with some reluctance, and relatively recently. What place does the city have in the Canadian psyche, and more particularly in Canadian literature? //

Atwood: That wasn't true in Canada until very recently. The great move off the farm, I think, came in the '30s, '40s—in around there. Before then Canada was largely rural. So that the big Canadian family saga is written in the '50s. I think I do have it in that book, in the chapter on the family. The grandfather who has the farm and stands for the old values and so on, the father who goes to the city for an easier life, and the son, who then makes connection with the grandfather in an attempt to recapture some of the values that he feels have been lost. That tends to be the pattern.

There have been sporadic movements towards "Let's have an urban poetry." And, of course, a lot of the novels now are set in the cities. But it seems to me that poetry at its core is anti-machine. And I think that is the problem: it's not necessarily anti-city, because there are models of cities that are not machine-ridden. But the city, I think, in the modern consciousness, is pre-eminently the place of machines. And it is only outside the city that you can find places where there are no machines. And poetry being primitive in its thrust and in its psychological origins, its connections are not really with the motor car, but with the heartbeat, the human body. I don't think you can ever alter that. And the metaphors one tends to find which correlate with the body are not machines, except in nightmare visions: it's only there that the body becomes a robot. In benign visions the body becomes an ocean or a tree or something like that.

Urban poetry is always quivering on the edge of being a nightmare poetry. It could have been different maybe in older times, when cities were smaller and more humanly scaled. But in modern times, if you actually look at the kind of poetry that comes out of cities, very little of it has to do with a beatific vision of any kind. It may be social observation, it may be a kind of horrific poetry, which is a poetry of real experience—you know, I think many people living in cities lead rather horrific lives, and I think poets have to write about that. But to get the transcendental vision, the beautiful vision as opposed to the ugly vision, you don't go to the city.

Davidson: That's obviously very important to you, and part of the pull of the North, presumably...

Atwood: Well, the North is to Canada as the Outback is to Australia, and as the sea was to Melville, and as...let me see now, as Africa is, shall we say, to *Heart of Darkness*. It's the place where you go to find something out. It's the place of the unconscious. It's the place of the journey or the quest. In nineteenth-century poetry, such as Tennyson's, it's the ocean voyage, or the quest for the Holy Grail, or whatever, that performs that function. And in Australia it's obviously the Outback, and that's why so many people have written about it as the thing you go into to have the spiritual experience, or the contact with a deeper reality in Nature. And it's a place of ordeal, and vision.

The usual model in Canada is related to Eskimo and Indian practice, which was that at a certain age you were expected to go off by yourself and fast. And in certain Eskimo cultures it was believed that a spirit would come to you, and you would then struggle with the spirit—Jacob and the angel—and if you overcame during that struggle, the spirit would be yours. But if it overcame you, you were in for bad times, trouble.

Defying Distinctions
Karla Hammond

Karla Hammond's interview was conducted July 8, 1978, and originally appeared in *Concerning Poetry.* Copyright © 1978 by *Concerning Poetry.* Reprinted by permission.

Hammond: In a *New York Times* interview, you spoke of your parents' support in expecting you to put to use your skills and intelligence and in not urging you to marry. What myths of patriarchy specifically did they work against?

Atwood: They didn't work specifically against any, because no one in the '40s thought in terms of patriarchal systems. Their attitude was that of Maritimers from Nova Scotia. Maritimers have a large number of universities per capita, and people tend to be readers there. For instance, my aunt, my mother's sister, was the first woman to get an M.A. in History from the University of Toronto. On the other hand, my grandfather felt that my mother was too frivolous to be sent to college. It wasn't that she was a girl; he just felt that she was too frivolous. So she ended up sending herself to college. My parents' attitude, then, was a Maritimers' one: use your intelligence. Indeed, it was a moral injunction; if you don't use your intelligence you're doing something wrong. Specifically and quite practically it was, use your intelligence to get a scholarship to university, because you can do that and we'll feel affronted if you don't.

The orientation of my entire extended family was scientific rather than literary, except for my other aunt, who wrote children's stories and encouraged me when I first began writing. So while the society around me in the '50s was very bent on having girls collect china, become cheerleaders, and get married, my parents were from a different culture. They weren't consciously women's lib. They just believed that it was incumbent on me to become as educated as possible.

Hammond: You didn't attend a full year of school until you were in grade eight. How was this an advantage?

Atwood: I'm very glad that I grew up that way. We spent six to eight months of the year in the bush, and the rest of the time in cities, where

I attended school. At that time no one seemed to object to the fact that children were pulled out of school early in spring and didn't return until late fall. No one thought in terms of "peer groups," or "socialization." School was still lessons and material that you learned. We were able to cover the school course, although we weren't attending the school, because our mother used to be a schoolteacher. She'd taught school in order to earn the money to put herself through college. So she taught us in the mornings and we were able to cover the material in a much shorter period of time than we otherwise would have spent on it. We got the afternoons off. So that was one advantage. The other advantage was that learning wasn't something that you did because you had to do it. I also escaped much of that peer group pressure on girls to be dumb—the idea that it wasn't chic to be intelligent.

The best learning situation for anyone is one-to-one, being taught something that you want to learn because you need the information and being taught by someone whom you love. Even Plato knew that. My brother regularly taught me the things that he himself was learning. The most extreme example of this occurred when he was in high school learning Greek. He attempted to teach me Greek, but it wasn't a success. My father also had a very instructive personality. He taught us informally —just what he happened to be doing at the moment. We learned by observation. We probably spent considerably more time with our father than other children would because he didn't go to an office. He was an entomologist and collected insects in the summer. He would take the family along. He'd put a rubber sheet under a tree, hit the tree with the back of an ax, and the caterpillars and other insects would fall down onto the rubber sheet. Then everyone would pick them up. He was a well-versed naturalist, too. So we learned a number of things informally that we would not otherwise have known. The main advantage was that I didn't feel learning was something that was imposed on me, by a system, from the outside. When I entered fully into the educational system, I resented having to sit in a chair all the time and all the other rules and restraints.

Hammond: You've taught in the "system" yourself—on the college level. How has this affected your writing?

Atwood: I haven't taught since 1972 and before then only sporadically. It affected my writing by giving me less time to write. I couldn't write prose because I couldn't block out those large portions of time that you need for prose. If I teach I prefer to teach a subject which is at some distance from my own concerns, like Victorian literature—the subject I know best.

Hammond: You've mentioned graduate school. Did you get a Ph.D. from Harvard?

Atwood: I've done everything except about a quarter of the thesis. Somehow things came along that I had to write and I did that instead. Also since teaching isn't my life's work, what would be the value of my finishing my thesis? It wouldn't have any monetary or practical value. I will, however, eventually finish it because I like finishing things. But I'd never turn down the chance to write a novel for the chance to finish my thesis. I'll do it sometime in a moment of emptiness or despair. //

Hammond: Did you teach creative writing?

Atwood: I have attempted to do that and it was quite enjoyable. I set up exercises, almost like experiments, to see what would come out. My students enjoyed that because they got things out of themselves that they never thought possible.

But if you're teaching subjects in which you're really heavily involved that you find painful, then teaching becomes an energy drainer. Teaching Canadian literature is painful. I didn't really enjoy writing *Survival*, but I felt that I had to write it because no one else had. If I teach I'd want it to be something unconnected with what I myself do. It's unlikely that I'll ever have that choice again.

Hammond: Earlier you mentioned escaping "peer group pressure," by virtue of your own liberal education, and you've spoken of teaching. As a writer, who are some of the women poets today whose poetry presents women with choices for self-definition in a largely male-defined world?

Atwood: I'm too ignorant to be able to name poets in any kind of categorizing way, but some of the women whose work I read and admire are: Anne Hebert, P. K. Page, Jay Macpherson, Margaret Avison, Phyllis Webb, Gwendolyn MacEwen (the preceding are all Canadian poets)... Adrienne Rich, Marge Piercy, Rosellen Brown, Annie Dillard ... any list I could give would be incomplete at best. I'm sure there are many, many more. This has been a hotly debated issue in the United States. In the United States you can say "feminism" and you can draw a line around it and go inside it and there you are. There are so many people in your country that you can form a fairly isolated subculture. In Canada it's much harder to do that because everyone's so saturated with the problems of Canada at the moment that it's difficult to pull away from that and say, "That doesn't concern me. I'm going to do

nothing but feminism." I see the two issues as similar. In fact, I see
feminism as part of a large issue: human dignity. That's what Canadian
nationalism is about, what feminism is about, and what black power is
about. They're all part of the same vision.

Hammond: How do you respond to feminist critics' conviction that men
are knowers and women are practical doers?

Atwood: I've never run across that one. I would think that most feminists
would object to that distinction. Women have been practical doers in
many societies, as have men. They've also been knowers. Anything that
states, Thus shall you be because of your set of genitals—whether it's said
by feminists or others—is going to be limiting. No society is above making
these distinctions. Earlier this year, I heard Margaret Mead give a lecture
in which she said that this is the first attempt that has ever been made
in the history of human society to say that everyone can do everything;
roles in previous societies have always been divided according to sex. It
wasn't always women who cooked and men who were merchants. She did
say, however, that few societies have given weapons to women and sent
them out to war. The division is there partly so that men can say they're
men. It's very easy to say that you're a woman. People use the term "real
woman," but it doesn't have the same connotation as "real man." If you're
not a "real man" you're not a man. If you're not a "real woman"—that
is, someone's idea of desirable femininity—you're still a woman. No one
says that you're a non-woman. "Real woman" may mean good woman
or acceptable woman. But if you're not a "real man," something's missing.
Men worry much more about their maleness than women worry about
their femaleness. We all know we've got femaleness. The question is
what to do with it. Many of these distinctions have been made by men.

Hammond: "Backdrop Addresses Cowboy" raises an interesting concept
of woman as space desecrated.

Atwood: That poem is about Canada. What is being desecrated may in
fact be female, but it's also a particular place. The cowboy is a familiar
symbol. The poem was written in the era of Lyndon Johnson, and the
border is more than just a decorative frame in the poem. It's an actual
border between one place and another as well as being a metaphor. So
it isn't just about women. //

Hammond: "Marrying the Hangman" is a poem which many people
familiar with your work frequently cite and are excited about. Could

you tell me something about the origin of this poem, how you came to write it, how long it took to be written, etc.?

Atwood: It's coming out in my new book, *Two-Headed Poems*, in the fall (1978) in Canada. It will be published later in the States. It will also be appearing in the October (1978) issue of *Ms. Magazine*. It's based on an actual historical event. In the eighteenth century, in Quebec, there were only two ways to avoid being hanged if you'd been condemned to death by hanging. One was to take the position of the hangman, if the position was vacant and if you were a man. The second was to marry the hangman, if you were a woman and the hangman was unmarried. You could not, however, become the hangman if you were a woman. There was a woman who was lodged next to a man in prison. She had been condemned to death by hanging for the offense of petty theft. The man, however, had not been condemned to death. He was only incarcerated for dueling. But she talked him into taking the position of hangman, which was vacant, and then into marrying her. So the poem is based on that event and it takes off from there.

A friend of mine saw the story in *The Dictionary of Canadian Biography* and sent it to me. I didn't do anything with it for a long time, but then one day a number of other things came together and I just wrote the poem in one fell swoop! It took me about an afternoon. I didn't revise it much. I added a couple of little clarifying details and I added one word to one of the catalogs, but apart from that it stayed the same.

Hammond: In *Survival* you've explained that Canadian poets prefer drowning as a "natural" means of dispatching their victims because it is useful "as a metaphor for a descent into the unconscious." Both your fiction and your poetry is characterized by drowning scenes, i.e. in *Surfacing* and in "This Is a Photograph of Me." Is it a way of cutting through false memories?

Atwood: Too complex a question. Canadian poets have used quite a few drownings. They also like freezings to death. Drowning and freezing. In Quebec they prefer people to burn up. It's just a very, very general statement. It doesn't really mean anything except in that general manner of critical statement that causes people to react and contradict you. I'd have to take each poem and point out the differences. //

Hammond: You've spoken of Poe as an influence?

Atwood: That's a joke. I usually say that in speaking of this high school period, when we weren't taught any Canadian literature or any modern literature. In writing poetry your idea of a poem is defined by what you've read, what has been given to you. So, in saying Poe, I also mean Byron, Shelley, Tennyson, and others whom we read at that time. I didn't get to T. S. Eliot until college. My early poems are all rhythmically regular. They rhyme. A number of them have the galloping rhythms of "The Destruction of Sennacharib."

Hammond: You've said, "I don't think of poetry as a 'rational' activity but as an aural one." Does the aural quality of a line alone determine line length and line breaks?

Atwood: Poetry is primarily oral in that it was oral first in human societies and it's oral first when a child is learning language. Children learn to recite, chant, and make up their own verse long before they learn to read. While speed reading may be very helpful for reading business reports, it's impossible to speed read poetry because you have to do the equivalent of moving your lips when you read. You're sounding out the poem and anyone who just scans it visually is missing the whole point. If you can't get the aural quality right, then the poem will be wrong; not that the play between the visual line, as it appears on the page, and how you hear it, isn't important—it is! //

Hammond: In any given poem are style and meaning inseparable—that is, if one changes, the other inevitably changes?

Atwood: Yes, that's why it's annoying to find that people, teaching our work in high school, say, "Make a précis of this poem, twenty-five words or less: 'What does it mean?'" That antagonizes the students because they think, "If all it meant was that love is difficult, spring is nice, or war is hell, why did the poet go to all this trouble to hide it from us?" Anyone who teaches that way doesn't take language seriously. They believe in abstractions.

Hammond: Does your work incorporate elements of surrealism, i.e. dream imagery, obscure humor, anti-rhetoric statements, fantasy land-scapes, obscure abstractions, a non-repressive vision of reality?

Atwood: You can have all these characteristics that you mention in work that's not necessarily surrealistic in the classic sense. Literature itself does these things. I try to avoid obscure abstractions when I can. Of course, every poet thinks they're being clear. But I would certainly never delib-erately be obscure. That's cheating. It's mannerist.

Hammond: In your Afterword to *The Journals of Susanna Moodie*, you explained that these poems were "generated by a dream." Have any other poems come to you in dreams or evolved out of dreams?

Atwood: Yes, I have several. I could tell you what they were if you felt it would be of interest; but it's not really very useful because it doesn't make the difference between a good poem and a bad one. Dreams, in themselves, are usually quite incoherent.

Hammond: Through what means other than dream have poems come to you, i.e., conversations overheard, dialogue, correspondence, research, pure observation?

Atwood: Those factors are more related to the way in which I write prose. I'm a magpie with prose. I collect little pieces of information, overheard conversations. A poem, however, is generated by a word or a phrase. I've said this before, but I'll repeat my metaphor. It's like dipping a thread into a supersaturated solution. If you do that, the supersaturated solution will form crystals on the thread. From the language the poem condenses. All these other bits and pieces, you mentioned, are floating in the language. So if they happen to attach themselves to that thread, yes. But that isn't what has generated the poem and it isn't what generates the novel. For me, a novel is generated by a certain vision, which may be a scene or a character. The things you mentioned are what I write down on scraps of paper and put at the side of my desk because they may come in useful sometime... road signs, brand names, lettering on people's tee shirts. They're of linguistic interest. There's a man here who has a tee shirt that says, "Occam's Razor."

Hammond: Stanley Kunitz has spoken of the originality of a poem determined by that individual discovering his or her own "key images." Would you agree that mirrors/glass, snow, green, maps, blood, totems, games are key images for you?

Atwood: They certainly recur. I don't ever talk about that because it's too determining of the future. Also since you've stated "key images," people are always using them against you. Once a statement to that effect has appeared in print you can never get rid of it. It follows you around forever.

Hammond: Is the poet, by virtue of the craft, part theoretician and part philosopher?

Atwood: I don't know. I try to avoid defining what the poet is. As soon as you define what the poet is, someone else comes along and contradicts it.

Hammond: When I asked Nancy Willard whether the advent of the prose poem had made it more difficult to discern what is prose and what is poetry, she said you'd given a good criterion.

Atwood: The unit of the poem is the syllable. The unit in a prose work—a short story or a novel—is something much larger. It may be the character or the paragraph. Formally it may be the paragraph, but then you're working with very large building blocks—things that may appear on page fifty and again on page one hundred. It's a very large structure. With the prose poem, the unit is still the syllable, but the difference between a prose poem and a short story for me is that the prose poem is still concerned with that rhythmical syllabic structure. You're as meticulous about the syllables in a prose poem as you are in a poem. If the syllables aren't right, then the whole thing is wrong. In prose fiction, the effects that are occurring are different. You may have someone saying something quite ugly that sounds ugly because that's the way people speak.

Hammond: What are some of the striking differences in approach to poetry and prose? Can one of the dangers of being both novelist and poet be that one may tend to write a poetic prose?

Atwood: I don't work on poetry when I'm writing novels. The verbal energy that would otherwise go into poetry goes into the novel. I have working habits when I'm writing a novel, but not when I'm writing poetry. I can't talk about theme and style generally.

As to the dangers, there's greater danger in being reviewed in a certain way. If reviewers know you write poetry, then they say, "This is poetic prose"; whereas, if you don't write poetry, they may never say that. For example, I can't remember ever reading that about *Ulysses*, in which Joyce used prose in a very rhythmic way. Unfortunately, you can't prevent the way in which your work is reviewed. If you're writing as a novelist, when you're self-editing you'll delete passages that don't fit the novel.

As for writing habits, my ideal place for writing is an isolated place. If I'm writing a novel I like to have at least two hours a day, hopefully four. Late in the life of the book, six to eight hours. I use pieces of paper, a writing implement which can be a pencil or a ball-point pen, and a typewriter. That's why people don't think that poets and novelists need very large grants. They don't have to buy paint. I write on scrap paper in longhand. The first step in revision is typing it. I'm a poor typist. Still, if I were a good touch typist, I'd miss a lot of things. As it is, I'm very involved in the texture of what I'm typing and have to look at it all the time.

Hammond: You've said that *Surfacing* "does not exist for the sake of making a statement but to tell a story." Is this true of your poetry as well?

Atwood: What I was trying to say was that it is a novel and not a sermon. The same applies to poetry.

Hammond: The characters in your novels have frequently been labeled as victims and survivors. Would it be accurate to ascribe such categorization to the speakers of your poems—in a volume such as *Power Politics*?

Atwood: People have taken *Survival* and applied it to my work. This can sometimes be bothersome because one doesn't always like one's insights as a critic being applied to one's work, from which they weren't drawn. They were drawn from reading books by other people.

For instance, take the woman in *Lady Oracle*; I don't think that she's either of those. She's not particularly a victim. Although she's a survivor, I wouldn't say that that's what categorizes her. Certainly many of her complicated problems are caused, not by her victimhood or her survivorhood, but by her romanticism. She's someone who is attempting to act out a romantic myth we're all handed as women in a non-romantic world. I'm interested in the Gothic novel because it's very much a woman's form. Why is there such a wide readership for books that essentially say, "Your husband is trying to kill you"? People aren't interested in pop culture books out of pure random selection. They connect with something real in people's lives.

Hammond: Science fiction, too.

Atwood: It's true of science fiction which is not particularly an inarticulate form anymore; it's become a fairly rarefied form. But it's certainly true of *True Romance* magazines which are—although sometimes in a more dramatic and bizarre form—about what happens in the lives of those who are reading them. There's usually an area of reality in popular literature that's hooking into the reality in the lives of the readers. Even Harlequin Romances. Those books are about the dream that we all secretly have—that everything can work out, that everything can be happy, that there is a Mr. Wonderful who does exist. The Gothic form centers on *My husband is trying to kill me*, and that's of great interest when you think about it. The story of *Jane Eyre* is really still with us, as are the four characters in it. The mad wife is still with us. The question is, at what point does the orphan turn into the mad wife? How long does she have to be married to Mr. Rochester before she turns into the mad wife?

Hammond: Would you comment on the theme of appearance and reality in your work?

Atwood: I'd prefer not to say anything about that because some poor teacher is going to have to wade through a number of badly written term papers that take off from whatever I might say. It's too general a statement. From my work and the remarks that I've made about it, you probably realize that I don't necessarily think there's only one appearance vs. only one reality. It's fun to write about Henry James's novels that way because people are always putting on social fronts in them; then you discover that what's really occurring is horrifying and appalling. But in our society people don't put on social fronts very much. They're likely to reveal their whole life to you in about the first half hour of sitting beside you on a bus. So it isn't that they're hiding anything; it's just that the true story of their life is used as a defense. No longer do we have those closets with skeletons in them which we had in the Victorian period. Everyone is quite fond of their skeletons. They take them out and parade them around so that everyone can commiserate with them.

Hammond: In what genre other than prose and poetry or critical articles, reviews, etc., have your written?

Atwood: Just about everything that you've mentioned except plays. I've never written a play set in modern times. I wrote them as a child. Nor have I written one of those factual nonfiction books like *How My Leg Fell Off and I Learned to Talk Again*, or a biography, or an autobiography. Don't know that I ever will.

Articulating the Mute
Karla Hammond

Karla Hammond's interview was conducted July 8, 1978, and originally appeared in *The American Poetry Review* 8 (1979). Copyright © 1979 by Karla Hammond. Reprinted by permission.

Hammond: You've mentioned in another interview a dark period between the ages of eight and sixteen when you didn't write.

Atwood: When I said a "dark period" between the ages of eight and sixteen when I didn't write, it was partly a joke. At four, five, six, and seven years of age, I was just writing comic strips, little poems, stories and plays. Between eight and sixteen I was interested in other careers. First, I wanted to be a painter. Next I wanted to be a dress designer. Then I went to high school and got hit with the concept of having to earn my own living. My extra option at school was Home Economics. I chose Home Economics because the guidance book presented five possible careers for women: airline stewardess, school teacher—preferably public—nurse, secretary, and home economist. Of the five, home economist was the least distasteful and the most sensible financially to me. It didn't occur to me that I might be a writer. In fact, at the time, I didn't really write anything except for school essays. At sixteen I started writing poetry. I don't know why I wrote; there certainly weren't any role models around.

Hammond: Did your early work come out of "nationalistic consciousness"?

Atwood: There was no nationalistic consciousness in Canada at that time. It didn't arise until the mid-sixties. We were taught very little Canadian writing or history in school. This is why nationalistic consciousness emerged. It's often difficult for Americans to understand because they've had the opposite experience. They've been so inculcated with the American ethic that their deepest wish is to become international. But, as Canadians, we were international already and still are. We receive more world news and more publications from different countries than you do. We're much more eclectic in our total behavior, so that a shortage of internationalism for us isn't the problem. The problem is nationalism. It isn't a question of dominating other countries; it's impossible given Canada's size. Someone who hasn't seen how close we came to extinction and how close we are to it now, just can't understand. They think we're being narrow or belligerent; whereas all we're saying is, "We exist." Not that we're better, just that we're different. Similarly women have been saying, "We exist. We don't wish particularly to be defined by you."

Hammond: Has life in the Ontario and Quebec northland given you a distinct sense of a personal mythology?

Atwood: The main thrust of Canadian poetry over the last fifteen or twenty years has been to articulate the mute; so I'm really not very interested in a personal mythology. If you were put down in a place where you'd never been before you'd probably be more interested in figuring out the place than you would be in figuring out yourself. You can only indulge in the luxury of figuring out yourself when you're oriented in space and time. Canada was a country that lacked such orientation.

Hammond: Winter is a frequent landscape in your poems. Is it because, as you explain in *Survival*, winter is the "real" season?

Atwood: Although it's not true in Vancouver, in the part of Canada in which I live and over most of the country, there are only three months of the year when it almost definitely won't snow: June, July and August. Most of the time the snow stops in April and doesn't start until October or November. But it may stop as late as May. It snowed on May 20th in 1976. Winter is the real season because it's the prevalent season in Canada.

When I was in India the people there asked me why green was so important a color in my poetry. I asked them what the opposite of green was for them and we concluded that brown was the opposite of green. When the foliage ceases being green it becomes brown. But when the landscape ceases being green in Canada it becomes white. So the visual alternation in Canada is not green/brown (or green/blue as it is in Hawaii), but green/white. Winter is important in my work because winter is important in the place where I write. Water is important in my work because if you look at an aerial map of Canada, you will see that there is more water per square mile there than in almost any other country on earth. Therefore, the key element for Canada is water. I suspect that the key element for the United States is fire.

Hammond: You have a number of references to maps. But do you have an interest in cartography apart from poetry?

Atwood: From what I've said about Canada you should be able to figure out why I have an interest in maps. The map is a usable metaphor for locating where you are. I suspect maps will become less important in my present and future work because of my past usage of them. I'm interested in geology and geography apart from poetry—not just the drawing of maps, but looking at maps and seeing where places are in relation to each other. That's often more important than you realize. For instance, if you look at Afghanistan (where Graeme and I were just before the coup) and if you can think of Afghanistan by itself that's one thing. But if you see that it adjoins Russia to the North, China to the East, the Indian subcontinent to the South, and Iran to the West, you'll realize that, in fact, it's a very strategically located country. I enjoy visiting places where historical events of significance have happened. I liked going to Kabul because one of the greatest military disasters of the nineteenth century, or indeed of modern times, took place there. Namely the retreat of the British from Kabul in 1842. Sixteen thousand men set out and one arrived. The rest were all killed.

Hammond: You speak of poetry as a lens—indeed, you use images of glass and mirrors in your work. How is your work a reflection of Canadian culture or consciousness?

Atwood: A lens isn't a mirror. A lens can be a magnifying or focusing lens, but it doesn't merely give a reflection. It gives a condensation. Mirrors are, in fact, quite tricky because they give a backwards reflection; whereas a lens does something else. So I think of my poetry as a lens rather than as a mirror, although the literary culture, as a whole, often acts like a mirror of the society. I recognize my work more as a distillation or a focusing. But that isn't the only level on which art should function, the national level. A novel, in order to be successful, has to first hold the attention of the reader; second, it has to function on the level of the language in which it's composed. If the use of the language is terrible you're going to have a poor novel regardless of the consciousness it's reflecting or focusing. The same is true for women's work.

No culture exists apart from the ground in which it's rooted, but it doesn't stay there. "Universal" literature is always rooted in the particular. Russian novels come out of Russia. Canadian ones come out of Canada! It seems very simple to say.

Hammond: In *Words and Women*, Casey Miller and Kate Swift have a chapter entitled "The Specter of Unisex," in which they are speaking of an unsexed tongue. Miller and Swift speak of a book such as *Charlotte's Web* which by its "male orientation and use of subsuming masculine terms" no longer reflects reality. Miller and Swift are arguing that women want a tongue that includes them as well.

Atwood: Unfortunately, we're stuck with language and, by and large, it determines our categories. Poets generally are working with the expansion and elaboration of the language. When the Anglo-Saxons didn't have a word for something they made one up. That's not outside the English tradition. It's also a matter of word arrangement. A word isn't separate from its context. That's why I say language is a solution, something in which you're immersed, rather than a dictionary. There are little constellations of language here and there, and the meaning of a word changes according to its context in its constellation. The word *woman* already has changed because of the different constellations that have been made around it. Language changes within our lifetime. As a writer you're part of that process—using an old language, but making new patterns with it. Your choices are numerous.

Hammond: Have any women influenced your consciousness of a poetics?

Atwood: Yes. Influences occur in your first ten formative years. In Canada, some of the most interesting and prominent writers are women, and this has always been true. It's impossible to teach Canadian literature and ignore women. I first read a Quebec poet, Anne Hebert, in French and in English translation. Her poetry is wonderful—and very un-English. It's highly surrealistic, characterized by marvelous condensed imagery. I recommend it—particularly a poem called "The Tomb of the Kings." Another poet whom I read was P. K. Page. If you could see her poems, you'd understand why she was an influence. Jay Macpherson, a personal friend of mine, influenced me in that she was there; she was visible. It's all very well to have Elizabeth Barrett Browning and Charlotte Bronte kicking around in the nineteenth century, but to actually be able to look at someone and say, that person has published a book! You can't imagine how important that was to a Canadian living at that time, because of the dearth of poets and books available. Jay had a library, and I read poetry that I probably otherwise wouldn't have been able to read or have known about. Margaret Avison published a book, *Winter Sun*, which I reviewed in 1960 when I was in college. She's a very accomplished poet. I should mention Phyllis Webb and Gwendolyn MacEwen, another contemporary. You notice they're all Canadian.

Hammond: Is there a particular woman poet with whom you feel any affinity?

Atwood: Tends to be Adrienne Rich. Partly because everyone in the entire universe seems to have decided that whenever Adrienne Rich publishes a book I must review it. I don't know why this has happened. But I've reviewed her frequently in Canada and in the States, most recently in *The New York Times*. I have all her books and I've followed her through the years. She's very good. But my reading of American poetry tends to be accidental—whatever comes through the mail. For obvious reasons I know more about the women than about the men. I've read and reviewed Marge Piercy's work. But I do read American male poets, for instance, Robert Bly.

Hammond: Has your work been compared to Marge Piercy's or Colette Inez's?

Atwood: No. It's been compared to Sylvia Plath's. For a while Sylvia Plath took the place of Emily Dickinson. You could tell when someone had read only one or two women poets. They would either say that you were like Emily Dickinson or you weren't like Emily Dickinson. Then they were saying that you were like Sylvia Plath or that you weren't like Sylvia Plath.

Hammond: When I interviewed Karen Swenson we both agreed that women are more aware of their personal relationships as daughter, wife, sister, mother. Karen said that men, on the other hand, are always writing about their relationship with Nature. // Is "Dream 2: Brian the Still-Hunter": "but every time I aim, I feel / my skin grow fur / my head heavy with antlers" meant to suggest male identification with Nature?

Atwood: Men don't have to write about nature either. They could always say, "blood flows through my toes. I'm part of the lunar cycle." Many women write about their relationship to nature. Women might be more likely to say, "I am like the pumpkin" rather than "I am like the porcupine." The only way that you would ever prove something like that is by taking all the poems written by men and women and running them through a computer. General statements should only be made so that other people can agree with them.

In the "Arctic Syndrome: dream fox" poem, "arctic syndrome" is the name of a specific kind of madness that occurs only north of the Arctic Circle, in which the person becomes a fox or a wolf. It's indulged in by

52172

men and women. Ways of going crazy are culturally determined. This
happens to be an Innuit form of insanity.

"Dream 2: Brian the Still-Hunter" grew out of an anecdote in Susanna
Moodie's first book. A man named Brian the Still-Hunter used to come
and talk to Susanna Moodie every once in a while and he said this,
although not exactly in those words. He said that whenever he was aiming
at a deer he felt that he was, in fact, related to the deer. // So "Brian the
Still-Hunter" isn't about male identification with nature, necessarily; it's
from a real anecdote. This man was suicidal. He was always trying to
kill himself by cutting his throat with a knife.

Hammond: "The Explorers" and "The Settlers" suggest the transformation that occurred in *Surfacing* in a passage such as "The animals have
no need for speech, why talk when you are a word I lean against a tree,
I am a tree leaning." "Resurrection" suggests a final vision of this: "at
the last / judgment we will all be trees."

Atwood: "The Explorers" and "The Settlers" were written around 1964.
I wrote *Surfacing* in about 1970. So they're spaced in time. The relationships to the landscape are very different in "The Explorers" and "The
Settlers"—when the people have become part of the landscape by being
buried in it. The same is true for "Resurrection." The only way the
speaker could actually get into the landscape was by dying. In *Surfacing*
it's a visionary experience in which language is transformed. There was
some Indian influence on *Surfacing* at that point. //

Hammond: Has Indian myth or folklore influenced your poetic vision?

Atwood: Yes, I'm interested in it. It's one of the ways of viewing woman
and nature now available to us. The view previously available was the
Biblical relation between man, woman, and nature. That certainly dominated Western society for many years. Now, living where we do, there's
another perspective, but it isn't the only other perspective.

Hammond: Is there anything that you'd like to say about female literary
myths?

Atwood: Myths mean stories, and traditional myths mean traditional
stories that have been repeated frequently. The term doesn't pertain to
Greek myths alone. *Grimm's Fairy Tales* are just as much myth or story
as anything else. But some get repeated so often in the society that they
become definitive, i.e. myths of that society. Certainly Biblical ones have

been very important in our society. We all know what the Bible's attitude toward women is. However, I wasn't brought up a Christian, so I wasn't deeply affected by those beliefs, except insofar as they were held by the general culture. If I were going to convert to any religion I would probably choose Catholicism because it at least has female saints and the Virgin Mary. It does have a visible set of sacred female objects, whereas Calvinistic Protestantism doesn't. It is monolithically male.

When I was visiting Mexico, sometime ago, I visited a church there. In this church there were about six Virgin Marys—one for every occasion: one dressed in white for when you're feeling happy, one wearing blue. You'd pray to each for a different reason. Then there was one in black and you prayed to her when all the others had failed. They all had little tin arms, legs, pigs, and cows pinned on them, which were offerings that people had made when the Virgin had saved something of theirs.

The other alternative would be to become a Quaker, because you're not given any images: you're given a relationship to the divine. While there is a God the Father, women do participate in the religion.

Really I'm a pantheist.

The unexpurgated *Grimm's Fairy Tales* contain a number of fairy tales in which women are not only the central characters but win by using their own intelligence. Some people feel fairy tales are bad for women. This is true if the only ones they're referring to are those tarted-up French versions of "Cinderella" and "Bluebeard," in which the female protagonist gets rescued by her brothers. But in many of them, women rather than men have the magic powers.

Hammond: In *Signs* you've explained that you're not a theologian and yet your poetry as well as your fiction is imbued with a sense of mysticism. If you feel any affinity to religion is it more a sense of ritualistic/tribal/primitive incantation than institutional allegiance?

Atwood: Yes, by default. I have no institutional allegiance. My background is scientific. Much of what you may interpret as mysticism is simply science translated into a literary form. In other words, if you take a physicist and push him far enough he will get to something that is pretty close to what you might call mysticism. If you take a crystallographer, working in the higher reaches of crystallography, you'll arrive at the same resolution where the difference between matter and energy ceases to exist; ergo, mysticism—if you wish! I could call it science and you would probably feel that's the opposite of mysticism, but if you went far enough left and far enough right you would probably meet because you'd have a circle. Still, no one knows whether the universe is circular or not.

Hammond: What bearing does the preceding question and answer have on your lines: "there is nothing for us to worship" and "my wooden fossil God"? Is this an indictment of patriarchal religion? What beliefs of a matriarchal religious consciousness might serve as a basis for a future feminist theology?

Atwood: The subject of matriarchal religions interests me, but it isn't something with which I'm preoccupied because I'm just not a theologian. These forms appeal to me mythologically. With a male theology you had an exaltation of men, placing women in a secondary position. Would a matriarchal theology exalt women and give men a secondary place? If so, I'm not interested because it would be the same problem in reverse. It wouldn't interest me to have all the priests be women and all the altar boys be men. I'd prefer an egalitarian or human religion. Women are interested in female religious figures now simply because we've starved for them, but that doesn't mean that we should desacralize men and that women should be made sacred. There's no point in destroying a male child instead of a female one.

Hammond: Suzanne Juhasz in *Modern American Poetry by Women: A New Tradition* writes: "To be a woman poet in our society is a double-bind situation, one of conflict and strain. For the words 'woman' and 'poet' denote opposite and contradictory qualities and roles. Traditionally, the poet is a man, and 'poetry' is the poems that men write." Could you comment?

Atwood: It's part of the American tradition. I can see why an American woman would say that, because I'm familiar with those university courses: Romantic writers, all men. Then they'd include Emily Dickinson. Even now American universities habitually ignore women writers in favor of men. It isn't that Canadian men are nicer or less sexist. They would have done that in Canada, too, if they could have. But they couldn't because the tradition was already fairly heavily populated by women. So while they might sneer, they couldn't ignore them. When you look at a Canadian anthology, it's usually a quarter to a third women. Now that's not a half, but it's a quarter to a third. It was similar in the nineteenth-century English literature that I studied. You couldn't teach the nineteenth-century English novel without putting in Jane Austen, the Brontes, and George Eliot. So I never had the feeling that women were excluded from literature by necessity or fate. I did, however, feel that there was a conflict in the woman writer's own life. You would come to a fork in the road where you'd be forced to make a decision: "woman" or "writer." I chose being a writer, because I was very determined, even though it was very painful for me then (the late '50s and early '60s), but I'm very glad that I made that decision because the other alternative would have been ultimately much more painful: it's more painful to renounce your gifts or your direction in life than it is to renounce an individual.

People a little bit older than myself wrote in cupboards at night because they didn't want anyone to know that they were writing or criticize them for taking that time away from their family. They tried to fulfill all their roles. When they gained recognition, they would immediately have marital difficulties because their husbands couldn't deal with their success. So I felt that if I were going to marry or form a permanent relationship that that individual had to know, from the beginning, who I was and what I was doing. I wasn't going to conceal it. Many people thought I was really quite cold and perhaps I am in a very specific way. It's a necessary protective device.

Hammond: You said *Surfacing* was reviewed in the United States "almost exclusively as a feminist or ecological treatise. In Canada it was reviewed almost exclusively as a nationalistic one." Has this been true of the poetry as well? How does the Canadian reviewer's consciousness of poetic issues differ from the American's?

Atwood: A Canadian reviewer is reviewing my work from within the culture in which it was written. An American reviewer is reviewing it from outside that culture. The difficulty arises when the American reviewer doesn't recognize that. Americans have a tendency to regard anything written in English, on the North American continent, as being essentially American, or even "universal." In encountering various cultures that write but don't necessarily speak English, you realize that there isn't only one literature being written in English. There's nearly thirteen. Canadian English literature is written in English, but it's also written in Canada. Although Canadian poets deal with so-called universal themes, our literature has a shape and direction of its own. When you have an American reviewer who is conscious of that, then you get an intelligent, informed review. When you get an American reviewer who doesn't know that, you may get an intelligent review but an uninformed one. Many American reviewers mistake poems that are, in fact, about the culture or about nationalistic consciousness for poems that are written as personal or confessional revelations.

In Canada you have a technology that comes into the country from the outside and is essentially a foreign technology. Not that Canada doesn't have a technology of its own, but not much of it originates there. There are many influences and physical objects introduced or generated by foreigners. It isn't that we aren't good at messing up our own landscape —we can do that adequately, given the opportunity—but much of that is being done for us.

But to get back to being reviewed... I've been reviewed in the most viciously sexist ways—more so in Canada than in the States because American reviewers are suaver about the way they attack people. I've been called a Medusa, an Octopus, etc. The attack being: here is a woman who doesn't use words in a soft, compliant way; therefore, she is an evil witch. And I'm tired of it; but it's impossible to educate them. You're getting someone who really has a tremendous fear of women.

Hammond: You have written: "The duty of the critic is to society, but the primary duty of the writer is to the thing being made." Can you elaborate?

Atwood: It's a statement about writing derived from my own background and the fact that Canada is a very political country where people frequently indicate what they feel writers ought to be doing. You always have to say first that a writer is a writer. A writer isn't a preacher, a politician, or a lawyer. If they're a bad writer—regardless of the attractiveness of their ideas—they're still a bad writer.

Hammond: In *Survival* you mention novels which deal with the situation of the artist attempting "to function in Canadian society." In each case the artist is portrayed as a handicapped individual. What changes in the last decade or so have made it possible for the artist in Canada to function more effectively or is exile still necessary for survival?

Atwood: There's been a tremendous change in the past fifteen years. The works I covered in *Survival* were written or conceived before that change took place. Before, writers lived in isolation and were ignored. Generally, they were one-book writers. Everything that Tillie Olsen discusses in her forthcoming book, *Silences*, happened not only to women in Canada but to all Canadian writers. With a large reading public now, that has changed. Writers know each other. Prose writers have a Union. Poets have a League. They get together once yearly. The country is small enough so that you can have them all in an organization and get them all into a room. It's now possible to have a sense of literary community. The artist isn't the isolated, invisible person whom I described in that chapter.

Society, however, although it has seen the possibility for change, has not effectively changed. Canada is still a colony, although now it has recognized its own colonialism. The parallel with the Women's Movement is pretty accurate. Now we've had all the definitions, but the wage difference between men and women is still very large. Canadians have had the books on colonization, but most of their industry is still owned by the United States. The power is held by people other than those having the realization. In the case of women, it's men; in the case of Canada, it's Americans.

Hammond: Political oppression and tyranny seem to be personal as well as poetic issues for you.

Atwood: It's almost impossible for a Canadian not to be involved in politics, because the place is saturated with it. If I lived in the States, I'd feel differently. Americans often feel that the system is so enormous that there isn't much they as individuals can do. In attempting anything individually, they get kicked around, bombed, maced, or else their candidate gets defeated. They can go off on a hill and meditate and everyone will approve of their uninvolvement in politics. In Canada you're involved because the climate is political.

Hammond: Could you speak about your involvement in Amnesty International?

Atwood: It's one of those organizations in which you're involved because although you realize that political imprisonment and torture may not characterize your own country, should it ever happen you'll want a neutral organization to speak for the victims. I'm not active at the organizational end. I'm a member-at-large.

Hammond: Is poetry a means of translating power into social and political forms?

Atwood: No, it's the reverse. Social and political forms get translated into poetry. If you want to change the world, you do not choose poetry as the means for accomplishing it. In Latin America, however, writing a poem can be an act of enormous courage because the penalty for doing so could be death. But let's not delude ourselves about the nature of the society in which we live. Here one doesn't get killed for writing poetry. As for "Poetry must be a weapon in the hands of the people," that's true only in certain countries where speech is controlled. Writing a poem against the government and circulating it is, in fact, an explosive act because it allows people to think differently. In our society everyone has numerous forms of thought available to them; thus, thought itself is not taken very seriously. Essentially, the government doesn't care what you write. It doesn't care about poetry. Canadian society, however, cares about poetry more per capita than American society does. American poets are often voices in a desert, shouting at the tops of their lungs, convinced that no one can hear them. Such a conviction affects what they shout. Certain women poets and black poets are different. They believe people are listening to them. In fact, people are listening to them. You can articulate change but it's already happening. You can make change a possibility in the imagination, but you can't effect change the way a law can effect change.

Hammond: Carol P. Christ has asked you: "Is the traditional identification of women and nature a legacy of oppression or a potential source of power and vision?" Comment?

Atwood: It's a potential source of power and vision. The oppression isn't in nature; it's in what people have done to nature. To ask that question is to also ask, Is being a woman necessarily to be oppressed? The oppression doesn't come from within the fact of being a woman. It comes from outside that fact. Of course that separation is only theoretical. The oppression is in people's attitudes towards nature. You aren't and can't be apart from nature. We're all part of the biological universe: men as well as women.

So my answer would be that it's a potential source of power and vision —partly because the alternative is to lock yourself away or become a machine. And that isn't practical or plausible for anyone—men or women.

Just Looking at Things That Are There
Alan Twigg

Alan Twigg's interview was conducted in 1979, in Vancouver, British Columbia, and originally appeared in his collection *Strong Voices: Conversations with Fifty Canadian Authors* (Harbour Publishing, 1988). Copyright © 1988 by Alan Twigg. Reprinted by permission.

Twigg: Did you come from a relatively typical liberal background?

Atwood: I came from a very isolated background. This is probably the key to some of my writing. I grew up isolated from society in a kind and non-violent family of scientists. When I hit society I was shocked. I'm probably still in a state of culture shock.

Twigg: And you always will be?

Atwood: Probably. Because I was only exposed to a small range of human behavior, the good side. But the bad side is pretty bad. If you grow up being told, "On Saturdays we burn crosses on people's lawns," then you can't be so easily shocked. You become numb to it. "On Fridays we go down to the corner bar and beat each other up and then we go and kill Jews or Catholics or Blacks or whatever." You can get hardened to that kind of thing. But I've never become hardened. So whatever radicalism I possess comes out of that.

Twigg: What's radical about *Life Before Man* is that it's the first Canadian novel I know of that seriously conveys an awareness that the human race can become extinct. Was that a conscious theme while writing the book?

Atwood: Yes. It's why the novel is set in the Royal Ontario Museum. And why Lesje is a paleontologist who studies dinosaurs.

Twigg: And why the characters exhibit predatory behavior?

Atwood: Absolutely. Not just the character of Elizabeth but also how our society encourages people to be that way.

Twigg: With a book like *Life Before Man* and a movie like *Apocalypse Now!*, I wonder if we're heading into an age of examining ourselves for evil.

Atwood: Being aware of how awful we can be might be a self-preservation technique. Certainly when you do that it stops you from turning other people into the devil. You're unlikely to say that everything is the fault of the Germans or any other group you want to use as a scapegoat.

Twigg: Our scapegoat in Canada has always been the United States. *Life Before Man* resembles *Surfacing* in that regard because it really helps dispel that pretension that Canadians are somehow morally superior.

Atwood: People can be morally superior when they are in a position of relative powerlessness. For instance, if you're a woman being victimized then you can afford moral superiority. But once you have power, you have to take responsibility. Some of your decisions may be harmful to others. I think Canada has been able to afford moral superiority because it's been relatively powerless. I don't think, and I never have thought, that Canada's inherently better. In fact, all you have to do is look at its past record. Scratch the country and it's quite a fascist place. Look at the attitudes to the War Measures Act or the RCMP opening the mail. Canada's not a goody-goody land of idealists. If we got to a position where we needed some witches to burn, I'm sure we'd find some and burn them. That's why I find Canada potentially a somewhat scary place. Underneath, we're not much different from anywhere else.

You look at mankind and you see something like Dante's *The Divine Comedy*. You see the Inferno at one end with everybody pulling out each other's fingernails, as in the Amnesty International bulletins. Or you see the Purgatorio, shaped like a mountain, with people climbing up it or sitting still. Up at the top there's what used to be called Heaven with what used to be called God. Only now we've replaced Heaven with a kind of Utopian vision of what humanity could be if only . . . Fill in the blank. The trouble with real life is once you try to implement Utopia, you end up with the Inferno. You end up pulling out a lot of fingernails from the people who don't agree with you. That is, as we say, the Human Condition. That was the catch-all phrase when I was in graduate school. Whenever you came to the point at which you didn't know why things were the way they were, you said that was the Human Condition.

Twigg: Was this new novel called *Life Before Man* from the start?

Atwood: No, it was originally called *Notes on the Mezaoic.* Mezaoic means "middle life." The novel is the middle of the lives of several people. And they're middle class. And it's mid-history. But the title was changed because everybody said, "Notes on the What?"

Twigg: Have you sat down and figured out all the possible interpretations of *Life Before Man* as a title?

Atwood: I think I've got the main three anyway. For Lesje, it refers to the pre-historic era. For Elizabeth, it means that her own life is given priority over any relationship with a man. For Nate, it's connected with his political idealism. That is, humanity right now, considering all the things it does, such as shooting children, is not yet fully human.

Twigg: That's actually a very optimistic idea.

Atwood: Very optimistic. Absolutely. Nate is an optimist at heart, but he doesn't want to admit it.

Twigg: But there are negative connotations to that title, too.

Atwood: How so?

Twigg: Meaning that life, in a holistic scientific sense, is always going to take precedence over the insignificance of man.

Atwood: That's William. He's more interested in the survival of cockroaches than he is in the survival of the human race.

Twigg: *Life Before Man* could also mean life before the eyes of man, as opposed to life lived before the eyes of God.

Atwood: That would fit as well.

Twigg: I read it mostly as *Life Before Ethics*.

Atwood: That would be Elizabeth. She has no interest in ethics whatsoever. "Morality" is your relationship with yourself. "Ethics" is your relationship with other people. The '60s confused people. They tried to enjoy themselves and not worry about restricting their lives in artificial, puritanical ways. The problem was, once you enter into social relationships, ethics has to come in. When they stomped on morality, ethics got thrown out too. I'm not a social predictor, but I do think that "morality" is going to come back in now. Unfortunately most people still aren't too equipped to think ethically!

Twigg: Do you think it's our swing back to conservatism that's going to solidify some standards of morality again?

Atwood: I don't know whether it's a question of standards. It might be more a question of fear. I think a lot of people do things because they're frightened. In times of stress, or what people think of as times of stress and hardship—because, of course, this country is not in stress and hardship, people are not starving in droves in the street, we're doing a lot of whining that would be pretty much sneered at in other parts of the world—people get frightened. They think they may not be able to get jobs. Or they won't be able to get the kinds of jobs that they might like to have. Whereas in the early '60s, people didn't feel like that.

So now we're retreating back into our rabbit holes. We're pulling in our tentacles so they don't get stepped on. When that happens, you want to form a monogamous relationship with somebody, hoping that it's going to keep you warm and safe.

Twigg: This runs all through your work. The idea that fear is more primordial than love.

Atwood: Yes. Because in a society like ours where people are pretty much out there on their own hook, there's no real social support system for them, no small tribe or clan or integrated structure that's going to support an individual in it; so fear is a real motivating factor. And because you don't really know where the danger is coming from, fear takes the form often of a generalized anxiety or paranoia. You don't know who the enemy is. You don't know what direction you'll be attacked from. So everybody ends up constantly swivelling around, looking for the next threat. People are afraid of whatever's out there. And rightly so.

Twigg: And that influences who you love and how you love them.

Atwood: Yes. Are you loving someone out of desperation and need, or are you loving someone because they're "them," as we say?

Twigg: The marriage in *Life Before Man* paints a pretty depressing example of what happens when domesticity and sexuality can't coexist under one roof.

Atwood: Yes, but now marriage is retrenching itself. People are getting married a lot younger again because in times of economic hardship, people retreat to the domestic burrow. But perhaps these marriages will be formed on more equitable terms. One hopes, with marriage in the '70s, people are going into it with different expectations. In 1955, the husband was the breadwinner and the wife would have children; the husband was the boss and the wife kept her mouth shut. I'd like to think that some of that has changed. But you tell me. You're young enough.

Twigg: I think maybe one of the problems now is that people may be getting married without enough expectations.

Atwood: Or without any.

Twigg: We're groovy, we're together, and if it doesn't work out we can always drift off somewhere else.

Atwood: None of this stuff would make much difference if it weren't influencing the lives of children. Society has always said, "You have to preserve marriage for the sake of the children." I've never really bought that one. But on the other hand, when breakups start happening on a large scale, you have to think of the consequences. We may be producing a lot of isolated, self-protective, narcissistic children.

Twigg: At least Elizabeth does genuinely care about her kids.

Atwood: Yes. Strange to say, many readers like Elizabeth. She doesn't take crap. She's not hypocritical about herself. She had a bad childhood and she got locked into a struggle with her aunt. When she is finally able, not exactly to forgive her aunt, but at least to go through the motions of giving human support, that's positive. Even though she doesn't *feel* compassion, she acts it out anyway. After that happens, there's a chance she will be able to get outside herself. She puts politics and the Women's Movement down at the beginning of the book because if there's nothing in it for her, forget it. But by the end of the book there's a possibility of change. I never make Prince Charming endings because I don't believe in them. But I do believe that people can change. Maybe not completely, but some.

So Elizabeth has a lot of fans. Especially women over thirty-five with two kids and a shaky marriage. They think Elizabeth is all right. She's ruthless in her dealings with other people, but then people have been ruthless in their dealings with her. Violence begets violence.

Twigg: What do you say to the argument that this book only adds to the ennui of the present? That bleakness begets bleakness?

Atwood: That's like saying everybody should write happy books. As far as I can tell, people in a crisis would much rather have that crisis admitted. When a friend of mine was dying, everybody tried to jolly him up. They said, "Oh, no, you're not going to die." The fact was he knew he was dying and he wanted to talk about it. I think people in a crisis would rather have somebody say, "This is a crisis, this is real." That's much more comforting than saying here are John and Mary, they live in this bungalow, they have a washing machine and three kids, and they're really happy. What could be less cheerful if you're in a bad situation than being told normal people are happy? A lot of normal people aren't happy.

Twigg: I agree. People always talk about censorship from the government or censorship through economics. But the main form of censorship in our society is really self-censorship.

Atwood: Exactly. People will say, "I don't want to hear about it" or "I don't want to read about it." But for me the novel is a social vehicle. It reflects society. Serious writers these days don't write uplifting books because what they see around them is not uplifting. It would be hypocritical to say the world is inspirational. It's not. These days the world is a pretty dismal place. You can blank that out. You can destroy your Amnesty International newsletter without reading it. But that doesn't make it go away. The less you pay attention to it, the more it's going to be there for somebody else.

We think we can go on playing with our toys forever. But if you're not aware of the fact that you may die, you're much less careful about other people. One of the crucial moments in any life is when you come to that realization.

Twigg: When did you come to that realization for yourself?

Atwood: Sometime in my twenties. I had had a romantic, adolescent notion of death earlier, but I hadn't really felt that solid moment when you realize your life is not going to go on forever, that people you know aren't going to be here forever, that we're going to die. What was it the Greeks used to say? "Call no man happy until he is dead."

Twigg: Do you think it was essential to you as a writer to come to terms with death?

Atwood: It's essential to everyone as a human being.

Twigg: But there's always been this particularly strong awareness in your poetry that life is transient.

Atwood: Life is transient. War is hell.

Twigg: Birds fly.... Do you get sick of hearing critics say your poetry is better than your novels?

Atwood: People often have difficulty handling somebody who does more than one thing. That's their problem. It's not a difficulty for me.

Twigg: Do you think it's been an advantage for you because you can carry into prose that poet's instinct to "make it new"?

Atwood: I don't know whether my poetry is an advantage to me as a novelist or not. For me poetry is where the language is renewed. If poetry vanished, language would become dead. It would become embalmed. People say, "Well, now that you're writing successful novels I suppose you'll be giving up poetry." As if one wrote in order to be successful. The fact is, I would never give up poetry. Poetry might give me up, but that's another matter. It's true that poetry doesn't make money. But it's the heart of the language. If you think of language as a series of concentric circles, poetry is right in the center. It's where precision takes place. It's where that use of language takes place that can extend a word yet have it be precise.

Twigg: That's one of the best things about *Life Before Man*. It seems in this novel you've dispensed with a lot of the trappings of a conventional novel and concentrated on writing more from your poetic strength. Many Canadian reviews have criticized *Life Before Man* for what it isn't rather than trying to appreciate what it is.

Atwood: Yes, I have that trouble. Some people always want to review the book that came before. When I wrote *Surfacing*, people wanted it to be *The Edible Woman*. When I wrote *Lady Oracle*, people wanted it to be *Surfacing*. With this one, some reviewers wanted it to be *Lady Oracle*. They thought it was supposed to be a satire. But this new novel is more like *Surfacing* than *Lady Oracle*. Maybe this is why many people have missed its social and political content.

I cannot publish a book in Canada today without getting a third bad reviews, a third good reviews, and a middle third that goes either way. I expect that. You can't be a writer of my visibility without somebody saying, "She's supposed to be such hot stuff. We think she's overexposed or overrated." That's going to happen every time.

Twigg: *Maclean's* praised the book as an excellent "women's novel." Were you aware that you lacked "the soaring perspective of the great novelists"?

Atwood: That definition of a women's novel as being a book fundamentally about human relationships has to include all of Jane Austen, all of the Bronte sisters, quite a lot of Charles Dickens, *Vanity Fair*, and *Middlemarch*—which to me is the best Victorian novel. Not to mention just about all of serious modern literature with the exception of spy stories, murder mysteries, and Westerns. Everything else fits into that "women's novel" category. Novels have people in them. You can see their society through their interaction. Some people just can't see very well.

Twigg: Or they don't want to see. Stories that are so modern can frighten people.

Atwood: Some people are frightened of my work, that's true. A real kind of heavy shock set in around *Power Politics* in 1971. But then three or four years after they appear, my books aren't shocking anymore. Because that's where people have come to.
   A lot of writers write about their childhood or what it was like in the small town where they grew up. Things that happened twenty years ago. On the pain level, these books are easier to read than something more immediate. When it's in the past, you know it's over. But the closer something is to you, the more shock value it can have. It could be you. That's why some people find me pretty terrifying. They confuse me with the work.

Twigg: Also people are still very wary of any woman with power. And *Life Before Man* is quite devastating.

Atwood: Yes, but I think more and more, as people get used to the idea that I'm around, some of that fear goes away. I can find there's more openness now to what I'm doing than there was before.

Twigg: My wife's comment on reading the book was that everyone can see themselves growing older in it.

Atwood: True.

Twigg: And that can make people feel very uncomfortable, too.

Atwood: Yes, I suppose the message there is, if you've got something to do, do it now. Everybody's going to croak sooner or later. Meanwhile you do have some latitude about what you're going to put into your life story. If you think about life only in terms of having a job, of future security, of doing things according to the book, you're probably just playing somebody else's script.

Twigg: Your *Survival* hypothesis has been rather fiercely attacked as "fashionably radical, bourgeois individualism." Do you take any of that Marxist criticism seriously?

Atwood: No, I don't have very much time for the kind of purist leftism that defines itself as the only true religion. It's like Plymouth Brethrenism. They're so puritanical that they don't even go after new members. They're just interested in defining their own purity as opposed to the evil of everybody else. That kind of leftism is useless in this country. It has no sense of its constituency. It doesn't know how to address them. So if they want to call me names that's fine, nobody's listening.

I work on a magazine called *This Magazine*. As far as I'm concerned it's the best of the small left magazines in Canada. One of the members, Rick Salutin, wrote a piece on *Survival* as a Marxist book. He was talking about how it had an awareness of historical development, how it took into account its place as a political instrument in that development, and how it made a connection between the economy and the culture.

Twigg: When you have a nation that is only two or three generations removed from the pioneer experience, is it really possible for us to have had anything other than a literature which is predominantly concerned with survival?

Atwood: That's one of the things I'm arguing. Although I don't think that's the only determining factor. In Western Canada that pioneer experience may be only two or three generations removed, but in Eastern Canada it's often eight or nine. So it's not the whole story.

Twigg: The whole story is that our colonial status as a nation has spawned a literature of failure.

Atwood: No, I said a literature of survival.

Twigg: Either way, being victimized politically has created a nation that is lacking in self-respect.

Atwood: Yes, Canada doesn't go for the brass ring.

Twigg: In the seven years since you wrote *Survival* have you become any more optimistic about Canada's progression towards attaining self-respect politically?

Atwood: Culturally, you could say Canada's doing O.K. Writers have a union now and they're standing up for their rights. We've even got a film industry of sorts. But that's a very small group of people. When you look at the economic situation you can see that things have in fact gotten worse. More of Canada is foreign-owned than when I published that book in 1972. So maybe our burst of culture is only a mushroom that will disappear in three or four years. Our entertainment market may be taken over by bigger interests now that Canada is becoming a more lucrative market. For instance, chain book stores now control forty percent of the business. If they control sixty percent, they will start dictating what will be published. Publishers will send them their manuscripts first and the chain will say what gets published. They will have a stranglehold on writing, and the market will be even more foreign-dominated and junk-dominated. This is not optimism or pessimism. It's just looking at things that are there.

Evading the Pigeonholers
Gregory Fitz Gerald and Kathryn Crabbe

The Gregory Fitz Gerald and Kathryn Crabbe interview is
a transcript of a videotaped interview conducted on Sep-
tember 13, 1979, during a visit of Margaret Atwood to the
State University of New York, College at Brockport, where
she was a guest of the Brockport Writers Forum and Vid-
eotape Library. The interview originally appeared in *The
Midwest Quarterly* 28 (1987). Copyright © 1987 by The State
University of New York. Reprinted by permission.

Fitz Gerald: There's an interesting pattern of color imagery in the poem
you just read, "You Begin." Would you tell us about your notion of that
imagery?

Atwood: I hadn't really thought about the imagery until you asked me,
but I took a quick peek and I see imagery of coolness—the colors are
blue and green. I build toward hot colors in the middle of the poem—
colors like orange and red—and then there are no more colors. The
word *color* is mentioned, but no specific color is named. The colors build
up to the midpoint of the poem—the most dangerous point of the poem
—and then there is a diminuendo.

Crabbe: The cool blue that starts the poem is familiar to a reader of
your poems; you do quite a bit with greens and blues, and with fish.
Could you comment upon the Canadian background for these images?

Atwood: As far as I'm concerned, life begins with geology, and with geography. If you look at a map of Canada, you'll see that it is one of the
most watery countries in the world. If you think of a map on which water
is blue and land is green, you'll see that much of Canada is blue. You
might say, then, that it's quite natural for me to use those color images
in my poetry, because that's what I'm surrounded by much of the time.
That may give the impression that Canada is nothing but a big stretch
of woods, but of course that's not true. My novel *Life Before Man* is set
entirely in the city; there is very little water, not much green, and no fish.

Fitz Gerald: One of your critics, Linda Rogers, has said that she finds a chill in your imagery.

Atwood: You're referring to that funny article called, "Margaret the Magician"?

Fitz Gerald: Yes, that's the one.

Atwood: She spent much of the article analyzing my cover photos, saying that I didn't smile in them. At the time I read that, I counted my cover photos and discovered she had missed a number of them. Some have smiles, some don't. But to base analysis of a writer's work on whether cover photos have smiles seems silly.

Fitz Gerald: You reject, then, the notion of a chill in your poetry?

Atwood: There is in some poems and not in others. Name one serious modern writer who's all sweetness and light. That reflects not one's personality or predilections but what is going on around the writer. The writer is a focus for what is coming in from outside. Looking around you, do you see much that would cause any writer with any seriousness to ignore completely the darker side of life?

Fitz Gerald: I don't see how one can.

Atwood: I think Linda Rogers's point was that I exert an hypnotic or mesmerizing influence upon the reader, presumably through the cover photos.

Crabbe: When I listen to you read, I hear an expression of consciousness of rhythm. Even when you read your prose, I'm impressed by an awareness of rhythm. There's also a concern for how the poem looks on the page—you're a very careful lineator. Do you think of a poem more as an aural or visual experience for the reader?

Atwood: I think of the poem as an aural experience; the visual experience is a notation. That's not an eccentricity of mine; many poets think of their poems that way. Any poet who is not conscious of rhythm probably would not be a very good poet.

Crabbe: Do you work from a principle in lineation?

Atwood: From a principle? No. Do you mean, do I have a theory? I probably once did, but it changes according to what I'm doing at the moment. No, I don't have a theory. All I can say is that sometimes the lines get longer, and sometimes they get shorter. Sometimes I'll go through a period in which I'm using rather long lines and writing prose poems. On the other hand, in *Power Politics* the poems are very aphoristic, short and condensed. If you write too long in that manner, you get yourself into a corner, and the result is silence.

Fitz Gerald: There has been a resurgence of interest among poets in metrics, as opposed to free verse. How do you react to that interest?

Atwood: I've never quite understood what "free verse" was. It doesn't seem to me that any verse is entirely "free." Very young poets think they are writing in free verse, yet slip into iambic pentameter because they have read so much Shakespeare in school. I did a great deal of formal pattern writing when I was quite young. Many readers think that modern poetry lacks structure, but they have not been taught to look for it. Then they either write iambics without recognizing them as such or slip into a kind of porridgy writing. Formal training doesn't hurt anyone; everyone should have to write a sonnet once, just to see what it is.

Fitz Gerald: There are more sonnets appearing than I can remember.

Atwood: I might add that to write a good sonnet today is very difficult, because the form has been used and used. It's like trying to paint a good landscape.

Fitz Gerald: Or write a few lines of good dramatic verse.

Atwood: That too. The problem for the twentieth century is that the Victorians were great experimenters with formal patterns, and they used them up, so that it became very difficult for the following generation to do anything in the same vein. I think that shoved poets into "free verse." It may be that "free verse" has now been used so much that poets are looking for some other source of energy.

Fitz Gerald: Syllabics have been tried, but they don't work so well in English.

Atwood: Yes, English is not that kind of language; it's still based on heavy Anglo-Saxon stress. Unless you have a language in which all syllables can get an equal stress, as in French, it doesn't really work.

Crabbe: Which of the poets that you have studied have been influential on your work?

Atwood: I kept away from the twentieth century to avoid the problem of influence. My field of study in graduate school was the nineteenth century. I studied Tennyson; that won't hurt anyone. I didn't want to do twentieth-century literature because I felt that something so close to me ought not to be done in the academic marketplace. My reading of modern poetry was done on my own time, so to speak.

I read Canadian poetry at a formative stage of my life, and I could name several Canadian poets who were influential—Margaret Avison, P. K. Page—people you probably have never heard of, but they're well known up there. I was coming along at a time of considerable artistic ferment, so I made contact with a number of my contemporaries— Gwendolyn MacEwen, Michael Ondaatje, George Bowering. Essentially a writer is not very much influenced after having written for ten years or so.

Crabbe: In studying Tennyson you were working with a poet who pays a great deal of attention to sound and to classical metrics. Did you find that background helpful?

Atwood: Yes and no. Among poets I know, it doesn't seem to make much difference whether they have been to university: some have been and are good poets, while others *haven't* and are equally good poets. One possible difference is that if you have been to university you are more critical of what you publish. That is, there are many "natural poets" who publish anything they write because they lack the critical ability to weed out the duds. However, having had a university education doesn't help in *writing* good poems. Poets are largely self-taught, but if they are conscious of quality in others' work, they may apply some of that consciousness to their own work. I'm fairly stiffly self-editing: I write about twice as much as I publish.

Fitz Gerald: That suggests considerable revision.

Atwood: Not necessarily. If a poem is going the way I want, it will sometimes stay just the way I wrote it; for instance, "You Begin" was published just about "straight." At the same time I throw out, or at least lay aside, quite a few poems, when they won't come right.

Fitz Gerald: Is there a danger in overrevising?

Atwood: Here again, there aren't any rules; you can only look at the result. Some schools of writing concentrate largely on process, but I'm not a member of that school.

Fitz Gerald: Was Gerard Manley Hopkins or Dylan Thomas an influence on your work?

Atwood: Probably not. Much of the impetus for my work was my experience during those "formative years" of which I spoke earlier, between the ages of sixteen and twenty-six. Poets of my generation were searching for an indigenous mode of expression as well as indigenous subject matter. We were heavily involved in developing our own publishing houses. In 1960 there were probably only five literary magazines in the whole of English Canada and maybe three publishers. You could read maybe five novels a year written by Canadians and published in English Canada and maybe twenty books of poetry, including mimeographed pamphlets. Poets of my generation published their own work before anyone else did—I set the type for my own first book—because we began writing in a vacuum. That's the activity I think of when people ask me about influences and my reading. All the expected things were interesting, but the important thing was discovering the fact of our own existence as Canadians. We weren't too eager to imitate English models any more, because Canadians before us had done that. Mine was the first generation that had enough poets right before it to start that chain reaction.

Fitz Gerald: A question about your fiction: how is the creative act different for you as a writer of fiction?

Atwood: Poems have immediate satisfactions to offer; that is, you have the first scene or the "kicker" or whatever it is you start with in about the same time it takes to write a short poem, but then you have to work very hard actually getting the material onto paper. The operative element, then, in writing a novel is willpower—aside from the obvious differences in form and what can be expressed in a novel rather than a poem.

Fitz Gerald: What do you think of those writers who attempt to combine the two forms to write poetic novels or prose poems?

Atwood: I write prose poems myself, and to me they're poems because the basic unit is the syllable. In a novel the basic unit is something much larger: it's blocks of imagery that connect with other blocks—character, plot. For me the novel operates much more solidly in relationship to the society in which it is written. Poetic novels—I'm not so sure what those are. You sometimes get stuck with that label because you write poetry as well as novels, but for me if the novel doesn't work as a novel it's probably bad.

Fitz Gerald: I was thinking about Joyce as a writer of poetic novels. For example, there is the Molly Bloom section of *Ulysses*.

Atwood: But that's definitely prose. It has rhythms, but for me they're the rhythms of prose.

Fitz Gerald: And Hemingway has a poetic passage in *For Whom the Bell Tolls*, for example, the first pages of Chapter XIII.

Atwood: What do you mean by "poetic"?

Fitz Gerald: The passage has a distinct rhythm that is no longer prose rhythm; it has a repetitive and impressionistic imagistic pattern, replete with poetic devices: alliteration, consonance, assonance, and so forth.

Atwood: People tend to compartmentalize. A student told me last night, "My thesis advisor won't let me work on you because you write novels as well as poetry." When I asked her what that meant, she said that people are now so specialized that they deal with either poetry or fiction, but not both. She finds people disapproving of me because I write both. I pulled Hardy out of the hat immediately!

Crabbe: Your poetry takes a more ironic point of view than your fiction, which seems comic, brighter in its resolutions.

Atwood: I'm not so sure I agree. The first novel has a circular structure; the woman at the end is essentially back where she started, except that she's been around once. I wouldn't call it exactly a "bright" ending. *Lady Oracle* is also circular; the woman is back where she started, but she does know more. *Life Before Man* is a different work altogether. The first three novels comprise a unit, and *Life Before Man* is the first of another unit of three.

Crabbe: Do you see something in the very form of the poem or novel that forces you to do very different things with each?

Atwood: For one thing novels are big; it's a matter of size. It takes a long time to read a novel, compared to a poem, unless of course it's a narrative poem. That takes us back to Poe's argument about the impossibility of a long lyric poem. He was after the immediate, evocative, hair-rising-on-the-back-of-the-neck response that the poet can achieve in the very condensed lyric poem and not in the long narrative poem with novelistic elements like character, setting, and development. In a poem you're working with syllables, rhythms in a quite different way.

Crabbe: Earlier you mentioned that the novel is more tied to the society in which it's written. Would you explain?

Atwood: Novels have people in them—or at least most of the novels I've read. Poems have a voice. You can have a narrative poem with personages in it, true, but people don't write those very often anymore. Even when the poem has a narrative structure, it usually contains a series of short lyric poems. You'll notice also when we're analyzing *Paradise Lost* we analyze it in much the same way we would if it were a novel: what was motivating Adam? what was Eve's character? Novels have people; people exist in a social milieu; all of the cultural milieu gets into the novel. You can put those things into a poem, if you like, but the lyric poem is so condensed that it's difficult to manage.

Crabbe: Does the fact that a novel has all these other elements make you think differently about the same issue?

Atwood: That gets into the question of a writer's relationship with an audience. In a poem you're taking much more for granted about the listener; in a novel you're addressing yourself to a readership also, but you fill in more information about your characters' backgrounds.

Fitz Gerald: How do you react to critics who label you a political writer?

Atwood: I *am* a political writer.

Fitz Gerald: Would you explain?

Atwood: The easy answer is that everything is "political." Any piece of writing can be analyzed as "political." The real answer is that it would be impossible to be a Canadian writer of my generation without developing a political consciousness, because even though we started out just wanting to be writers we found out immediately that access to our own audience was denied us. The publishing houses were controlled by foreigners, or were very timid about publishing Canadians because they felt Canadians were not reading Canadians. We were up against what we call the "colo-

nial mentality," which believes the "great, good place" is somewhere else
—New York or London. None of us was born with that mentality, but
we all developed it. My predilection is *not* to be political. I'd like all those
problems to be solved so that I wouldn't have to deal with them, but
those problems *do* exist, and we have to confront them merely to keep
ourselves viable as writers. We have to deal with the fact that at any
moment all of our publishing houses may go broke; you don't have to
cope with *that*. //

Fitz Gerald: One critic finds in your work a dichotomy between the
American and Canadian images: the American image is dehumanization
or excessive technology; the Canadian image is nature, land, open space.

Atwood: Perhaps, but in *Surfacing* there is a scene in which all these
images are going strong and people think certain acts have been done
by Americans until they meet them and find out they're Canadians. It's
not a question of the Big Bad Wolf and Little Red Riding Hood.

For us it's normal to use images of dehumanization to represent
America. For a Scottish person the same images would be applied to the
English. If you were a black in America, you'd apply those images to
the white man. If you were an Indian in the Canadian North, you would
apply them to the white man—Canadian, American, or whatever. If you
were in Quebec, you would apply them to the English—the Anglos. It's
a matter of who you're up against. If you were a woman, you would
apply them to men.

There is always a danger in that way of thinking, however, in that
you confuse individual members of the group with the group as a whole.
You say, "I don't like you because you're American, a tin woodsman
with a little motor inside"—which may be entirely unfair to the individual
American in front of you. At the same time, you have to face the facts:
we *are* dominated by the Americans. They use Canada as a branch-line
economy. Our workers *are* laid off before yours. We *are* dominated by
American unions. I didn't invent these facts; they are part of the society
in which I live.

Fitz Gerald: You are merely describing the reality of your situation,
then, not necessarily taking a position?

Atwood: Absolutely! Of course, I'm taking a position by choosing to
describe that reality, rather than some other reality. However, I did not
invent the reality I describe, and I cannot make it go away.

Crabbe: We have been dwelling on what it means to be a Canadian artist.

Atwood: Yes, but no one knows what a Canadian artist is. We *do* know that we encounter certain problems as Canadian artists.

Crabbe: Not only are you a Canadian artist, but you are also, according to some of your critics, a feminist writer. How do you react to that designation?

Atwood: We are great categorizers and pigeonholers in our society, and one reason is to put people safely into pigeonholes and then dismiss them, thinking we have thereby summed them up. "Feminist" is to me an adjective that does not enclose one. It's not enough merely to say that someone is a feminist. Some people *choose* to define themselves as feminist writers. I would not deny the adjective, but I don't consider it inclusive. There are many other interests of mine that I wouldn't want the adjective to exclude. People who understand my viewpoint tend to be women from Scotland or black women in America who say, "Feminist, as it is used in America, usually means white middle-class American women saying *they* are *all* women."

I get arguments from feminists from the States who say, "Why do you bother with this nationalism? It's all patriarchal, male-dominated boys' games. Why don't you just play girls' games?" Someone who understands my position would more likely be from a peripheral culture such as my own, someone from Scotland or the West Indies or a black feminist in the States. I read a piece by Alice Walker that said a great deal to me.

What the term "feminist writer" means to certain American feminists cannot mean the same thing it means to me. They are on the inside looking at each other, while I am on the outside. Certainly sex cuts across national boundaries; feminism is in some sense international, but it can only be international in the same sense that anything else is international if you want it to work. It must be a meeting of nationalities, not the submergence of one nationality in another. One cannot be a Canadian feminist writer exclusively in the same way one can be an American feminist writer exclusively. My country is simply too small, and we have too many problems just as Canadians. We *have* to work with men.

Crabbe: You would say, then, that you are a Canadian artist first?

Atwood: No, I wouldn't say that. I would say that all these factors connect with each other. Canadian nationalism is merely another form of a general human rights interest. Probably in your country I would be called a pinko socialist as well, since Canada is a much more socialist country than the States. It has had to be.

Using What You're Given
Jo Brans

Jo Brans's interview was conducted at Southern Methodist University where Margaret Atwood appeared as part of the University's eighth annual Literary Festival in 1982. The interview first appeared in *Southwest Review* and also appeared in Jo Brans's collection *Listen to the Voices: Conversations with Contemporary Writers* (Southern Methodist University Press, 1988). Copyright © 1988 by Jo Brans. Reprinted by permission.

Brans: Are you a feminist writer?

Atwood: *Feminist* is now one of the all-purpose words. It really can mean anything from people who think men should be pushed off cliffs to people who think it's O.K. for women to read and write. All those could be called feminist positions. Thinking that it's O.K. for women to read and write would be a radically feminist position in Afghanistan. So what do you mean?

Brans: Let me try again. What I meant by asking that question was whether you think that you espouse a feminist position or propaganda in your writing.

Atwood: I don't think that any novelist is inherently that kind of a creature. Novelists work from observations of life. A lot of the things that one observes as a novelist looking at life indicate that women are not treated equally. But that comes from observation. It doesn't come from ideology. I started writing in 1956. There wasn't any women's movement during my writing life until 1970. That's fourteen years of writing. Now, on the other hand—and you have to try to define this very clearly—I'm not one of those women who would say, "Well, I made it, therefore anybody should be able to do it, and what are they whining about." That's not the point. Nor am I against the Women's Movement. I think it's been a very good thing and I was happy to see it. But it's very different from saying that what you write is embodying somebody's party line. It isn't. And none of the women writers that I know, including ones who are regularly defined as feminists, would say that they are embodying somebody's party line. It's not how they see what they're doing.

Brans: You have gotten crossways with some feminist groups, particularly with *Surfacing*, where a woman character wants to undo the effects of an abortion.

Atwood: To me that is just what that character would do. The abortion was coerced—it was forced. That's not an "antiabortion" stand. It's an anticoercion stand. I don't think even women who are in favor of freedom of choice would say abortion is a good thing that should be forced on everyone. And if they've read the book—you sometimes feel these people haven't, or they don't know *how* to read—that is what they would see, the negative effects that happen to the character are connected with the fact that the thing is forced on her by the circumstances.

Brans: What does pregnancy mean in your writing? There are so many places, for example, in *Life Before Man*, and then the little story called "Giving Birth," where pregnancy seems to mean something profound and various.

Atwood: Well, girls can have babies and boys can't. The fact has been noticed by more people than me. In the story "Giving Birth," giving birth is wonderful for the woman from whose point of view the story is told, but she mentions this other shadow figure for whom it's not wonderful. It's awful. I think one of the things the story says is that there is no word for forced pregnancy in the language. We don't have that concept, although the fact itself exists. So, there again, I wouldn't say that pregnancy is wonderful for everybody. We know that it isn't. It can be wonderful for a person who wants to go through it. But you could say that of every act in life.

Brans: What about a girl like Lesje, for example, in *Life Before Man*, who becomes pregnant in order to prove a point?

Atwood: Once upon a time more women than we would like to admit got pregnant to prove a point. In fact, they got pregnant to get married. Remember shotgun weddings? I'm sure that still happens. I don't think it's tiptop for the children who are involved. //

Brans: Yes. But Lesje doesn't have that in mind.

Atwood: No, no. She's tired of being put down for not being the mother. You can't say that pregnancy is one thing. It's many things, like making love. I mean, it's not just one thing that ought to have one meaning. It's one of those profoundly meaningful human activities which can be very multifaceted and resonant. It can have a very positive meaning for some people and a very negative meaning for others.

Brans: Which is the point of the extra woman in "Giving Birth."

Atwood: Remember that I'm old enough to remember the time when women were told they had to get pregnant and have babies in order to "fulfill their femininity." And I didn't like that either. Nor do I like women being told that they oughtn't to get pregnant, they can't get pregnant, that it's antifeminist to get pregnant. I don't like that line either.

Brans: So you're really defining your feminism for me, I think, right now.

Atwood: Yes, I'm defining my feminism as human equality and freedom of choice.

Brans: What do you think an ideal relationship between a man and a woman would be?

Atwood: A happy one.

Brans: I was thinking of your poem "Power Politics."

Atwood: That talks about all kinds of different ways in which marriage isn't happy. You may often define a positive by defining negatives.

Brans: What I like most in "Power Politics" is the wit. It is the sharpest and wittiest poem. There's a lot of anger in it, and frustration because of the impossibility of communicating.

Atwood: But there again, that doesn't rule out the opposite pole. I'll read some love poems in the reading tonight to show it can be done. I'm not a pessimist. People sometimes read my poems and think, oh, this is a pessimist.

Brans: Anyone who thinks that should read "There Is Only One of Everything." I love that poem, and it is a love poem—wonderful. But it's not only a love poem, it's also a poem about observing the world, and the particularities of the world, I guess. What effect has being Canadian had on your writing?

Atwood: There's a funny poem in Canada called "Recipe for a Canadian Novel" in which it's recommended that one take two beavers, add one Mounty and some snow, and stir. I'm not in favor of anybody consciously trying to be the great anything, but every writer writes out of his or her own backyard. I give you William Faulkner as an example. There's a genre of writing we call "Southern Ontario Gothic," which is something like Southern Gothic. The South has often had problems of making itself felt as something other than a region—it so often just gets called "regional," doesn't it?—whereas, in fact, Southern writers are doing what all writers do. They're writing out of what they know.

There's a story you'll appreciate. When I first met our mutual friend Charles Matthews, who, as you know, is from Mississippi, I said, "Oh, I so much admire William Faulkner. He was so inventive, and he made up all these funny and grotesque things." And Charles said, "He didn't make anything up. He just wrote it all down." That just proves my point. That's what writers do, and Canadian writers are no different from other writers in that respect. They write about what they know. Some of what they know is Canadian. When they travel, or when they think in other terms, then the terms become larger. But the base, the way of thinking, remains Canadian, just as for the Southern writer the way of thinking remains Southern. So to me it's not a question which is particular to Canada; it's a question that's about all writing and all writers.

Brans: And how to transcend region somehow?

Atwood: I don't think you transcend region, anymore than a plant transcends earth. I think that you come out of something, and you can then branch out in all kinds of different directions, but that doesn't mean cutting yourself off from your roots and from your earth. To me an effective writer is one who can make what he or she is writing about understandable and moving to someone who has never been there. All good writing has that kind of transcendence. It doesn't mean becoming something called "international." There is no such thing.

Brans: So you don't think then that there are national literary qualities, even though you wrote a book about Canadian literature?

Atwood: In any transaction involving a book there's the writer, there's the book, and there's the reader. The writer can write the book and make it as good a book as he or she can, and it can be a pretty good book. That doesn't mean the reader is going to understand it, unless the reader has receiving apparatus that's equal to the product. //

I write for people who like to read books. They don't have to be Canadian readers. They don't have to be American readers. They don't have to be Indian readers, although some of them are. I'm translated into fourteen languages by now, and I'm sure that some of the people reading those books don't get all the references in them, because they're not familiar with the setting. I don't get all the references in William Faulkner either. That doesn't mean I don't enjoy the books, or can't understand them. You can pick up a lot of things from context, even though you may not understand that it was that family in Oxford, Mississippi, that was being talked about.

Brans: But as an educated reader you still would have this human rapport with the book.

Atwood: An educated reader has a rapport with all books, depending on taste to a certain extent, but an educated reader would never *not* read a book because it wasn't by somebody from his home town, right? or because the person was a different color, or because the person was a woman or a man. I've had women say to me that they just don't read books by men anymore. I think that's shocking. I've had that said to me by several people within the last couple of weeks. //

Brans: Do you have any problems in portraying a character of the opposite sex in your writing?

Atwood: The same problem I would have portraying an English person, or somebody that was just enough different from me that I'd have to do research. So, with men, it depends on what kind of man you're doing, of course; but just to give you an example, writing *Life Before Man* I showed the manuscript to a man (I showed the manuscript of *Bodily Harm* to a West Indian, and that was helpful, too) because I wanted to just have a read on the details—the accuracy of the details—and he caught me in one major mistake, which a man would never have made. He said you cannot shave a beard off with an electric razor. You have to use a straight razor. An electric razor will just get all clogged up if you're trying to shave long hairs with it. Little things like that. I think men have often portrayed women characters, and sometimes they slipped up on those kinds of details. Unless they go do the research on how you put on panty hose, they aren't going to know.

Brans: But you don't think there's anything intrinsically different in the mind of a man and a woman?

Atwood: Sure, lots of things. But I know a lot of men. I talk to a lot of them. They're not foreigners. They really can be conversed with.

Brans: You wouldn't agree with the poem by Adrienne Rich, "Trying to Talk to a Man," where she says you're talking across vast distances in a desert area.

Atwood: You're still talking, and, of course, it depends partly on what you're talking about and what your attitude is and who the man is. That does make a difference. I don't think that all men are the same, any more than I think all women are the same. And there is such a thing as an intelligent, cultivated, well-read, and sensitive man. I find it just absurd these days that I'm having to stick up for men. I find that such an absurd position to be put in. I've been doing the other thing for years, I mean, telling men that they ought to read books by women. Here I am suddenly feeling, out of a sense of fairness, that I have to say not all men are pigs, some of them write good books.

Brans: Do you get attacked when you have a character like Nate, for example, in *Life Before Man*, who's sort of wimpy, as a man?

Atwood: I don't think he's that wimpy. He's having trouble making a decision, but that's a decision a lot of men have trouble making, namely, whether to leave their kids because their marriage is rotten, or whether to stay with the marriage for the sake of the kids. Any man leaving kids and a wife is going to have residual guilt feelings which he's going to have to work out and expiate and get rid of. And Nate is observed at the time during which he's caught in the process, but it doesn't mean he's a wimpy man.

Brans: Well, I'm glad to have you defend him.

Atwood: There again, people, even women, expect men to be better than they are, and better than women. Now, notice what you did. You came after me for Nate, who's actually the nicest person in the book. Now, Lesje is a wimp. Nobody ever attacks Lesje for being unrealistic and wimpish and so on, because they expect girls to be like that. Hardly ever at all has anybody ever said that. Nobody comes after me for Elizabeth being a bitch.

Brans: Well, I would have come after you for that.

Atwood: Next? It's always Nate. And I think the truth is that people expect men to be supermen. Even women—even feminists—take points off them when they aren't. They don't take equal points off the women for having failings, because women are expected to be imperfect.

Brans: Well, I thought of Elizabeth as having a bad childhood, and of Lesje as being young, and so I was willing—you're right. That was prejudiced of me.

Atwood: Women are supposed to be imperfect, but they are also expected to be supermoms, so you can't win, either way.

Brans: What did you have in mind about the dinosaurs in *Life Before Man*? Do you think we've lost something by becoming overly civilized?

Atwood: I don't like to close my symbolisms.

Brans: But you were suggesting something about a sort of purity of action and motive in the dinosaurs?

Atwood: No, they're Lesje's escape fantasy, among other things, but I don't like to explain and pin down things that I've put in my books. They have multiple meanings. One of the meanings is that all kids love dinosaurs, and I was no exception.

Brans: You have such diversity. All of the novels are very different from each other, and then, of course, I love your poetry, which is quite different from the fiction. Do you consciously put on different hats? Do you set out, say, to write a comedy of manners (and I think those terms are too constricting)? Are you consciously doing a particular kind of thing with, let's say, *The Edible Woman* or *Lady Oracle*?

Atwood: Yes, both of those, definitely.

Brans: Were you working for a genre, or did you start with an image that lent itself to that sort of treatment?

Atwood: I start out with an image, and the book develops around it. Yes, I always start with images, and the tone of the book comes later. //

Brans: You're so caught up with the transformation/metamorphosis/ rebirth idea. Does that have anything to do with your having studied with Northrop Frye? Did he shape your thinking?

Atwood: No, I think it has to do with the fact that my father was a biologist. I had the kind of reading childhood that Norie Frye would advocate. But he hadn't advocated it while I was having it. In other words, I read very early *Grimm's Fairy Tales*, Greek mythology; I was familiar with the Bible, and so on and so forth. Norie Frye didn't enter my life until the third year of university, when I had already been writing for four or five years. // My interest in metamorphosis may have come from *Grimm's Fairy Tales*. People are always having rebirths there. The culture is permeated with rebirth symbolism. It's Christian, among other things. And it's an idea that is very much around. If I were in India, they would say, Do you believe in metamorphosis? Do you believe in metempsychosis, do you believe in the transmigration of souls? But it seems to have been a concept in one form or another that has been run through the sausage machine by many different human cultures.

Brans: But it's clearly so central to you.

Atwood: It's central to me, but it's also central to lots of other people. It's central to any novel. Usually in a novel the central character changes. That's one of the things that happens in novels—the person learns something or they become something more, or they become something less, but they always change. They're not the same at the end as they were at the beginning. If you did write a novel in which they were exactly the same, you would probably find it either terribly experimental or terribly boring or possibly both.

Brans: It seems to me all your novels are affirmative, in a sense. // I was struggling very hard with *Bodily Harm*, because it did seem to me, with the political satire...

Atwood: You made it through to the last page, though.

Brans: But in the last page I thought I found this rather guarded affirmation, because she's "paying attention," that was a phrase that you used, which to my mind is a very affirmative statement. And then, something like, she's flying. And her luck is holding her up. So it seemed to me that of all the books you have written, this would, on the surface, be the least affirmative, and yet...

Atwood: I think it's actually the most affirmative, because you can only measure affirmation in terms of what it's set against. Having hope for the human race in India is a really different thing from having hope for the human race in Texas. In Texas you don't have to deal with massive poverty and people dying in the street and starvation and beggary and so forth. It's easy to be optimistic here.

Brans: I was thinking too of her personal trauma, because the loss of the breast seems to be . . .

Atwood: That happens to a quarter of all women over the age of forty. That's what the statistic is right now, so people better begin to deal with it. But part of what the novel does is set our way of thinking, which is an affluent way of thinking. We can afford to worry about our personal health and our fitness and our personal romances, and what we're eating, and whether we're fashionable, and whether we look good, and personal change and growth and all of those things we read about in women's magazines—that's in the forefront of our lives. //

Brans: Why are Americans often so hateful in your books?

Atwood: I don't like American foreign policy, in many instances. But neither do a lot of Americans. Nor do I confuse individual people with decisions made by governments. I think it's wrong to do so.

Brans: But, for example, in *Surfacing*, when the Americans come in they're so clearly the enemy. Or the CIA in *Bodily Harm* . . .

Atwood: All that stuff is realistic. It's not made up and it's not my attitude. I'm just writing it down. People sit around in bars and discuss who the CIA is this month.

Brans: Are you serious?

Atwood: Absolutely.

Brans: I didn't read *Surfacing* at all on that level. I thought the Americans were a symbol.

Atwood: No, no. No, no, no, no. // I was just writing down people's conversations. That's how people, at least some people, talk about the Americans. But you notice that the guy who talks about them that way the most is also the most spurious person in the book. And the people he thinks are Americans actually turn out to be Canadians, so you have to watch that kind of playing around.

Brans: And in *Bodily Harm* it's the CIA.

Atwood: Yes, in *Bodily Harm* they really do sit around in bars and say, So and so was the CIA, but they've moved. And who is it now? Well, I hear they're using locals. And there's a lot of speculation as to just who the CIA is, and the CIA is known for knowing who's doing the drugs, but not being concerned about turning them in, because that's not what they're interested in. They're only interested in the political stuff.

Brans: And if they leave them alone, they can find out more.

Atwood: And if they leave them alone, they can find out more, that's right. But a lot of people doing the drugs are Americans as well.

Brans: Do you have a specific political position?

Atwood: Politics, for me, is everything that involves who gets to do what to whom. That's politics. It's not just elections and what people say they are —little labels they put on themselves. And it certainly isn't self-righteous puritanism of the left, which you get a lot of, or self-righteous puritanism of the right, I hasten to add. Politics really has to do with how people order their societies, to whom power is ascribed, who is considered to have power. A lot of power is ascription. People have power because we think they have power, and that's all politics is. And politics also has to do with what kind of conversations you have with people, and what you feel free to say to someone, what you don't feel free to say. Whether you feel free during a staff meeting to get up and challenge what the chairman has just said. All of those things. //

Brans: You don't belong to a political party?

Atwood: Not any political party. I belong to Amnesty International, which concerns itself with torture and political imprisonment. I belong to the Canadian Civil Liberties Union.

Brans: So you maintain then a kind of writer's immunity.

Atwood: Nobody's immune. I don't endorse political candidates.

Brans: But in your books you're not attitudinizing at all? You're simply showing the world as you see it and sense it and feel it?

Atwood: Let me just think about that. I don't think people are morally neutral, O.K.? But that does not have anything to do with labels. That is, if you call somebody a democrat, if they say they're in favor of democracy, you then have to find out what they're actually in favor of by asking them a number of specific questions. Only then do you find out what's under that. If somebody says they're socialist, same thing. You have to ask different questions to find out what they really mean. The same with the feminist. And what you're really trying to put your finger on is, how will this person behave in this situation or that situation? Is this going to be somebody who's going to vote for burning witches, is it going to be somebody who's going to vote for fair trials, or is it going to be somebody who's going to vote for shooting people?

Brans: And those are not the things you learn by looking at a label.

Atwood: You don't learn those by looking at a label. People use labels for their own purposes—either to put on other people so they can line them up against the wall and shoot them, or to put on themselves to make themselves feel good. So that's why I took you through the mulberry bushes when you asked me about feminism. It's a label.

Brans: And again about politics.

Atwood: That's right. I think when you say "political writer" you usually mean either somebody who writes about doings in the White House or somebody who has a particular ax to grind in that they think everybody should vote for so-and-so, or that the world should be such and such a place, and that this is the way to get it. I don't have any surefire recipes like that. I am, of course, somebody who would vote, as I did recently in the Toronto election, in favor of an East/West nuclear arms freeze. That to me isn't even politics. It's survival.

Brans: You've been writing for so long. Apparently there's a very great need for you to write.

Atwood: It's very enjoyable for me to write. It's a pleasure. I bet you've never heard a writer say that before.

Brans: Writers say various things, but for a lot of them I think it is a torment, but a necessary torment.

Atwood: Don't ever believe that. If they didn't enjoy it on some level they wouldn't be doing it.

Brans: What do you think you accomplish for other people with your writing?

Atwood: It's not my business. That's their business. They are the receivers. They are in charge of their own equipment.

Brans: So you simply do it out of a love for it.

Atwood: Partly. I don't rule out communication, and reading a book is, according to the neurophysiologists, almost the equivalent of having the experience, on a synaptical level, what happens in your head. In fact, you could think of a human being as an enormous computer that you can run programs through. But if you think of a book as an experience, as almost the equivalent of having the experience, you're going to feel some sense of responsibility as to what kinds of experiences you're going to put people through. You're not going to put them through a lot of blood and gore for nothing; at least I'm not. I don't write pretty books, I know that. They aren't pretty. //

Brans: Always, in your books, there's this sense of making do. You have a phrase that runs throughout your poetry and your novels. Something like, it's your life and you're stuck with it. You have to make do.

Atwood: That's a negative line. But there's another way of putting it, which is this: some people, by "freedom," mean freedom to do whatever they want to, without any limitation whatsoever. That isn't the pack of cards we're dealt. We are dealt a limited pack. So I would see freedom more as the power to use what you're given in the best way you can. It doesn't mean that you're given everything. You aren't. Nobody is.

More Room for Play
Catherine Sheldrik Ross and
Cory Bieman Davies

Ross: We know that there is more than one Margaret Atwood. The
Margaret Atwood that we'd like to interview is Margaret Atwood, the
children's author. Could we start with your own reading as a child?

Atwood: What I read? Beatrix Potter, very early on. A. A. Milne. These
are books that were read to me. *Winnie the Pooh, Alice in Wonderland,
Alice Through The Looking Glass*—children's classics, in other words, of
those times. When I started to read myself, I remember being impressed
by E. Nesbitt and Edgar Allan Poe that some fool had put in the children's
library. I terrified myself in grade six with Poe. *Grimm's Fairy Tales* I had
very early—the unexpurgated complete version which my parents
bought by mistake, not realizing that it was full of people being put into
barrels full of nails and rolled down the hill into the sea.

Ross: Not to mention incest, illegitimate babies, and so on.

Atwood: Well, those things didn't really bother me at all. In fact, none
of it bothered me at all. I found it quite fascinating. But my younger
sister, who is twelve years younger than me, didn't like that at all. So for
some children it would have been too much. I have only the vaguest of
memories of Dick, Jane, Spot, and Puff. I know we had them at school,
but they didn't leave much of an impression. There were a lot of collections of fairy tales—*The Yellow Fairy Book*, all the Andrew Lang books.
I read all the ones I could get my hands on, that they had in the school
library. I probably read books that were somewhat too old for me at the

time. I remember reading *Moby Dick* early on, not really understanding it that well but finding it quite fascinating. Things like *Robinson Crusoe* and *Gulliver's Travels*, which were originally written for adults, but people put them in children's libraries because they don't have any sex in them. Fenimore Cooper, of course—I read some of those. Mark Twain I liked a lot—*Tom Sawyer* and *Huckleberry Finn*. Again, *Huckleberry Finn* is an adult's book; it's very scary in parts. And I read comic books. It was the comic book generation. My brother collected them, so we had a huge number, somewhat disapproved of; but our parents knew we read other things too, so it wasn't a problem. People traded them a lot. Saturday afternoons we sat around and traded comic books and read them.

Ross: This would be Marvel comics and *Superman?*

Atwood: The Marvel group was a bit later—that was *The Hulk* and *The Fantastic Four*; they came later. I read *Batman, Superman, Captain America, Wonder Woman, Donald Duck, Mickey Mouse, Little Lulu.* All of that I read, and Archie and Veronica and Betty, *Casper the Friendly Ghost.* He was actually a bit later than our generation. Then there were some crime comics that were kind of bloody and there were horror comics. But I think my favorite was Plastic Man who could transform himself into anything, but you could always tell because it was red and blue.

Ross: So, in fact, a lot of fairy tales and romance.

Atwood: Yes, a lot of fairy tales and romance. I was never big on *The Little Engine That Could* and that kind of morally encouraging tale about machinery.

Ross: Stories about staying on track and moving in the right direction.

Atwood: Protestant ethic, goal-oriented books I wasn't so keen on. I was much more keen on dragons and magic and those things. And some of the comic book stuff fed right into that, because that's exactly what it is.

Ross: And then there are origin stories...

Atwood: Yes. Rudyard Kipling for sure I read, and that kind of origin story. The Bible I was familiar with because of Sunday school, translated into cute little fables—people in bedsheets. Remember the colored pictures that they used to give you? That was quite useful in later life, although I didn't think so at the time. I read the *Boys' Own Annual*, with all those stories; old, old copies of it are in my grandfather's attic. About the turn of the century they had all those stories of adventures in caves and recovering lost treasures—the Rider Haggard, *Allan Quatermain*, *King Solomon's Mines* kinds of boys' adventure stories, really. Nobody ever told me they were supposed to be for boys only. So I read them. I read some Ernest Thompson Seton and animal stories—Sir Charles G. D. Roberts, *Wild Animals I Have Known*, *Kings in Exile*. They were quite sad. The animals always died. They were quite depressing. I used to cry over them—it was terrible. I read *Little Women* at one stage. And Arthur Conan Doyle; at about age ten or eleven I devoured all of Sherlock Holmes and some of his other knights-in-armor fraudulent historical romances. I also read a lot of "classical Victorian fiction." I read *Pride and Prejudice* at an early age. I read *Wuthering Heights*, of course. And I read Dickens. I read some things that were too old for me that I didn't really understand and that depressed and upset me. Victor Hugo was too depressing. What else?

Davies: Did you read *Anne of Green Gables*?

Atwood: Yes, I read *Anne of Green Gables*. I like it. I didn't read all of the sequels. *Anne of Green Gables* is the only really interesting one, I think. The others are about when she's grown up, and for kids that's just not as interesting.

Ross: The only things that are Canadian in your list are the animal stories and *Anne of Green Gables*.

Atwood: Those were the only Canadian things around.

Ross: George Woodcock has said that it doesn't matter what kids read up to the age of twelve—that Canadian kids have imported books but that that doesn't matter. After the age of twelve, he says, it becomes important for us to have our own writers. I wonder how you feel about this?

Atwood: I don't really know how I feel. I've talked to a lot of people about it hither and thither about the globe. I know that West Indian people feel that having children's books that are produced in England is confusing to their children, because they say "A is the apple" and the West Indians don't have apples. "Apple" to them means something else. They see a picture of a thing that to them isn't an apple and they've never seen it before and it's called an apple. And what they call an apple doesn't look like that. I think on that level—on the level of what is observed reality—it is helpful to have some books that name your own reality. If we had to read all books in which there was never any snow, the kids would find it very confusing. Now English literature is close enough to Canadian in climate and language and so on that there isn't a huge gap in understanding, although some of the things are obviously English and kids know when things are foreign. It is just that if your own reality is never named, then it leaves you with a curious feeling of non-existence. It's not that foreign books should be excluded; by no means. They feed the imagination, and I think a literature that confined itself to nothing but *The Little Engine That Could* and Dick and Spot and Puff and Jane, in the Canadian equivalent, would be very boring. I want books with dragons in them, even though I've never seen a dragon. So I think a judicious mix...

Ross: Was it having a child and wanting that child to have Canadian books that got you into writing children's books?

Atwood: No, my writing children's books wasn't politically motivated. *Up in the Tree* was one of about six rather nonsensical books that I wrote in fairly quick succession during a period when I was feeling quite dippy. I didn't have a child at the time. I was just writing them. I do write rhymed Christmas cards for people, rhymed birthday cards, rhymed satirical verse, and that kind of thing. So writing children's books was not completely out of the question. The other book, *Anna's Pet*, which was prose, I was approached to write, and I wrote it along with my aunt, who had been one of the first people to encourage my writing. So I thought it would be fun to do a book with her. She had the knowledge of how to write with a limited vocabulary for kids because she writes children's books.

Ross: And you were given a limited vocabulary?

Atwood: Well, they gave us a grade level, and she was used to writing for grade levels, so we worked it out together. She said, "You can use this word; you can't use that one; we can use this tense of these words but not those tenses" and all that, which I knew nothing about.

The story itself has an interesting history. It's based on a little story that she had written many years ago in phonetics because someone had asked her to do that. And she has based the story on my brother, who did take worms to bed and who hid snakes under his pillow and things like that. She had been visiting us at the time when my brother had taken a snake to bed and it had gone away, unknown to my mother. It had crawled into the wood stove to be where it was warm, so that when my mother opened the stove to light the fire in the morning, there was the snake. She said, "I think the snake would be happier outside."

Davies: What made you change the boy to a girl in the story?

Atwood: It didn't really matter whether it was a boy or a girl. Obviously I thought it would be more interesting to have a little girl who dug up worms than to have a little boy who dug up worms. I dug up worms. Lots of kids dig up worms. It is stereotypical to have little boys who dig up worms, but little girls do it too and I saw no reason why not.

Davies: You mentioned that you wrote *Up in the Tree* along with five other nonsensical books. Does the genre of children's literature allow you a particular perspective on the world that you want at the time that you are writing?

Atwood: You can only have that optimistic, happy-ending perspective on the world in children's literature. It doesn't ring true in serious adult literature because we know the world isn't entirely like that. We know that we would like the world to be like that, but we know that there is a gap; whereas in children's literature you can wholeheartedly endorse that optimistic perspective because you are dealing with wish-fulfillment. You can give full play to your wish-fulfillment and have everything turn out absolutely right and nobody's ever going to die, there's never going to be any tragedy, the princess will be rescued, and the prince will be restored to his right mind. Have you ever noticed how often the princes go out of their minds in *Grimm's Fairy Tales*? But it will all be set right and that's very reassuring. I think that it's reassuring for kids to be read that kind of book, because, Lord knows, they'll have the unhappiness soon enough. So better they should have a foundation of happy endings in childhood so that they can have some kind of feeling of cessation of anxiety and of expectations fulfilled which will carry them on through later life when things don't always work out that neatly.

Davies: So it permits you to use comic structure or romance structure?

Atwood: That's right, without any qualms. I use comic structure and romance structure anyway, but very, very modified.

Davies: More ironically?

Atwood: Yes. And with not quite so exultant rewards at the end of the book, shall we say, to put it mildly.

Davies: In "Production Problems," you say that you can do things in writing children's books that the age denies you when writing adult fiction and poetry. What else can you do in children's books—can you use words differently?

Atwood: You can be definitely sillier. There's more room for play. I play around quite a lot anyway. But you can do it in a more overt and simple-minded way, I think. At least I can. We're talking as if I write a lot of this and in fact I don't. There's a certain delight in complicated triple-syllable rhymed endings. There's a delight in doing those kinds of things with words. Kids have that delight and they will do it themselves.

Davies: Almost like sheer celebration.

Atwood: Word play and experimentation and fun and enjoyment, really.

Davies: And nonsense?

Atwood: A certain amount of nonsense, although there's no such thing as real nonsense, of course.

Ross: Do you want to elaborate on that?

Atwood: Every word has a meaning. You can't make up a word that doesn't convey something to the listener. It may not be a set meaning, but it has a meaning. The human mind makes meanings out of what it perceives. You can't make something with no meaning. Even if the meaning is, This doesn't have a meaning, that in itself is a statement and has meaning.

Davies: To get back to "Production Problems," in that article you talk about the economics of publishing children's literature in Canada.

Atwood: Yes. When I published *Up in the Tree*, which was a while ago, I certainly ran into the fact that we couldn't have full-color illustrations, because if we did it would make the book too expensive and so on. What you're up against is the fact that Puffins and kids' books produced in large countries can be produced for a price that is going to undercut most Canadian children's books, unless they're published abroad. So you run into things like *Bonny McSmithers* being in black-and-white drawing. I like *Bonny McSmithers*, by the way. Kids like it. In *Up in the Tree*, I lettered the whole book. It wasn't even typeset and I used two colors, red and blue. We were able to get a third kind of weird color by overlapping the other two, but essentially it's two colors.

Ross: This constraint reminds me of the narrator's situation in *Surfacing* when she is illustrating Quebec folk tales. She wants to use red because red is a sacred color, but she has to use yellow to suit the publisher and extra colors aren't allowed, to keep the costs down. Did this situation come out of your own experience?

Atwood: No. I wrote *Surfacing* long before I wrote *Up in the Tree*, I think. No, just a minute now. I wrote *Surfacing* before I was aware of that problem, but I think I wrote *Up in the Tree* about the same time as I was writing *Surfacing*. I wrote it in England, I remember that. Then somebody twisted my arm to actually publish it later on.

Ross: So the production problems came later when you were illustrating the book for publication?

Atwood: Yes, I illustrated it later. Laying it out determined how many lines got put on the pages. Some of the pages have only two lines on them, others have four, so that the thirty-two page book effect could be achieved by arranging the pages.

Davies: The production of *Anna's Pet* must have been a different sort of thing.

Atwood: I had nothing to do with production. I had a word length, but I didn't have to worry about layout or illustrations. My aunt and I collaborated on the text together. We did it by mail, back and forth in successive drafts, with different suggestions added in by other people and by each other. It was a very easy process. We said, "Let's do this," "That's a good idea" and so we did it. She's really quite wonderful and a very nice person, easy to get along with. And so am I, of course.

Davies: Can we talk about the illustrations? Ann Blades did the watercolors for *Anna's Pet*. Did you have an idea in mind beforehand of what kind of illustrations you wanted?

Atwood: I knew her work. I knew the way she illustrates things and she was proposed to us. We accepted her because we knew her work already, and we were very pleased that she did it.

Davies: I talked to her last November about illustrating *Anna's Pet*. She said she enjoyed doing the book but that she had troubles with the tadpole, trying to give it personality. Were you pleased with the illustrations?

Atwood: Oh yes. Let me have another look. . . . I think the illustrations are quite charming. She gets very serene expressions on the faces of the characters. Did you know that *Anna's Pet* has been turned into a puppet show? I haven't seen it yet, but my aunt has and she says it's a smash.

Davies: Who's doing the puppetry?

Atwood: Mermaid Theatre of Nova Scotia, who work with people and puppets. They do children's theater with puppets essentially. . . . I think that's charming. That's the worm. Anna looks so entranced by it, which is the proper way to look when you look at a worm. That's my mother and the stove, and that's exactly the kind of thing that my mother would do, as my aunt well knows. So there is a kind of family background to the story.

Davies: Since Ann Blades hadn't talked to you before she did the illustrations, the text must have inspired her to come up with a visual reproduction of your feeling of the book, which is splendid, really.

Atwood: It is. It's a different kind of house than any that I've ever lived in, but it looks a lot like the architecture of my grandparents' house in Nova Scotia—that white frame kind of building.

Davies: Before we end the interview, can we talk about the choice of animals in your books? In *Anna's Pet*, the animals are not cuddly.

Atwood: It depends upon your point of view. They are, however, animals that you would be able to come across quite easily at a farm. Nor would it take any great skill for a child to be able to apprehend them. Whereas, if she had to chase a rabbit all over the place, she never would have caught it.

Ross: You're stuck with realism and plausibility in *Anna's Pet*.

Atwood: I'm stuck with realism and plausibility wherever I go.

Davies: In *Up in the Tree*, you have the beavers...

Atwood: Those are porcupines.

Davies: Porcupines?

Atwood: I think they are porcupines. Let me see the book. They're porcupines. Look, they don't have beaver tails. Porcupines are things that come and chew off your ax handles and eat your toilet seat. Beavers mostly cut down trees; they're not interested in ladders. Porcupines are, alas. Anything with sweat on it they will eat.

Davies: Why did you choose these particular animals—the porcupines, the snail, the lizard, and the bat?

Atwood: I draw them quite well. Part of the explanation for choosing those animals is really quite ordinary, like what you can draw. I have spent a lot of time with snails in my life. Snails, lizards, frogs and toads, snakes, worms, and all those kinds of things. I, in fact, was the nature counselor at Camp White Pine, where the sun will always shine in beautiful Haliburton. I spent a lot of time with those creatures because the kids would catch them and they would come up to me and say, "Look what I caught," and there it would be, all over their hand. I spent a lot of time rescuing creatures from kids who clutched them too tightly.

Ross: A few final questions. Do you see any patterns in writing for children in Canada?

Atwood: I don't know enough about it. I can say that it was the Canadians who invented the real-life stories about animals, from the animal's point of view.

Ross: Roberts and Seton?

Atwood: Yes. When the English put animals in books before that time, the animals were usually dressed-up Englishmen in furs. Even in the Mowgli books, the animals have military rank. Or in the English books, like *Wind in the Willows* or *Alice in Wonderland*, the animals have social status. Human beings cannot write about animals without anthropomorphizing them a little bit, or else projecting their own fears and fantasies onto them. It's no accident that Greenpeace is Canadian. Save the whales; save the seals—it's a very Canadian thing to do. *Never Cry Wolf* is a very Canadian book. *A Whale for the Killing* is classical. An American story about animals is much more likely to be about killing them, catching them and killing them.

Ross: Do you have any plans for other children's books?

Atwood: Not at the moment, but you never know. I don't consider myself a professional children's book writer. If I do it, it will come out of left field, the same way that it did before.

Witness Is What You Must Bear
Beatrice Mendez-Egle

Beatrice Mendez-Egle's interview was conducted for the Living Author Series in November 1983 and originally appeared in *Margaret Atwood: Reflection and Reality* (Pan American University Press, 1987). Copyright © 1987 by Pan American University Press. Reprinted by permission.

Mendez-Egle: When John Gardner was here in 1981 he said that feminist writers have now moved into a second generation. He referred to these writers—and he included you in this list—as "smart girls." He described "smart girl" fiction as a new kind of fiction where the writer is "free to bat her eyelashes." He described it as a "skirt-swinging feminine prose which has the veneer of ladies' fiction but which is also profound and very real." What is your reaction to his categorization of you?

Atwood: Oh, I'm not that; I'm "pre-feminist." I've been around for too long to be a "smart girl." I started writing in 1956, and there wasn't any feminist movement, really, that I noticed, until about 1969. I guess what he was doing was contrasting fiction of the late '70s with fiction of the early '70s. Female fiction of the early '70s was very "head of the brigade"— you know, "Charge of the Light Brigade"—and there was a certain kind of plot that I remember: it was the harassed housewife who is having all of these problems because her husband won't let her do this, that, this, that, and isn't communicating; and the happy ending, which used to be marrying Prince Charming, is leaving your husband and getting a job. Well, I never wrote those, and I haven't written them since. I think probably my first novel, *The Edible Woman*, which I wrote in 1964, would as easily fall into his category as anything I've written since.

Mendez-Egle: Gardner also mentions a "veneer of ladies' fiction"—is that a certain avoidance of blood and guts and action?

Atwood: I did have a number of men say that they liked *Bodily Harm* the best, and I have the sneaking suspicion that the reason was that it had guns and war in it. Could that be?

Mendez-Egle: Possibly. I've found that some students who encounter some of your more vivid poetry—if we may use that term—more graphic poetry, have a negative reaction: "What's a woman doing writing about things like that?"

Atwood: Women get killed too. They don't usually do as much of the actual killing themselves. Take a visceral image like a dead rat and put it in a poem by a man and nobody would blink an eye, but put it in a poem by a woman and everybody feels suddenly that there's something wrong with her mother.

Mendez-Egle: Exactly. Some have observed that this kind of poetry is brutal.

Atwood: It's about brutal things. I don't think the stance of the poetry is brutal. If the stance of poetry were brutal, the voice in the poem would be applauding brutal things.

Mendez-Egle: "Notes Toward a Poem That Can Never Be Written" says, "The facts of this world seen clearly, are seen through tears," and ends, "Witness is what you must bear." I find many rather averse to bearing that kind of witness. Students seem to want to know about joy and hope and wonder and all those things.

Atwood: They're young. Those things exist, and I write about them as well. In fact, if you didn't write about them as well and only wrote about the dead rats, it would be an unbalanced picture and also pretty depressing. Generally the reason for working against brutality is that something else is possible. If you didn't think that something else is possible, you'd just join right in and shoot lots of people, wouldn't you?

Mendez-Egle: Seemingly, then, you feel a great sense of responsibility as a writer.

Atwood: No, not as a writer, as a human being. I don't think writers are the only people who should uphold this kind of thing; I think everybody should. I would feel the same way if I weren't a writer.

Mendez-Egle: You said that you started writing when you were sixteen. What was it about writing at that age, when you were sixteen, that made you realize you wanted to be a writer?

Atwood: I started writing. There was no *a priori* vision at all. I didn't think, I would like to be a writer, and now, maybe later, I'm going to write something. I started writing; it was more interesting than anything else I was doing. It was obviously a vocation.

Mendez-Egle: Can you describe the writing process you go through from the time you get an idea to the actual working out of the idea and maybe even putting it in manuscript form?

Atwood: I don't "get an idea" for a novel and then start translating it into something else. I usually find that I have collected a number of compelling images or that a voice starts operating, somebody starts talking, and I want to know more about him, find out about him; or possibly even a chance encounter with somebody will snap the whole thing into focus. *Bodily Harm*, for instance. I had been collecting some of these scenes and images, but it didn't fall into place until I met somebody on a beach in the West Indies who told me the whole story of her life—none of which got into the book—but that story just made a few things fall into place. I suddenly saw how I was going to proceed with the novel, how all these disparate elements were going to start fitting together. Just something like that can trigger it. Once you decide to start, you can think about things for years. I thought about *Surfacing* for five years before I actually started it. I'd written about two pages of it in 1965, but I didn't actually sit down and write the book until 1970. Starting a book is like jumping off a cliff. You're never ready, but you just feel that you have to start sooner or later. So you start and you know that it's probably going to be bad, but it doesn't matter: you have to start anyway. //

Mendez-Egle: What about the sheer mechanics of it? Do you have set working hours?

Atwood: I have set working hours. I usually try to have a separate place to write in, and the best thing is to just be able to go there and shut the door and write.

Mendez-Egle: Do you get writer's block and if you do how do you work yourself out of it?

Atwood: Because I'm multi-media, because I write in numbers of different things, I may block in one area. Then, instead of stopping altogether and chewing my fingers down to the bone, I switch into something else. If I'm blocking on a novel, I switch off and write maybe a travel piece or something like that, which is more mechanical and sort of like practicing the piano.

Mendez-Egle: What advice would you give to a person who wants to write poetry or fiction?

Atwood: I'd say, read a lot. People think that they can be writers without ever having read anything, and they think that writing is essentially their expression of their own emotions, period. It's a lot more than that, and sometimes it's something quite other than that. It doesn't matter what they read, but by reading a lot they'll find out what things they have affinities with. If they read a lot of things they don't like or don't particularly connect with, that's O.K. All writing is really learned from other writers, to begin with. //

Number two, write a lot. Try to write every day, even if you don't feel like it and even if you feel you're blocking. You should get to that piano and sit down and just get your hands on the keys and start playing because otherwise you're just going to start putting yourself into a metaphysical spin and sit there wondering about the meaning of life and who you are and all those other things that interfere with writing. //

Mendez-Egle: When you started writing what goals did you set for yourself?

Atwood: When I started writing in Canada in 1956, there was no cultural milieu that indicated to me I would ever make a living as a writer, that I would ever be known as a writer. I'd thought that my future would be to publish in little magazines. That's what was available. Maybe, if I was very lucky, I might be able to publish a book. I didn't have, therefore, a reasonable, realistic goal. I didn't have in view ever being able to support myself as a writer, and that was probably good for me. In other words, my goals were idealistic and writing-centered. I wanted to be a great writer. That's what people in their adolescent years want, and I think it's a pretty good thing to want.

Mendez-Egle: At what point did you know you were going to be successful as a writer?

Atwood: Probably when I was about thirty-two. I had published before that. I published my first book of poetry when I was twenty-five, and I immediately won the major Canadian literary prize. People aren't usually that young when they win that particular thing, so I think it was a bit of a fluke.

Mendez-Egle: How did it make you feel?

Atwood: I was stunned. I was also poor. I was very glad to have the money. I was very stunned, and my roommates lent me a dress, made me get my hair done to go and collect it. It was quite funny. All of that was very nice, but it was so unreal to me that I didn't really have any context for it. After that, it was quite easy for me. I didn't have any difficulty getting published. But I still wasn't financially in a very good position; I still had to have jobs.

No writer ever feels successful, as someone producing quality writing, unless they've decided to retire. You always feel that what you've done isn't what you can now do. You never feel that your best work is in the past unless you're getting to a point where you're really thinking of giving it up.

Mendez-Egle: The last poem in *True Stories* says, "each poem is my last and so is this one," and that seemed to me to indicate a little bit of uncertainty about whether the muse will remain constant throughout your life.

Atwood: Every writer has that uncertainty. You always know that this may be the last thing you'll ever write. Something else may not arrive. If I say that to my friends, they make disgusted noises, but it's true.

Mendez-Egle: Writer's insecurity then.

Atwood: No, it's just that if you didn't have that insecurity, you'd get very sloppy and lax, and it would become routine. And you wouldn't become excited about it anymore, and you wouldn't be putting all of your energy into it. It would just become a kind of routine thing.

Mendez-Egle: Do you think that creative writing can be taught, as we try to do in the classroom sometimes?

Atwood: You can't ever turn somebody who isn't a writer into somebody who is. But you can bring out latent potential; you can provide some shortcuts. You can teach people who may not be writers a lot more about the processes, and they then have an enhanced understanding of what they read. That's a valuable spinoff for those courses.

Mendez-Egle: In your poems, short stories, essays, and novels, you've been rather transparent in telling us who Margaret Atwood is. Can we depend on that portrait?

Atwood: I'm not in my novels. I often have people confusing me with the characters in my books. Because of *The Edible Woman*, they wonder if I'm anorexic or if I have an eating problem. Because of *Lady Oracle*, they think I once was much larger than I am, and they write me for my formula, how I did it. And they think my parents are dead because of *Surfacing*; my parents aren't dead. In fact, the characters in my novels have such diverse life histories I don't know how anyone could think I'm all of them. Some novelists do put themselves into their books a lot, but when I'm writing a novel, I'm consciously creating a character. I may use some things from my life, but I'm not the characters in the books.

Mendez-Egle: Which one would be your favorite character?

Atwood: My favorite character as a roommate or as a creation?

Mendez-Egle: As a creation.

Atwood: As a creation, I probably did the best job on one of the most unpleasant characters, namely Elizabeth in *Life Before Man*. As a roommate, I would prefer Joan Foster from *Lady Oracle*. She seems to me the most amiable of those women.

Mendez-Egle: I've heard someone mention that since Joan was a closet writer of Gothic romances, perhaps Margaret Atwood might be too.

Atwood: Alas, it is not so.

Mendez-Egle: What effect do you think the reading of so much escapist literature has on our consciousness?

Atwood: I don't think that most people feel when they read one of those books that that is real life. Most people find real life sadly lacking because it doesn't measure up. Escape fiction, or Louis L'Amour's Westerns, is a kind of wide-awake dreaming. It's the enactment of a plot that is quite basic to a lot of people. The plot of a Western is, I will be virtuous and a hero and conquer evil. Evil is in the form of some other man who wears a black hat as opposed to the white one you happen to be wearing. A little escape reading isn't bad for anybody; if we all had to read nothing but serious, realistic fiction, we would feel quite cramped.

Mendez-Egle: Do you think perhaps for the average reader there is a sense of impotence in the face of evil?

Atwood: Name me one person who doesn't feel that. We all can envision a world better than the one we live in, but we don't know how to transform the one we live in, to deprive it of hydrogen bombs.

Mendez-Egle: One of the stories many students have read in preparation for your visit is "When It Happens," and . . .

Atwood: That was not necessarily or specifically an atomic explosion. It was more like general collapse. But certainly there is the feeling in the corner of everybody's mind that the future may not continue to be like the present. It gives people the feeling of unreality in relation to their own lives. Even though they may continue to have their bungalow, their marriage, and their kids, they feel those things are under threat.

Mendez-Egle: Some writers continue mentally to revise their works throughout their lives. If you revised any of your works, what one would you target and why?

Atwood: It's not my impulse to revise books. I generally feel that when I finish something it's finished, and I don't wish to revise it. There may be things about it I think I could have done better, but it's too late now.

Mendez-Egle: To what extent do you consider the reader when you write? Do you have a specific audience in mind? How does the reader fit into your writing process?

Atwood: The writer can never know the reader. You may meet specific readers, but specific readers are as different from each other as you can imagine. To try to tailor what you're doing to some idea of the reader is futile. I don't consider the reader at all because the reader is many people. I do consider the great Reader in the sky who is the Ideal Reader. The Ideal Reader is the reader who reads what you write according to the text, just what's on the page, is conscious of everything that you are doing in a literary way, responds on an emotional level at the right places, laughs at the jokes, doesn't mistake irony for straight comment, gets the puns: all those things the Ideal Reader does. The Ideal Reader for me is somebody who reads the book on the first read-through to see what happens. I think that if you read a book at first with your term paper in mind, you miss the book because you're looking for the water symbolism or how many times people wear shoes. I read books to see what happens to the people in them. And after that I can sit back and admire how well it was done and what great skill was brought to bear. But the first time through I want to read the book.

Mendez-Egle: How do you feel about your novels and poetry being taught in English classes? Many people think once you put a literary work into a classroom you turn it into a textbook rather than into a form of art.

Atwood: I would rather have the students locked in a library and not let them out until they'd read so many books. If you like reading, it's pretty hard for any classroom experience to "ruin it" for you. People who don't like reading are usually resentful anyway. But sometimes you can convert people who don't like reading, and that's a real plus. Reading is different from television and movies in that you can do it at your own pace, you can turn backwards, you can be reflective about it, and it allows for many more dimensions of experience than do movies or television. The writer suggests some things to you and helps you fill in, but really you're supplying all that sensory information yourself. I can describe in a book what a heroine looks like, but that's something that the reader fills in according to what the reader thinks and the reader feels. So the reader is actually participating in the creation of the book. Every time someone reads a book, a new book is being created in the reader's head. Reading is a creative activity.

Mendez-Egle: Would you go so far to say then that once a book is written, a writer simply becomes another reader?

Atwood: That's absolutely right. I seldom do, but when I do go back and read things I've written a long time ago I'm often surprised. First, I can't remember having written them. Second, I think either Hey, that's pretty good or Oh, come on. //

Mendez-Egle: To what extent is your writing autobiographical?

Atwood: What people don't understand about writing is that if all the writer were doing was writing about him- or herself, he'd do one book. What you're doing when you're writing is putting yourself in the position of another person, which you can do yourself in real life. You can say, "Gosh, I wouldn't like to be in her shoes because it must be horrible what has happened to her," or, "He certainly is lucky." We do that all the time, except that a writer raises that to a conscious level and works it out in detail.

Just because some of the points touch our lives doesn't mean it's autobiographical. I've never had cancer. I wrote a whole book in which the character has had and probably still has. People who have had and possibly still have say, "How did you know? How did you get it so right? This is how I feel." That's writing. It's flattering when people think that: "You must have had it; how could you know?" But it doesn't mean that it's autobiography.

Mendez-Egle: "A Travel Piece" seems to be like a prelude to *Bodily Harm.* Is that correct?

Atwood: Yes. The short stories sometimes connect with novels that I later do. "The Man from Mars" connects with *Lady Oracle*; "A Travel Piece" certainly connects with *Bodily Harm.* In both cases they're about travel writers. Some poems overlap with some of the novels that I later write. Some of the pieces in *True Stories*, particularly the ones about politics and the ones about the West Indies, fed into *Bodily Harm.* But I was going to the West Indies for years before I ever wrote a thing about it.

Mendez-Egle: So you would say then that a writer takes bits and pieces of imagination and experience and turns them into a creative whole for the reader?

Atwood: Yes. It's all your real life in that it has all passed through your head, but what is real life? Is it something that you read in the paper that happens to be real to you, or is it something that happens in your family?

Managing Time for Writing
Sue Walker

Sue Walker's interview was conducted in February 1985 while Margaret Atwood held the Endowed Chair in Creative Writing at the University of Alabama and originally appeared in *Negative Capability* 5 (1985). Copyright © 1985 by *Negative Capability*. Reprinted by permission.

Walker: Do you consider yourself primarily a poet or novelist—or both?

Atwood: I consider myself a writer.

Walker: I was thinking of how you divide your time as a writer.

Atwood: First of all, poetry and fiction aren't the only things that I write. I also write literary criticism, and I write travel pieces when I want to keep my hand in and I don't have anything else going. It's also a convenient way of getting about in the world. I have also written screen plays and TV screen plays. Of all of these things, I put poetry and prose fiction at the top.

Now, how do I divide time? It takes me anywhere from nine months to three or four years to finish a novel. And while I'm working on a novel, I usually don't write much of anything else. I might write the occasional review, but that's usually an interruption, and I prefer not to. When I have finished a novel, I am usually exhausted. I have exhausted my fiction energy, and there comes a period during which I don't write much. After that, if I'm lucky, I start to write poetry. I'll keep going with that for a period of anywhere from two to three years until I've exhausted the poetry. Then I start writing fiction again. That's not a decision. It just seems to be the way my life arranges itself. I did find it difficult to write fiction while I was teaching at the university and also while I was a full-time student. With fiction I need a long uninterrupted phase of time.

Walker: What do you think about combining writing, a marriage, and a career? For men and women—because you are married to a writer.

Atwood: I think it works out very well. People often think that it won't because it is some kind of competition. But we write such different things in such different ways. There were no surprises. We knew we were writers when we met. We had already published, and we were both quite well known. So it wasn't the usual situation in which the marriage has been contracted with one partner or the other not admitting to being a writer, or not knowing it, or not yet having been published. When that happens and the person starts writing and becomes published, it can upset the understanding in which the marriage was arranged. The good thing about writers' marriages is that they can live anywhere without being tied down to a job. We can spend time at home because our time is flexible. This is important when you have children.

Walker: You make it sound easier than *Life Before Man*. That novel seems to portray relationships pessimistically.

Atwood: It may not be pessimistic enough if you look at the statistics.

Walker: I have just finished reading E. L. Doctorow's *Lives of the Poets* and it interests me the way he interweaves the psychology of relationships with the political. Maybe he's political about relationships...

Atwood: I think the word *political* tends to be weighted in the United States in a way in which it is not in other countries in the world. // It got shoved over to the side as something that didn't belong in art, and if you started putting it into your work, you were somehow sullying yourself. To say that politics is dirty or that politics is dangerous and only dangerous people get involved with it is to isolate yourself from your environment. It might have happened just before Hitler in Germany; young people, respectable people, high-minded people did not engage in politics. They thought it was a dirty game. //

Walker: Well, I'm Southern, and I think Southern writing often includes an element that is *political*.

Atwood: I think that Faulkner was a very political writer and, in fact, he was very inspirational as an influence on Latin American writing and to a certain extent on Canadian writing. He was the big influence from the United States.

Walker: Faulkner influenced you?

Atwood: Among others. Yes, absolutely. But his work is not non-political. We don't see it that way anymore because it's about the past. His work is old enough now so that we can take the same attitude towards him that we take to Charles Dickens, another very political writer. Isn't Oliver Twist wonderful—dancing and singing up there on the stage? Well, when Dickens wrote *Oliver Twist,* he didn't think it was quaint. He was writing about real life then, and so was Faulkner. //

Walker: Do you feel that your books are autobiographical?

Atwood: No, but the settings are accurate. I don't write about places that I haven't been to, and when I put a place into a book, I try to make it as real as possible. But the details of my life are not in the books.

Walker: How do you feel about posterity? How much information do you feel the public is entitled to about your life?

Atwood: My life is very boring. I don't see why anybody should be vitally interested in it.

Walker: No chosen biographer?

Atwood: Oh no, what would they put in? It's like people who approach you and say they want to do a television show on you, and you say, "What can you possibly put into it?" All you would see is a person sitting in front of a piece of paper, because what really goes on is in my head.

Walker: What you're telling me is that you're really a very private person.

Atwood: I think you would say "private." I might just say "boring." The first person who did an interview with me back in 1967 when I had just won some sort of award had just come back from Vietnam, where he had been a war correspondent; and because he was traveling in my direction, they asked him to do an interview with me. He could barely keep himself awake, and he finally said, "Why don't you say something interesting?" //

Walker: Do you follow a schedule? And is discipline very important to you?

Atwood: I have a schedule that I follow every day. What I am saying applies to prose fiction, because it doesn't apply to poetry. I can't will myself to write poetry, and I doubt that many people can. They can provide themselves blank time and hope that the poetry will come into it, but they can't say, Now I am going to write five pages, which is what I say to myself every morning.

Walker: So you think of poetry as a gift?

Atwood: Well, I think it's all a gift, but it comes in different packages.

Walker: How do you see the difference—in writing poetry and prose, a novel, for instance?

Atwood: The process is very different. Since I write lyric poems, they are not very long. You can have the idea for a novel in the same amount of time that it takes you to "have a poem," and it can be a very short stage of time, but then you have to put the work in. You have to sit down and write the novel, sentence by sentence, and page by page, and chapter by chapter, and that takes a lot of time. So you're talking about a continuous process that may take you anywhere from nine months to three-four years. And that means a daily immersion which can be very tedious. That's when willpower comes in. It's important to keep going even if what you did today is bad. At least you'll be sticking to it. I think that attitude wouldn't work with poetry. If you don't have poetry to write down, you can spend your time rewriting what you have already done or indeed typing it out. That could give you a sense of accomplishment.

Walker: Can you define a good poem? I'm thinking of elements that can be taught, common elements that separate what is publishable from that which is not publishable.

Atwood: One can say, "Does it contain an element of bathos?" Are you dealing with language inappropriate to the occasion being described? I think an anthology of bad verse is enormously useful for young students to read because then they can scan their own poem to look for ridiculous moments that they did not intend. I used to edit a poetry magazine when I was a student, and I once had a poem that was submitted that had in it the line, "The evergreens dark behind." Now what the poet meant was that there were evergreens behind the house and they were dark, but that wasn't what the line actually said. You have to watch if a poem has that kind of error. Or if it has lines like this: "I sweep the dust of my dismal vision under the rug of night." That again is a quote. So we rule out all those and then get to the finer points. //

Walker: When you went to college, did you go with the idea of becoming a writer?

Atwood: Absolutely. In fact, college was about my third choice. I first thought that I would become a journalist. I talked to some people about it; this was in the '50s and they said, "Girls who work on newspapers end up writing the obituaries or the ladies' page."

Walker: What did you take in preparation for being a writer?

Atwood: I ended up in Honors English, but that wasn't to prepare myself for being a writer; it was because I was good at it, and I thought I could get a job. I didn't have any idea that I would ever be able to support myself writing. It wasn't done in Canada at the time. So I didn't have grand visions of success; I had the idea that I would be a kind of starving artist in a garret turning out masterpieces that possibly two hundred people would read because that was the size of the reading audience for Canadian poetry at that time. And in order to support that, of course, I would have to have some kind of other job, and I thought I could do English literature. I did think at one point of becoming a waitress. But I tried that, and it was very exhausting. You lose your appetite, and you don't feel like writing at the end of the day.

Walker: Did you have any significant mentors?

Atwood: Yes. Where I went to college at the University of Toronto—in Victoria College, which is one of the colleges within that University— there were several people whose attitude was very positive. One was Northrop Frye, who was not breathing down my neck, but he did take writing seriously, and he didn't giggle openly at the people who did it. Remember, this was the '50s and not very many people were writing. But we wrote out little things, and we published them in our little magazines. It made us feel that being a writer wasn't a completely discard-able thing, and that was important for me then. It's very important to give young writers that opinion. //

Walker: Are there any other writers in the family?

Atwood: There is a funny thing about my brother and myself—we both wrote as children. We are both interested in science. Our marks graduating from high school were about the same in both subjects. He became a scientist, and I became a writer, but he reads a lot for recreation, and

I read popular science as my recreation. He is a neurophysiologist—head of the University of Toronto Physiology Department at the Medical School.

Walker: What do you plan to do now that you haven't done?

Atwood: There are about three books that I have lined up. I'm finishing one, and I know what the next one is going to be. Then I have another one I tried to write in 1968 and didn't complete. I'm going to do that one again.

Walker: What is the difference in coming at it now after the gap? After it's been on the back burner all these years?

Atwood: It's been on the back burner, but my technical approach to it was wrong. I tried to tell the story from the point of view of too many characters at once. It became too unwieldy and large; it lost narrative momentum. In writing a novel you have to give the reader enough reason for turning the next page—apart from your delightful prose. //

The Empress Has No Clothes
Elizabeth Meese

Elizabeth Meese's interview was conducted in April 1985 at the University of Alabama and originally appeared in *Black Warrior Review* 12 (1985). Copyright © 1985 by *Black Warrior Review*. Reprinted by permission.

Meese: Has there, from your point of view, been any good criticism on your work? Or do you read criticism about your work?

Atwood: There's been an awful lot of criticism about my work, and I've ceased to read it because I find it inhibiting. You find yourself arguing with this or that little point and the fact is that you can't spend your time doing that. I will look at the biographical material to see if it's accurate, which it never has been. And I can't understand why that is.

Meese: What kind of problems have there been?

Atwood: Wrong places of residence at wrong times...you know, just ordinary stupid things like that that get into circulation and other people copy them because it's the printed word and they think it's true. Once one of those things gets into print circulation it's awfully hard to get it out. But then new ones keep appearing. So I *will* look at that, but the nuances of interpretation I don't look at any more because it could take up all my time.

Meese: So then you haven't looked at Jerome Rosenberg's book? Or did you work with him?

Atwood: He came to visit us at one point, but I haven't looked at it yet. I will look at it later for the biographical material. And I think it's probably frustrating for people who do work on me to have me *not* read it.

Meese: I was curious about Rosenberg's view of *Power Politics*. I didn't know until I read his book the sort of controversies that surrounded a lot of your work.

Atwood: Controversies have surrounded *all* of my work.

Meese: So it seems. That surely didn't occur to me. I guess there have been fewer controversies about it here in America.

Atwood: There have been controversies here as well. Back when I was still reading criticism there was a feminist controversy about *Surfacing*. Some people thought that it was about mother-goddesses and other people thought that it was anti-abortion.

Meese: What about *Bodily Harm*? Do you know if there's been much attention to that?

Atwood: Quite a lot. The older a book is the more attention there's been paid to it, as usual. The one thing they have the most trouble with is *Life Before Man*. Why could that be? Because it's a novel novel. It stays very firmly within the boundaries of realism and the people who do criticism on my work have been attracted to it through the other books, and therefore they didn't know quite what to do with that one because it didn't have the things in it that they were looking for. And so there's a controversy about *that*. Some people loved it and other people hated it. I suppose that's better than lukewarm or "isn't this nice, dear."

Being misinterpreted used to bother me. But I now realize it's inevitable, and it's probably inevitable for just about everyone. Except that since all this lands on your own doorstep, you don't see all that's written about other people. But once you start talking to other writers and hear *their* stories, you realize that similar things have happened to them. But why should it be otherwise? Because every reader is different and readers bring who they are to a book.

Meese: Well, they're really in a position of reproducing your text. Like it or not.

Atwood: You mean recreating...yes. "Recreating" I would say, rather than just "reproducing."

Meese: Well, I mean that, I guess, in a very particular way. That it *is* a product of their own labor, not just your labor. In the kind of dichotomy that Barthes makes between the reader as consumer who reads it, throws it away, and gets another one off the shelf or at the bookstore, and the readers who really have to somehow labor to produce your text for themselves. I like that image of the reader.

Atwood: Yes, and it's borne out by the neurologist who hooked up people's brains and gave them books to read and sat them in front of television sets. In fact the brain works harder when reading; it's more fully involved.

Meese: What kind of changes are *you* aware of, or what do you see as the *shape* of your fiction over time?

Atwood: You think of a stone thrown into a lake. I would say that the first novel is that little ring. And then you have another one after that, a bigger one. So I would say that the range of vision, the area of society or life or even language has expanded. But I think that happens to people as they grow older; it ought to, or there's something very wrong. And as you go on, the writing itself will lead you into areas where you never expected to go.

Meese: How does that work out, say, in a concrete example? When are you aware of that?

Atwood: Well, if you had told me in 1960 that I would sometime be writing a novel about human rights violations in the West Indies I would have told you you were crazy. //

Meese: What about your own politicization?

Atwood: If you grew up in the '50s, even in Canada, it was better than the States in that respect. The States went through an intense period of Freudianization in the late '40s and in the '50s, which had something to do with men returning from the war and wanting jobs and people deciding that women should all go back to the house and free up the jobs. So there was a lot of propaganda floating about, and I have had women from the States *tell* me that they were taught in college, in college where they were supposed to be learning, that if they used their brains, they were defeminizing themselves. I find that so shocking. We were still in the "old tradition" of tough old female deans and dons telling us not to pay attention to boys and do our studies. So we had that. Anyway, I don't remember getting all this Freudian stuff. I think it just wafted over the border in American women's magazines. Any imported culture is always fantasy land to a certain extent. You may pay attention to it, but you know that it's not real. Your granny is more real than *Redbook*. So even in Canada there was a certain amount of cultural pressure. Although not from my immediate family. They came through the Depression.

They know the value of the dollar; they thought people should have jobs. "Just in case, dear."

So it was none of this "get a good man to support you." They didn't believe in that. But writing was something else again because there weren't many visible writers. In fact, there weren't *any* visible writers in Canada at that time. But in a way that was an advantage because it was not an area monopolized by men. It was free for all, really. And what writers there were felt so isolated and beleaguered that they were happy to welcome anybody that showed any interest in it. So I didn't have the experience of being put down by men, or being told I couldn't do this because I was too feeble. There were a couple of male writers who gave out noises like that, but nobody paid that much attention to them. And the others were really very supportive and helpful; "be as you like, but write" was the message, because the view was more writers against all those people out there who weren't buying our books than men against women. The urge to develop a national literature was very strong, and that's why the Writers' Union, which I helped found, has not had chauvinist problems. Because the people in it know, whatever their private predilections, that if they start behaving that way, half their membership would leave. Because half are women. So it's a different balance of power. Not so among the poets. The poets' union, for whatever reason, has more men in it. And they have those problems, and they have a women's caucus which was organized some years ago because people felt that men were controlling magazines and grants. Part of the problem was, of course, that men were willing to do that kind of horrible work, and women weren't. // The poets organized first, but they weren't practically oriented. Why? Because nobody makes any money out of poetry anyway. So the fiction writers were formed as a craft union, really. And that's why they call themselves a union rather than an association or a guild. And they were very much involved in contracts and things. Why? Because there were no literary agents in Canada. You either had to go outside the country, in which case your agent probably wouldn't understand the Canadian situation and you had to do it yourself anyway, or you didn't have an agent. So that was one of the big things that caused its formation. //

Meese: Well then, back to your own process of politicization that leads you, say, into Amnesty International and human rights work.

Atwood: It probably began back in the '50s when I, number one, was a member of the United Nations club in high school. I don't know how I get into these things; I tended to get into things like debating in college.

Again, I don't know why. Some friend says you have to do this. That's how you get into it. But it's stood me in good stead because I can now do those things. I know how to run a meeting according to *Robert's Rules of Order*. It's very useful. And then I was the nature instructor at a Jewish summer camp, although I'm not Jewish. This was a reformed, liberal Jewish summer camp, and they hired a certain number of non-Jewish people every year to expose the children to them, because the children were from a quite rich area of Toronto which they never went out of and they just didn't see people who weren't Jewish, except the cleaning ladies. One of the first things the seven-year-olds asked me was "Are you Jewish?" I said, "No." And they said, "Are you the cleaning lady?"

And at that camp a lot of the programs—I think it was still close enough to the '40s and possibly even the '30s—were quasi-political. By that I don't mean "late-'60s politicized" in that way. I mean that we were all supposed to believe in the brotherhood of man. There was a big thing every year called the Camp-Wide Program. That was always started off by some exciting, dramatic event. Sirens would go off in the middle of the night and you'd have to get all the kids out of their beds and you'd go to the football field and people would be going around saying, "The Martians have landed."

And you get there and there would be a big bonfire and here would be two men standing in the middle of it looking like Martians. Actually, they were wearing asbestos suits. And they would say, "We're from the planet so-and-so," and the little kids would start to cry and the big kids would say, "It's only Phil." And then they'd say, "We have decided that the Earth is behaving very badly and we have given you seven days to make peace."

And it was a very strange situation because it was several generations of Jewish people. The generation older than mine was quite political. They were the inheritors of '30s populist Depression politics. Then there were these kids who were affluent '50s kids. So you would have this spectacle of the older people teaching the kids to sing songs from the Spanish Civil War. The kids had no idea what it was.

That's probably where all of that dates from, although at the time I just thought it was a skit. It was really funny, because my own parents are not political at all. They're scientific instead.

Meese: And not religious either?

Atwood: Well, my mother went through all of that small-town religion because it was the social form then. And also she tells me that she was very religious as a child and thought that wings would grow out of her shoulder blades if she prayed for them, because you were supposed to be able to pray for things and get them. She cut little holes in the back of her nightgowns so that the wings could come out.

But I rebelled against the family and went to Sunday school. My father was quite against it, but my friends were going. That has been very valuable because I know the Bible, which is useful for anybody in literature, among other things.

My brother is a scientist, and I don't think he ever has a political thought in his head. I wouldn't say that I'm hardline anything. I have a great distrust of ideological hardlines. They make me shudder because the other thing that I grew up on, of course, was a lot of history. My father is a history nut. The basement is full of it. So I read the biography of Rommel when I was twelve. I read Winston Churchill's five volumes on the war when I was fourteen or fifteen. At my Jewish summer camp in the '50s, people didn't talk about the war or the concentration camps. There was a period of time that was repressed. It was too close and they just wanted to forget it.

There was a man who peeled potatoes for the kitchen. He did nothing but peel potatoes. And he had a number on his arm. He was obviously a shell-shocked survivor that the camp had hired. Everybody knew he was there. Nobody talked about him. He was the "forbidden man."

On the other side of things, in college I taught what we call "English as a second language." You could volunteer to teach people to speak and read. One of the people I taught was an older woman who had been a professor in Czechoslovakia and so she had lots to say about the Russians. You read the histories of McCarthyism or witch hunts—those things scare me.

Meese: So you see the development of your political consciousness as being a continuum?

Atwood: Absolutely. When I first started to write, I didn't connect the writing at all with any of that. It was very much art for art's sake, personal. That may be the way you have to learn to write. I'm suspicious of people telling people what they have to write. I'm very much against that in any way. It's like telling people when they're twenty, before they learn the scales on the piano, that they ought to be composing *The Magic Flute.* They have to learn that themselves. //

Meese: Do you think that the way you write about women's identity or sexual relationships is political as compared with, say, the human rights issues of a novel like *Bodily Harm*? I mean, do you separate those?

Atwood: I think they're all political, but it's all nonpolitical as well. In the pragmatic sense, you save people by raising money, writing letters, in a very concrete kind of way. On the other hand, you can't raise money to do those things unless people agree with what you're raising money for. But I'm an artist. That's my affiliation, and in any monolithic regime I would be shot. They *always* do that to the artists. Why? Because the artists are messy. They don't fit. They make squawking noises. They protest. They insist on some kind of standard of humanity which any such regime is going to violate. They will violate it saying that it's for the good of all, or the good of the many, or the better this or better that. And the artists will always protest and they'll always get shot. Or go into exile.

Meese: I think one of the messiest subjects that seems to recur is your attitude toward the political, or toward the monolithically ideological. And you talk about it a lot. You talk about yourself in that essay "On Being a Woman Writer: Paradoxes and Dilemmas." And it *does* end up being a set of paradoxes and dilemmas. But sometimes it sounds like you're just totally resisting it and denying, for instance, feminism, but then there is the example of Adrienne Rich, whose work you praise and admire.

Atwood: Sure. But if practical, hardline, anti-male feminists took over and became the government, I would resist them. Why? Because they could start castrating men, throwing them in the ocean, doing things I don't approve of. But any extreme group is likely to behave that way. Why? Because they think they have the true faith. And, like Ayatollah Khomeini, if you think you have the one true faith and you are dedicated to it, you'd feel that any action you may do is justified. It's the end justifying the means. In other words, I think that fanaticism—as apart from belief—is dangerous. Now belief in the rights of women is another thing.

Meese: That's where it gets messy.

Atwood: Belief in the rights of women. Absolutely. Women are human beings; they are equal human beings. I happen to believe that. And I will fight to eliminate inequalities as I have done. Look who I contribute money to, endorse, support, go to the meetings of, and all that. It's all on record. But once they start saying, "Thou shalt write about this" and "Thou shalt not write about that," "Thou shalt not say, 'The Empress has no clothes.'" "Thou shalt not say, 'This was a stupid, pigheaded way to behave,'" then I say no. You know, women are equal human beings. That also means they're equally fallible.

Meese: ... and diverse. What one does is end up denying the specificity of women's experience by homogenizing it.

Atwood: I deny the homogeneity of it. Subject to the same kinds of pressures, yes. I too have had trouble getting a bank loan because I am a woman. People whistle at me in the street. Yes. Yes, all of that. But you can *not*, therefore, go on to say that everybody who writes about flowers is out the window. You know, "We're not going to allow you to listen to those people; we're only going to listen to people who write about masturbation."

Meese: Well, then you'd finally end up with one story and one heroine. I mean...

Atwood: There isn't just one story; there are lots of stories. It's the same thing that black women writers complained of early in the movement. They were saying, "This is a white, middle-class women's movement. You are trying to tell us that our experience is like this, and it is *not* like this. It's like that." And that's what you have to keep on saying. Because, yes, the experience of an Australian feminist is not the same as the experience of an American feminist. An English feminist is something else. They have their own set of circumstances to deal with. And what any women in any culture have to deal with is the attitude of the men in that culture, which differs vastly. Even in English-speaking cultures it differs vastly. If I have anything to say to the American feminist, it's that they've been too parochial. America is very big, you can get lost in it, but they haven't looked enough outside.

Meese: We, furthermore, haven't done a good job of accommodating the diversity within.

Atwood: I think that's happening. I think people are aware of it. There's a group of Chicano women in New York now that's put out a book, for instance, and their experience is something else again. There are certain common denominators, but they're very specific to the situation and what would be seen as retrograde and a step backwards for one group is seen as a huge advance for another group.

Feminism for women in India, for example, starts with getting them jobs and money. It starts with setting up little weaving projects in the villages so that they can demonstrate to their husbands that they're worth something. I'm involved in something called the Canada-India Village Aid Association. It takes a total view of the culture, rather than just put in medical clinics or whatever. The thing about India is that there's no pension plan. There's no welfare of that kind, and your children are your future. So you can't say to a couple, "Only have two kids." Especially with the infant mortality rate the way it is. You're telling them to throw away their old age. There won't be anybody to support them. You just can't do that unless you lower the infant mortality rate and give them some more secure way of existing. They'll go on having as many kids as they can to see if any will survive to take care of them when they're old.

Meese: It must be really hard to teach writers or to work with young writers around that issue of politics, because there's a lot of support for the notion that what one does as a writer is apolitical.

Atwood: That's only in this country. It's not true in England. It's not true in Europe. It's not true in Canada. It seems to me to be mostly in the United States.

Meese: Why do you think that is?

Atwood: I think that it is for two reasons. One, McCarthy scared people. Two, there was a period at the end of the '60s when there was a lot of strident, "political" writing that got very rhetorical and bored people. And the '70s and '80s have been a reaction against that.

Meese: Do you think that might also have to do with some sort of cultural imperialism? That there is a homogeneity? The classical tradition the Academy wants to maintain is an appearance, an illusion of homogeneity?

Atwood: The classical tradition in America is political. I studied this with Perry Miller. It was a big eye-opener to me. But from the Puritans on down, practically until the '50s, there was a great deal of what would now be called "political." *Moby Dick* was a political book. Thoreau, Lord knows. Whitman. You know, the classics. You can't say that those had no political interests, no vision. And what do we mean by "political"? What we mean is how people relate to a power structure and vice versa. And this is really all we mean by it. We may mean also some idea of participating in the structure or changing it. But the first thing we mean is how is this individual in society? How do the forces of society interact with this person?
The Man in the Grey Flannel Suit is political. To my mind, a lot of John Updike is political. It's just that people don't analyze him that way. In a very large affluent society, you can afford to go out in your own little boat and think about the infinite. Men can afford that more than women can. I would love to just sort of drift around and look at waterlilies.

Unfortunately, I can't afford to. Wouldn't it be nice if we had a world in which all we had to do was contemplate nature? Meanwhile this is the world that we live in. And it's all very well for some fellow to go sauntering off into the woods by himself. A woman thinks twice before she does that. Either she thinks twice or she's a nut. //

Meese: I'm interested in what sort of background you bring to questions of character. And particularly I notice that you make disparaging remarks about Freud. You don't seem to make such disparaging remarks about Jung. I wondered whether you've done reading in those works that you would count of any importance?

Atwood: I think Freud was a seminal thinker of the twentieth century. He just happens to be very reductionist about women.

Meese: So not much help if you're a woman?

Atwood: Well, a lot of things aren't much help if you're a woman. All they do is relegate you to some little straitjacket that you don't particularly feel you fit into, or else, if you try to believe that you do, you'll end up with several fewer limbs than you ought to have. Sure, a lot of Freud is valuable. He was very much a product of his own time and culture, and therefore, he, of necessity, saw women in a certain way. He also dealt with only sick people. Any theory derived only from sick people is bound to be somewhat truncated.

Meese: Have you read any of the French deconstructionists or the post-structuralists? Are you interested in that?

Atwood: I am not a literary theorist of that kind. The English tradition from which Canadian writing derives, I think, is Lockean. It begins with the noun. It begins with the concrete noun and the concrete verb. The French are going in a lot more for the abstract. You can say things in French that sound just wimpy in English. And as for the Germans... the way their language is constructed means that you can bring a thing into being simply by nounifying it. You cause it to become a noun and, lo, it is. You can make a noun out of an adjective by capitalizing it and putting *heit* onto the end of it. *Schonheit.*

Meese: But you seem so abstract in certain ways, too. Your books are full of it. There are so many invitations to mostly abstract philosophical speculation from the critic in reaction to your books.

Atwood: I have an ambidextrous brain. My early background in university was philosophy. I went into philosophy originally because I thought if I went into English I would become too limited, and I quickly realized that, in fact, it would work the other way around. So I switched in a jiffy over to English, but I kept philosophy as what you would call a "minor," my principal areas of interest being aesthetics and ethics. I keep my hand in it to a certain extent, although really it tends to aggravate me a lot. Kierkegaard would never have been a woman, you know. And I think a lot of the speculation about the void and things like this are very male. Why? Because they could afford to do that, again. I think women are much more grounded in the world because they have had to be.

Meese: Is it true of people like Susan Langer?

Atwood: I'm not saying here that this is gender-specific, that women can't think abstractly. That's not what I'm saying at all.

Meese: I just wondered if you thought that there were any women that produced a different sort of aesthetics.

Atwood: I would say that it is coming. It's on its way. Do you know Annette Kolodny? She's very smart. I like her work.

I don't want to give you the impression that I'm completely cut off from these lines of thinking. I just don't think that they're a primary concern for the writer. The primary concern of the writer is to write. And if you get too snarled up in those things, it will inhibit your writing. Or else make it very shrunken and problematic. I'm sure of it for me. //

Meese: I'd like to return to your novels. When you wrote *Bodily Harm*, did you have any conscious awareness of things like body as body, body as text, and body as body politic playing together in relation particularly to disease or dis-ease?

Atwood: The body as a concept has always been a concern of mine. It's there in *Surfacing* as well. I think that people very much experience themselves through their bodies and through concepts of the body which get applied to their bodies. Which they pick up from their culture and apply to their own bodies. It's also my concern in *Lady Oracle* and it's even there in *The Edible Woman*.

I'm interested in where you feel your body can go without being conspicuous or being put into danger. How you see the adornment of your body, which every culture does, to some extent, in different ways.

Whether you see that as something forced upon you or as something that you do of your own free choice. Whether you see beauty as a tool, which, of course, women in this country are taught to do. Whether you see it as part of your stock in trade that you have to use to get what you want. All of those things. And it is very central to everybody. It came home to me down on Gulf Shores when I saw the Southern Belle contingent in their beach makeup. O.K., come on. This is going too far. Makeup for the beach. I said to somebody, "How early do these women start putting on this makeup?" And somebody said, "Sun never touches their faces." All that is very central to a culture. And if you travel to other cultures and see which parts of the body are considered exposable and which parts are not, then you realize a lot of things about your own culture. The fact that we go around with parts of our bodies sticking out is very interesting. In India I always take care to have several long cotton wrap-around skirts because if I tried to give a reading or anything with my legs showing nobody would hear a word I said. They'd all be so aghast. They'd all be looking at my legs. Not out of lust but just out of horror, that I would be allowing these parts of my body to be exposed. So I think, there again, when you travel you have to take a lot of care to know those things in advance, otherwise you're going to get stoned, as my friend who wore shorts in Jerusalem was stoned by some Arab boys.

Meese: Are you working a lot with the problem of the committed life or engagement?

Atwood: The problem is, why did George Eliot never write a novel about a famous English novelist who succeeded?

Meese: Who'd want to read it?

Atwood: Wrong. Wrong. Anybody would if it were written properly. But she never did. These women all don't amount to much. They drown, or turn into Dorothea, or marry Ladislow. The answer was that she was so atypical that she didn't feel, obviously, that such a character would have been central to the concerns of her society. It's like, for instance, Alice Walker. Her characters are not successful, black female writers. They're people who are struggling for some sort of minimal achievement. There are several ways of approaching that. We had some stuff in the Women's Movement early on. We wanted strong, successful, earthy women who fight and achieve, and succeed. I think, well O.K. You fight, struggle, achieve, and succeed, and what are you in the terms of this society? Well, maybe you're an executive in an ad company. Meanwhile, everybody else is still on welfare. It's a difficulty where to place your character in the society. And I think I would rather take a character who is not on top of the heap and go with that person some distance. In some cases it's a very small distance; in the case of Elizabeth in *Life Before Man*, it's a very small distance, maybe, for you and me. But for her it's a very big distance. And this is a lesson I learned very, very early on. I went to a very early women's consciousness-raising session for people in the arts, and there was one really nifty woman there who was a set designer, and she was worth listening to because she was old. But a lot of them were just little artists, little young actresses and things. And they were talking about whether it was or was not liberated to wear false eyelashes. I was so pissed off that I went and talked to my friend, Rick. And I said, "What are these people? What was this?" He said, "If eyelashes are where they're at, that's where you begin." And a lot of people are still at eyelashes. //

Meese: You write multiple endings. In fact I think *Surfacing* had even more of a suggestion of the ending.

Atwood: Have you read *Survival*? Go back to the part about the victim position. It's all there. You cannot create a character who is fully liberated in every sense of the word in a society which is not. Unless we make that person a mystic and withdraw them from the society.

Meese: I thought it was interesting that in *Surfacing* you took a more mythic course, or allowed your character to do it.

Atwood: But she only goes up to the point where she is going to go back to society.

Meese: But you even took a more realistic course, though again through multiple choices, at the end of *Bodily Harm*. You're moving that limit a little bit.

Atwood: O.K. The Americans believe in free choice, and they think that what that means is that you have a choice of everything. You don't. You have a very limited smorgasbord. You have a choice between A, B, or C, and that is it in your own life. And anybody who thinks otherwise is just indulging in the most wishful thinking. Utopian. Millennialist. To me, American thinking. I mean, you don't say to an Indian woman who is starving, "Become liberated and be an ad executive." She can't even *read*. What you're talking about is something, to you, very small; to her, very big. When people are making daily wages the equivalent of two cents, adding a third cent is very big. It's all very well for these people to sit around theorizing in their living rooms. But that's *their* living rooms. Lucky they should have living rooms and the time to do it.

Meese: Well, it's on that basis that I believe Rennie makes a very big move.

Atwood: Rennie makes a very big move. She accepts responsibility for another human being, which this society does not encourage. This is a society of individuals. You're supposed to be "me first." Right?

Meese: But it's also her mother, it seems, that helps her understand that.

Atwood: The mother, yes, with the grandmother. That's right.

Meese: In the same way that the mother carries a very special message in *Surfacing*. It seems to be preoccupied with the father, but it really is also preoccupied with the mother.

Atwood: It absolutely is, if you go back and look at it. And the mother is the one who appears at the end first. And the image in that book for the mother and the father is that little barometer that has the two figures of equal size balanced.

Tightrope-Walking Over Niagara Falls
Geoff Hancock

Geoff Hancock's interview was conducted December 12 and 13, 1986, at Margaret Atwood's home in Toronto and originally appeared in his collection *Canadian Writers at Work* (Oxford University Press, 1987). Copyright © 1987 by Geoff Hancock. Reprinted by permission.

Hancock: Interviews can take many forms. They can act as an adjunct to literary criticism, or they can act as literary biography. An interview can get inside a writer's work. Do you think I might learn something about your work which isn't readily apparent from an interview?

Atwood: Interviews are an art form in themselves. As such, they're fictional and arranged. The illusion that what you're getting is the straight truth from the writer and accurate in every detail is false. The fact is that most writers can't remember the answers to some of the questions they get asked during interviews, so they make up the answers. A lot of the questions are about things they don't usually think about, or if they do think about them, they don't think about them at the time of writing. Any memory you have of what you did at the moment of writing is just that, a memory. Like all memories, it's usually a revision, not the unadulterated experience itself.

   Also, writers quite frequently conceal things. They either don't want them known, or they think of them as trade secrets they don't want to give away, or they are hooked on some sort of critical theory and they wish to make it appear that their work fits inside the perimeter of that theory. Let's just state at the beginning that interviews as the truth, the whole truth, and nothing but the truth are suspect. They're fictions. //

Hancock: With Robert Weaver, you've recently collaborated on a short-story collection, *The Oxford Book of Canadian Short Stories in English*. Do you still see yourself as part of what you once called "our tough and somber literary tradition"? The anthology covers a century of writing. Or, and here's the flip side of the question, do you see a number of writers working in a variety of different directions not connected to a tradition? //

Atwood: You were thinking about *Survival*, I guess. That was an attempt to say, quite simply, that Canadian literature is not the same as American or British literature. That is now known in the world at large. It wasn't known then, in 1972, not even in Canada at the time. If you read the reaction to *Survival*, some people asked, "Why is she writing a 300-page book about something that doesn't exist, namely, Canadian literature?"

You must believe it exists, because you publish *Canadian Fiction Magazine*. There must be some reason for calling it that, and for putting stories by Canadians in this magazine. If Canadian writing were the same as British or American writing, why put it in a separate magazine? You can say, there's this difference and that difference, and it's changed and gone off in various directions. But you are probably not going to say, "There's no such thing as Canadian literature." That was the attitude of a lot of people only sixteen years ago. The mail I got from ordinary people was, "Gee whiz, I never knew. My high-school teacher told me there was only Stephen Leacock and that was it."

This situation—the need to struggle to assert the mere fact of our existence—is no longer with us. As a Canadian writer, you no longer have to say, either, "I'm going to leave the country to become a real writer in England or the States," or, "I'm going to stay here to fight and struggle to become known as a writer in a society that thinks art in general is suspect, and Canadian art is doubly suspect, because it's inferior." That battle doesn't need to be fought any more.

Hancock: To change subjects here, the imagination of Canadians takes us North.

Atwood: For Canadians, North is a constant. It's one of those ideas that's reinterpreted generation after generation, and by region after region. The idea of North is probably quite different for Quebeckers. But "North" is still the thing that's being considered. When the Americans send icebreakers through the Northwest Passage, why do Canadians get so stirred up about it? Not many people go there. It's not as though it happens where they are physically. It happens in their minds. It's a violation of their mental space.

Hancock: Though Canadian literature has made great steps forward, in some of your stories you've satirized the Canadian literary community.

Atwood: Literary communities are always comic, when they're not tragic: that is, when writers aren't being tortured, shot, and imprisoned. If you take "comic" as that which is divergent from what "normal," "average" people think you ought to be doing with your life, then you, Geoff Hancock, are a comic character. Here you are, running this magazine, devoting your life to this thing which is never going to make any money. It's quixotic of you to do it. You are the Don Quixote of the Canadian literary scene, and so is anybody who runs a literary magazine or a small press in this country. If the society in which you live thinks you should be making millions of dollars playing the stock market or being a doctor and playing golf, which is considered average and normal, then all us artists are defined as whacko. We ourselves may not think that. We may think that we—in general—are the sanest thing around—which I happen to believe. But from the point of view of society—and comedies always take place in that context—we are the "funny people," the eccentrics, the ones who are not in step. And we do have our eccentricities.

Hancock: You like to work in a variety of areas. Do you try to understand the processes of each piece of writing, whether it's a poem, a cartoon, a short story, an essay, a novel, a screenplay, or a theater piece?

Atwood: This word "process" is very fashionable. All it really means, as far as I can tell, is "how do you do it?" You have to understand something about the form before you can do it at all. We might include puppet plays, which was one of the things I started out with. Puppet plays for children's birthday parties. Every one of those art forms has a certain set of brackets around it. You can say, "This is what happens within this form," and, "These are some of the things that don't happen within it." Some of the most interesting things happen when you expand the brackets. For instance, when we do puppet plays, we don't usually show the live people who run the puppets. What would happen if we mixed up live people with puppets? What would we get then? We would get the Mermaid Theatre, one of the most intriguing puppet theaters around. The brackets were moved over to include live people. We've moved the borders, we've changed the rules.

It's the same with any form. You have to understand what the form is doing, how it works, before you say, "Now we're going to make it different, we're going to do this thing which is unusual, we're going to turn it upside down, we're going to move it so it includes something which isn't supposed to be there, we're going to surprise the reader."

For instance, in the novel, for a while it was the fashion not to show the author at work. Before that, it *was* the fashion to show the author. Now it's the fashion to show the author again. It was a new thing for the 1960s and 1970s of the twentieth century. It was standard for 1850s novelists to say, "Now, Dear Reader, let me tell you what I think about these goings on. Dorothea didn't know this was happening. But I, the Author, am going to let you, the Reader, in on the secret." If you go back before then, you have the author talking about himself, saying why he decided to write the story in this way and not some other way. Letting the reader in behind the scenes. All of those things are ways of moving beyond the conventions to include things not considered includable. The kind of material thought to be suitable for novels is constantly changing.

This is one of the things that happened to Canada. For a long time, Canadian material was not thought to be suited to "great literature." You could not make a "real novel" out of Canadian material. You had to go to the States or England to make a "real novel." Canadian novels *per se* were considered second-rate pastiche, or imitation or embarrassing. John Robert Colombo's poem about "How to Make a Canadian Novel" summarized that attitude. Put in some beavers and Mounties and you get boredom. Similarly with women's material. What-you-do-in-the-kitchen-when-the-boys-aren't-there. That kind of stuff was considered not suitable for great writing. It was always dismissed or not used. Then Margaret Laurence, Alice Munro, Margaret Drabble, Marian Engel, and others started using this stuff, and making it work. Lo and behold, it *was* usable, as it had been all along, except that nobody had noticed. //

Hancock: How do you keep track of where you are in a longhand manuscript?

Atwood: I usually start at the beginning and barrel straight through. It's like CBC "Coast to Coast." I start in Newfoundland, and then roller-coaster across the country according to the time change. If I'm working on a novel, I'll write maybe twenty pages in longhand. I start transcribing that longhand into typing, while at the same time on the back end of the novel I write more. I'm always catching up to myself in the typing while continuing on with the writing. That reminds me of what I just wrote the day before and allows me to keep track. But some of the stories I'll write in one sitting. When I'm feeling good I can write twenty pages longhand in a sitting, and transcribe ten on the typewriter. But, of course, there's a lot of revision.

Hancock: Is this a constant method of composition?

Atwood: I don't always start at the beginning and go through to the end. Sometimes I'm going along and I'll come to a scene which is out of sync. I know it comes near the end, but I'll write it down anyway. It's become quite immediate and I want to get it down before I forget about it. I will have little patches here and there. It's like coloring in a map. It's a form of exploration. You're going along a river. This is "explored territory" and this is "unexplored territory." But from what you know, there's a pagoda which you should be coming up to, though you don't know what's been here and there. You know you'll be coming to some things you already know about. But you don't always know how to get there. //

Hancock: Are you a severe critic of your work-in-progress?

Atwood: Let us put it this way. People have often asked me which of my editors is "the real editor." Is it my Canadian editor, my American editor, or my English one? The fact is, it's not any of them. By the time they get the work, it's been through six drafts usually. I used to be an editor with the House of Anansi. That taught me something about editing. Although I write quite quickly in the first instance, I revise slowly.

Hancock: Do you find your works "link" together? Is there a larger narrative framework?

Atwood: Do you mean does this novel and that novel have something to do with one another? Well, they all have women in them. In *Life Before Man* a male tells one-third of the story. Some of the stories are told from the point of view of men. "Uglypuss" is a case in point: most of that story is told from the man's point of view. The woman comes in at the end. But by and large my novels center on women. None of them are about all-male groups. None of them are about miners in the mines, seamen on the sea, convicts in the jail, the boys in the backroom, the locker room at the football game. Never a story have I set in those locations! How come? Well, gee, I don't know! Maybe it's because I am a woman and therefore find it easier to write as one. Few male writers write all their books from the female point of view. That doesn't mean they hate women.

Hancock: You also like paired characters: mothers and daughters, nieces and aunts, such as Elizabeth and Muriel in *Life Before Man*, the Handmaid and her sinister aunts, Joan of *Lady Oracle* and aunts Lou and Deirdre. Could you comment on this?

Atwood: Most novelists work in pairs, triplets, quartets, and quintets. It's hard to have a novel with no characters in it except the protagonist. But I am *interested* in the many forms of interaction possible among women—just as I am in those possible between women and men. I'm

interested in male-male interaction but can have no first-hand experience
of how men relate to one another when women aren't present. For that,
you have to ask men.

Hancock: Can a fiction be ideal?

Atwood: Do you mean perfect? Oriental carpet makers weave a flaw into
the design on purpose, because nothing on this earth can be perfect.

Hancock: Some of your books have come out in elegant and expensive
limited editions, like Charles Pachter and Glen Golusca's Salamander
Editions.

Atwood: Charlie made most of those as an art student. But books as
objects have nothing to do with perfection of writing. Perfection is a
non-existent thing on this earth. Perfection is an idea. I'm thinking of
the uncertainty principle in physics. Even the physical universe is not
"perfect," that is, wholly symmetrical, closed, finished. There's something
in the nature of things that's against closure. Here's the latest from my
nephew—he's the mathematical physicist. They now think the universe
is made of little strings, in thirty-two different colors. I said to him if
the little pieces of string are so small, how do they know what colors
they are? He said, "It's just a manner of speaking."

Hancock: A "string" is supposed to be a quintillion quintillion times
smaller than the smallest part of an atom, if I remember correctly. The
concept was thought up by a Russian physicist. Along with it goes what
he calls the TOE Theory, the theory of everything.

Atwood: Even better, there's supposed to be seven dimensions, four
more than we usually think of. Let's not even ask about perfection!

Hancock: Which aspect of fiction writing do you find most interesting
or challenging?

Atwood: It's all pretty difficult. The most challenging is to do something
that surprises me, the writer, and therefore, I hope, will surprise you,
the reader.

Hancock: Do you like to deal with the large format of a social mythology
through fiction?

Atwood: I think I used to like that idea. I don't like ideas as a rule—not as *a priori* determinants of fictional modes. Let me put it another way around. I started out in philosophy and English. Then I switched.

If you're an academic, you have to concern yourself more with "ideas." Ideas make the material a lot more teachable. People find it easier to sit in a classroom and abstract things or turn them into ideas, or consider them from the point of view of ideas. There's not a lot you can say from total immersion in the text. About all you can say are emotional things, like "Wow, it really grabbed me!" Or other reactions that come out in that banal way: "I hated it," "I loved it," "It didn't do anything for me!" Whereas if you deal in "ideas" you can analyze the structure, the prose, the style, or this and that. But as soon as you do that, you're analyzing, making an abstraction from the actual thing.

Academics have to do that at one level or another. They are in the business of teaching people. One of the things that happens when you teach people is that you say, "Let's look at it this way. Let's look at it structurally. Or mythically. Let's look at the prose, the punctuation, the texture." But if you are not an academic, you don't have to spend a minute of your time thinking about those things. If you are a practicing writer, and that only, your engagement is with the blank page and only with the blank page. You never have to toddle off to school. You never have to divide yourself in that way, the blank page at home at night, the daytime at school, where you point out how Marianne Moore's poems have little white spaces in them. You don't have to think about that unless you want to.

I used to teach, so I know whereof I speak. I thought differently when I taught. I think differently when I teach from the way I think when I don't teach. It alters how you perceive what you're doing. The mere act of teaching any kind of literature to anybody does that. I'm not making any value judgments here. This is merely an observation on the texture of the inside of your head.

Hancock: Do you prefer people to just experience your work?

Atwood: No, I don't have any of those preferences. It's not a value judgment. You were asking how I went about it, and what my experience was. When I'm not teaching, I don't have to think of my own work in terms of ideas or large social things or any of those concepts. I get right down in the mud, which is what engagement with the page is. It's mud.

Hancock: What makes fiction dramatic for you?

Atwood: Fiction has to surprise me. If a character is going along doing only what such a person would do, I get very bored. I want to know more. Or to have them come to a point where they're not what I thought they were. Or that they're not what they thought they were. It's probably a form of childish curiosity that keeps me going as a fiction writer. I probably want to open everybody's bureau drawers and see what they keep in there. I'm nosy.

Hancock: Whose fiction do you admire?

Atwood: Lots of people's! It's the question at readings that always stops me cold. I feel as soon as I start picking those lists, people are going to be hurt because I didn't include them—but it may just be because I haven't thought of them at the time. If you are wondering what I read recently that zapped me out the most, I can tell you three books. One was J. M. Coetzee's *Foe*. That was zappo! The other was Primo Levi's *The Periodic Table*. Another was Ireni Spanidou's *God's Snake*.

Hancock: Do you learn anything from books you admire?

Atwood: You learn something from everything. But *what* is the question. You often don't know for twenty or thirty years what you've learned. It may appear suddenly a year or two or five years later that you learned something back then that was important to you. I read for pleasure, and that is the moment at which I learn the most. Subliminal learning.

Hancock: Could you say something about the writer's "voice"? Is there a distinctive Canadian voice? Could you say something about your own voice?

Atwood: I hope there is more than just one distinctive Canadian voice. It would be so boring otherwise. I came across a funny thing I wrote some years ago. The Writers' Union of Canada thought it would improve its fortunes by having all its members write a piece of pornography. Andreas Schroeder was going to put these together into an edited book. This was the genesis of Marian Engel's novel *Bear*, by the way. It started out as a piece of porn about a woman fornicating with a bear. The Union gave up the idea because they felt from the submissions that serious writers weren't any good at writing pornography. But I think they were looking for the wrong thing. They should have been looking for the kind of parody serious writers tend to produce when they try their hands at this. They would have got more usable material. I wrote a piece called

"Regional Romances, or, Across Canada by Pornograph." It's five different pieces, starting with the Maritimes, then Quebec, Ontario, the
Prairies, and B.C. Each one is written in quite a different voice, but quite
recognizable. You would know the general area of literature that was
parodied. There is not one Canadian voice. There are various voices.
But none of them sound particularly British, and as a whole, they don't
sound very American either.

It all depends on where you stand in relation to the forest. If you
stand very close, you can see the molecules inside the tree. Move back,
you see a green thing in the distance. Where are we standing here? Are
we right close to the individual author? In which case, it's the author's
voice, not the Canadian voice. Do we stand back a little bit and see a
region? Do we say there's a Quebec voice, an Ontario voice? Do we put
Alice Munro's stories, Matt Cohen's *The Disinherited*, Robertson Davies's
novels, Graeme Gibson, James Reaney, and Marian Engel all together
in a corral and say "Southern Ontario Gothic"? This I've done. I've
taught such a course twice, once in Alabama, and once in New York.
Very teachable. There they are, and yes, they have something in common.

Hancock: Would you include yourself in this group?

Atwood: No. I'm not from southern Ontario. My roots are the Maritimes
and northern Quebec, not Ontario small town. But these writers are
different from the West and from B.C. and the Maritimes.

In the West, Edna Alford, Sandra Birdsell, John Newlove, Sinclair
Ross, Margaret Laurence are part of a group you might call "Western
realists." Then someone like Gloria Sawai flies in from left field and
writes "The Day I Sat With Jesus on the Sundeck and a Wind Came Up
and Blew My Kimono Open and He Saw My Breasts." That's an interesting story because the texture of it is like those other people. The woman
talks in the vernacular, very detailed about laundry and household goods.
But then in comes Jesus Christ. Within the compass of Western realism,
this is a variation on it. But it's somebody playing with the convention;
it's not a different animal.

And in B.C., there is more than just one group of writers. The Canadian voice contains all these different things. But if you stand back from
it all, you can ask, "Are these the same things that are happening in the
United States or England or Australia? Are Quebec stories and poems
like the ones from France?" Not from what I've read.

English fiction is all about social class. In English life you can't get
away from it. Canadians have a great advantage in England because
nobody can tell who they are just from talking to them.

Standing quite far back, you can say, "Yes, there is a Canadian voice." Standing further up, you would say no: only voices.

Hancock: And your own narrative voice?

Atwood: I would hope it's different in various stories. It's not that I manipulate it. That would imply something a great deal more conscious than what I do. I can't talk a lot about how I write, because I don't think about how I write when I'm writing. That's why interviews are suspect. I could make something up for you, but it would be made up.

Hancock: What do you think your strengths are as a writer?

Atwood: I used to say, in the usual Canadian way, "Well, aw shucks, I don't know." We're trained to be modest. But now that I'm middle-aged I'm going to allow myself to say, "Well, maybe I'm good." Not all the time, but enough times, I can get the words to stretch and do something together that they don't do alone. Expand the possibilities of the language.

Hancock: And your weaknesses?

Atwood: Weaknesses? We can't afford to think about those kinds of things. Most writers are tightrope-walking over Niagara Falls all the time. Look down and you've had it. If I thought too much about weakness I'd block. //

Hancock: Do you ever discuss works-in-progress?

Atwood: Hardly ever. I discussed bits of *The Handmaid's Tale* with Graeme. He thought I was going bonkers, I think. That's the problem with discussing works-in-progress. They always sound somewhat crazier than they may turn out to be. He kept saying. "You're going to get in trouble for this one." But he egged me on, despite that.

Hancock: Do you see your work as successful in terms of its intention?

Atwood: If I didn't think it was somewhat successful—and let us keep in mind my remarks about perfection—I wouldn't be publishing it. Success is different from perfection.

Hancock: You don't think afterwards, say, at a reading, that you should have taken something out through another draft?

Atwood: The book I would write this year is not ever the same as something I would have written twenty years ago. I wouldn't be writing that book now, whatever it is. I've changed and so has the world. My interests and perceptions have changed. What was of interest to me then would not be of interest to me now. My intentions don't remain constant, so how can a book be expected to live up to my intentions in 1986 when I wrote it in 1964?

Hancock: Do you find with each book you learn some new aspects of fiction? How to use backgrounds, foregrounds, language?

Atwood: No. I don't think you ever know how to write a book. You never know ahead of time. You start every time at zero. It doesn't count for anything that you were able to pull it off before. It means nothing. A former success doesn't mean that you're not going to make the most colossal failure the next time.

Hancock: Does part of the problem perhaps come with the dubiousness of imposing form on the material? One of the great things about the novel is that it ultimately has a form.

Atwood: It can't help but be a "form" because it is smaller than its container, which is the universe. Which is itself a form.

Hancock: Do you like form? Or are you suspicious of form?

Atwood: I don't see why it can't be both at once. That's how I feel about many people, liking and suspicious at once. Why shouldn't I feel that way about form? Let us say that part of the joy is learning to do something you didn't know how to do before. But once you know that and keep repeating it, the joy goes out of it.

Hancock: What is the novel to you?

Atwood: I'm very suspicious of anything beginning with a capital letter, like Man. Or Woman. Or the Novel. I seem to think from the ground up, rather than from the top down. // The "Novel" for me is the sum total of all men. Therefore, I have a lot of problems with making general statements about them. As for Woman, capital W, we got stuck with that for centuries. Eternal woman. But really, "Woman" is the sum total of women. It doesn't exist apart from that, except as an abstracted idea.

Hancock: When you sit down to write a long fiction, which eventually reaches three or four hundred pages in manuscript, do you stop to think about a series of characters in a number of situations that have to be shaped somehow?

Atwood: "Material" has to be shaped because eventually somebody is going to have to read it. Everything has a shape. An amoeba has a shape, though it's rather malleable. There is no such thing as a thing with no shape. It may be a more contained or less contained shape, or an awkward shape, or a graceful shape. It may be sprawling or rectilinear, but there's a shape of some kind which can be described.

Hancock: I bring this up, of course, because the novel, or long fiction, or long narrative, as recently as the 1960s went through a phase where it was considered dead and defunct as a form. Then it got revitalized.

Atwood: But did that ever really happen? Wasn't it just what a few people were saying? They said the same thing about God. Prove it. They claimed all this dead novel stuff, and all the while people were writing and reading novels, as usual.

Hancock: *Life Before Man* struck me as particularly interesting for its narrative strategy. You had three principal characters, with specific dates as an organizing device. Did you get that right the first time?

Atwood: I got part of it right the first time. Some books are a "good read." Part of that book was a "good write." I didn't have to go back to square one as I did with several others. I wanted a triangular structure. From the point of view of A, B and C were wrong. From the point of view of B, C and A were wrong. From the point of view of C, A and B were wrong. I wanted a nice little triangle. That part was not difficult to do.

But *Lady Oracle* was originally written in the second person. It was written as a letter to Arthur. But I realized I couldn't do that, because Arthur already knew a lot of the stuff that had happened to him. I would have been in the rather stupid position of having the narrator tell Arthur things he already knew. It does end up being a story told to somebody else, but you don't figure out who that person is until the end. It isn't Arthur; it's the guy she beans with the bottle.

I took a couple of runs at *Surfacing* in 1964 or 1965. It was the same time I was writing *The Edible Woman*. I've got several beginnings of what eventually turned into *Surfacing*. It was quite different. It was in the third person. The characters were different, though there were four of them. The woman was older. The other woman was her sister. The first complete write-through was quite bad. I had to go back and rearrange things so that there was more going on. My problem is that I get so fascinated by description and details I forget about anything happening; I have several unfinished novels with that problem. They have wonderful descriptions of things, but nothing actually occurs for a long time.

Once I tried to write a novel from the point of view of eight different characters. That was dandy and I had nice descriptions. But after 250 pages, no events had occurred. If I had followed out my scheme, the novel would have been about 1,500 pages long. It wouldn't have worked.

The Handmaid's Tale is organized partly by the repeated "Night" sections. There are periods of action, punctuated by periods of reflection.

Hancock: Does there have to be event in a novel?

Atwood: Yes, if you want people to actually read it. You can do various "theoretical" works and experiments which will be of interest to a very few people interested in dead ends and what doesn't work. The Andy Warhol movie about sleep is more interesting as an idea than it is as something you'd want to sit through for twelve hours.

Hancock: To deal with events, do you have to look carefully at your characters, their motivations, their psychological makeup?

Atwood: Characters don't just sit in a chair. Everybody has to get up to pee once in a while. Unless, of course, you want to write a novel from the point of view of someone who has had a total lobotomy. Or has no brain and is immobile. Or is in a catatonic trance. In those cases, if you have anything in the novel at all, it has to be unconscious inner event. But it's still event. Something is still happening.

Hancock: Do you try for what T. S. Eliot called "the objective correlative"? To try to reproduce in the reader the same emotional state as the characters?

Atwood: That's evocation, rather than representation. Certainly, that's what any successful piece of writing does. It evokes from the reader. It's not a question even of self-expression, of the writer expressing his or her emotions. Who really cares? You can say the writer felt this, the writer felt that. But unless you can evoke that emotion from the reader, it's merely a statement. //

Hancock: Does a novelist have a social conscience?

Atwood: I never met one without. Even Robbe-Grillet, who was some-body who tried for pure objective value-free depiction, is making a state-ment. You can't show a character doing anything without expecting the reader to have some view about that, because readers live in a society and make moral judgments. "John took an ax and he chopped off Mary's head." For you, the reader, is that good or bad? You are going to react one way or another. The way you react to it is going to depend upon what you already know about Mary, about John. You cannot put those words on paper without in some way engaging the reader's moral sense—supposing the reader has one, and I've never met a reader yet who had no moral sense at all.

Hancock: Does art have to be moral?

Atwood: It is, whether the artist tries to be or not. Even Oscar Wilde was making a moral statement when he said, "Morality is boring, and what I'm after is the beautiful." That in itself is a statement about morality. I'm afraid that engagement is unavoidable. How you handle or approach it is something else again. You can take the Oscar Wilde stance. Or you say, "What I'm after is pure form." By saying that, you imply the moral dimension is not important to your art. Or you can say, "The social conscience is innate; therefore, I will be out on the table about it, and these are the bad guys; let's all spit on the bad guys." However, the closer you get to that view, the closer you get to propaganda. That doesn't mean that art with some moral sense is inevitably propaganda.

Hancock: That argument between form and morality created a tremen-dous debate in American literature.

Atwood: I know, but I found it so unnecessary. Apostles of the obvious. Even fabulist fictions are moral. They are among the most moral of things. What's more moral than a fairy tale? Science fiction is dripping with message. But if something is only that, then we feel we're being preached to and we resent it. //

Hancock: I just read "Walking on Water" the other night, in *Chatelaine*.

Atwood: That's one of the "Emma" stories.

Hancock: Could you tell me a bit about those stories?

Atwood: Emma is a character who doesn't think a lot. She does things, but she doesn't think about them in great detail. She's not an internal character. Sometimes one gets tired of writing the various ratiocinations of the characters and wants to show a character in action, as it were. The Emma stories are very heavy on event, light on Emma's inner world. I have known women like this. Usually, we think of female characters as fearful and timorous. But I have known women who really would do anything. Walk up cliffs, and other foolhardy things. It was interesting to write about something like that. Such people interest me, particularly when they are women, because it goes against their socialization. I don't know if I could write a novel or a whole book of stories in that way.

Hancock: Would that be because of market demands?

Atwood: Nothing I do has anything to do with market demands, except in the TV script department. That's my substitute for teaching at university. Teaching university has a lot to do with market demands! But I've always felt my writing was somewhat eccentric. It has been *strange* that I have acquired the audience I have. Or the audiences, whoever they may be. Literary writers don't usually get those audiences. But I'm not in the position, for instance, of going to magazines or publishers and asking them what I should write fiction about. I've never done that. I've never had to.

Hancock: The story collections seem carefully structured. For example, *Bluebeard's Egg* is nicely framed with the two parent stories. Among many things, these are stories of the natural world framing the urban world of the other stories. Was it planned that way?

Atwood: I wrote all the stories before I arranged them. It's not a question of having to write this or that to make it nice. I usually spread them all out on the floor and see how they look best to me. It seemed evident those stories should be like that. It's like those psychological tests they give you, with different shapes and colors which they ask you to arrange into a pattern according to shape, color, and size.

Hancock: Would you find the main drama for your characters is in their anxieties?

Atwood: The Emma character isn't very anxious. But she gets into situations that would make us anxious. In one story, she almost drowns. In another story, her boyfriend almost drowns. I don't know why they are always almost drowning. Why can't they burn up?

Hancock: I was going to ask you a drowning question. Drowning occurs in *Surfacing*, "This Is a Photograph of Me," "Walking on Water," the other Emma story, "Death of a Young Son by Drowning," "Procedures from Underground," *Lady Oracle*. It seems a powerful image for you.

Atwood: I grew up by a lake. People drowned in it. I know some people who have drowned, or nearly drowned. Canada is full of water. There's just a lot of drowning going on. Now, if you have your choice about how people die in natural accidents in Canada, it's most likely to be by drowning. Look at the statistics. But you don't have to look at them. Look at your own life. How many people do you know who have burnt up in a fire, compared with those who have died in plane crashes, compared with those who have drowned or almost drowned? Is it not so?

Hancock: The women in both *Dancing Girls* and *Bluebeard's Egg* are rich in anxieties.

Atwood: Show me a character totally without anxieties and I will show you a boring book.

Hancock: This in itself raises questions about what is the nature of fiction.

Atwood: What is good fiction? Well, first it has to hold the attention of the reader; not all readers, but what we can call the suitable reader. Once upon a time, a long time ago, I took a course in the eighteenth-century novel of sensibility. I read all kinds of things of the period. One of them was *Sir Charles Grandison*, by Richardson, who had previously written *Pamela* and *Clarissa*. *Sir Charles* starts out at a cracking pace. The heroine is almost abducted from a stagecoach. Unfortunately, to the reader's great dismay, she gets rescued by Sir Charles. For the rest of this 600-page novel, Sir Charles is perfect. The heroine notices this and that instance of his politeness, his gentleness, his generosity, his perfection, his chivalrousness, but that's about it. I think I've met only one other person who has finished it. I finished it only because I was not going to let this defeat me; I was going to jolly well get through to the end to see if anything of any interest happened whatsoever.

People ask me, "Why do your characters have these problems?" If the characters have no problems, what's the book going to be about? The problem has to be an internal one, or a problem with another character, or an external problem like the Great White Shark, or the end of the world, or the people from Mars, or vampires. Something has to be there to disturb the stasis. Think of a play in which the characters do nothing at all, ever, throughout the whole play. The question then becomes: granted that something has to happen in a novel, why do certain kinds of things happen in my novels, while other things happen in other people's novels? That's the question, not why does *anything* happen.

Hancock: From a content point of view, something has to happen. The "and then, and then," and how and why.

Atwood: The "and then, and then" is basic. But if you don't do that well enough, the how and the why aren't going to interest anybody because there will be absolutely no reason to keep reading the thing.

Hancock: Do you concern yourself with getting the right scenes in the right order and then the right words in the right order?

Atwood: Probably the two things happen at once. I seem to write in quite different ways. Some stories are beginning-to-end straight write-throughs. Others are built up bit by bit. You can tell by looking at "Significant Moments in the Life of My Mother" that the writing of it was episodic. Sometimes you wake up in the middle of the night with a wonderful phrase or sentence or paragraph. You write it down, but you're not sure where it's going to fit. You find out later, or not, as the case may be. My life is filled with pieces of paper with things written on them that I've never used.

Hancock: Do you block out the action after you've got all those notes?

Atwood: Take, for example, *The Edible Woman.* I wrote it on University of British Columbia exam booklets. There was going to be one booklet per chapter. The booklets were white. I wrote that novel in four months, I find with horror in looking back. Then I revised it. Every day I would ask myself, What is going to happen today to these people? In the place where you plot out your exam question, on the left hand side, I'd make a list, a few notes, on what she does today. Then I would write the chapter.

But the point to remember is that nothing works, necessarily, dependably, infallibly. No regime, no scheme, no incantation. If we knew what worked, we could sell it as an unbeatable program for writing masterpieces. Writing is very improvisational. It's like trying to fix a broken sewing machine with safety pins and rubber bands. A lot of tinkering.

Hancock: Your short stories are all different. You're not writing the same story over and over.

Atwood: *The New York Times Book Review* called them "wilfully unfashion-able" or "wilfully eccentric." But I'm not too sure what is fashionable in the short story these days, nor do I much care.

Hancock: The American story writers move in schools, like fish. Right now, it's minimalist fiction, or "dirty realism," as in the works of Raymond Carver and Ann Beattie and Tobias Wolff.

Atwood: But as soon as that gets defined, it's already on the fade. To call this the "new fiction" is a marketing strategy. But Canada doesn't work this way. Everyone is equally weird.

Hancock: In rereading the stories, I was amazed to find a lot of writing about writing. "Giving Birth" for example, has a strong passage about the problem of communicating through language. That's a central con-cern with *Murder in the Dark*.

Atwood: So it was in *Surfacing*, and to some extent, *The Edible Woman* as well.

Hancock: Is that all interest in theory, or postmodernist concerns?

Atwood: None of the above. As I've said, I'm not very theoretical in my approach to what I do. As a theorist, I'm a good amateur plumber. You do what you have to do to keep your sink from overflowing. I tried for the longest time to find out what *deconstructionism* was. Nobody was able to explain it to me clearly. The best answer I got was from a writer, who said, "Honey, it's bad news for you and me."

Hancock: That's because the text is often deconstructed back to the author.

Atwood: What it also means is that the text is of no importance. What is of interest is what the critic makes of the text. Alas, alack, pretty soon we'll be getting to pure critical readings with no text at all.

I don't have to do that, because I don't have to sell my bod on the academic market. I'm not going to get tenure depending on whether or not I'm in the swim. I think I'd just embarrass everybody by asking those kinds of questions.

Let me put it this way. One of my early jobs was taking those recondite, verbose market-research interviews written by psychologists and translat-ing them into language that the average person interviewed could under-stand. So it was breaking down "psychologese" into simpler units that could be understood by somebody not a professional in the field. That's impossible to do with certain kinds of things. You can get a rendition of advanced physics, but it is just a rendition.

With literary criticism, I really feel that it ought to be graspable. It should not be full of too many of those kinds of words which only the initiated can understand. It's fun for the initiated to have a language which means something to them and to them alone. It means you can one-up people, and it's a closed circle; you can be declared in or out depending on whether you are using the current language. These things do have a habit of rolling over about every five years.

Hancock: That criticism aside, with all its inherent truths, your work is starting to be read that way.

Atwood: You can read any text any way. You can read it standing on your head. You can use it for toilet paper. It's not a statement about the text. It's a statement about the user.

Hancock: To come back to *Surfacing*, or "Giving Birth," or *Murder in the Dark*, your own prose draws attention to more than just the story, with a character and a particular situation. The prose itself says there's a problem of communicating through language. It implies a distrust of words, that there's a distrust of language, that language is a distortion.

Atwood: Language *is* a distortion.

Hancock: Do you mean we can't trust language to get through to "truth"?

Atwood: That's true. Although I've used language to express that, it's true. I think most writers share this distrust of language—just as painters are always wishing there were more colors, more dimensions. But language is one of the few tools we *do* have. So we have to use it. We even have to trust it, though it's untrustworthy.

Hancock: That's an interesting paradox.

Atwood: The question is, How do we know "reality"? How do you encounter the piece of granite? How do you know it directly? Is there such a thing as knowing it directly without language? Small babies know the world without language. How do they know it? Cats know the world without language, without what we would call language. How are they experiencing the world? Language is a very odd thing. We take it very much for granted. But it's one of the most peculiar items that exists.

People start to feel that there's some kind of inherent meaning in a particular word. Like "apple." People start to think there's something of *an apple* in the word "apple." But if so, why is it called something else in fifty-seven other languages?

Hancock: As *The Feminist Dictionary* points out, language is now being reevaluated, to find out how language has been maligned and changed through usage. For example, the word "gossip" was originally the dialogue between mother and a midwife. And "trivia" is derived from Trivia, Goddess of the Crossroads, where women traditionally exchanged news. But "gossip" and "trivia" are now seen as negative terms, when they were once positive.

Atwood: Not only is language slippery, but it's limited. The vocabulary we have is limited. There are a lot of things we don't have words for.

Hancock: Perhaps there is something "universal" beneath language? Gabriel Garcia Marquez's *One Hundred Years of Solitude* had an equal impact on Michel Tremblay in Quebec and Jack Hodgins in B.C. (not to mention other writers around the world), though neither read it in Spanish.

Atwood: How did it do among the Innuit? Or the Chinese? It's true you can translate things, sort-of, so that they can kind-of be read. But efforts to translate *haiku* have always frustrated me. I know perfectly well that the English translation of the Japanese may give the literal words. Yet the piece is totally lacking in the resonance you get from a knowledge of the tradition, a knowledge of the culture. "Plum blossoms floating down the stream." What does that mean to you? Not a great deal. It lacks a rich cultural compost. Every piece of writing exists in its surround. It comes out of that surround. It has meaning in the surround. You can take it out of there and look at it? An Assyrian sculpture, a figure of a winged bull with the head of a man, is interesting to look at. But it has nowhere near the meaning for us that it had for whoever made it. We don't know who that person is. We don't know his story. We don't know what magical powers he may have thought the figure possessed. It still has some meaning for us. But it's a different meaning for us. //

Hancock: We don't even know how to "read" a Chinese restaurant in Toronto. The dragons on the wall, the Fo dogs which represent Yin and Yang, the tree figures that represent health, wealth, and longevity. There's something tricky about language.

Atwood: There's something tricky about "reality," let alone language. Insofar as language relates to a cultural experience of reality, to what extent is that transmissable? To what extent can you translate that into another language and have it understood? I'm now translated into over twenty languages, only two of which I can read, more or less. I have no idea what those other versions are saying, to the people who read them.

Hancock: *Murder in the Dark* doesn't have a "plot," but it does have a "character" in the narrative voice in the four parts. Did you make a decision not to plot the book?

Atwood: I was just having fun. Sorry to be so idiotic about this. I know "serious" writers aren't supposed to say things like that. I started writing these little mini-fictions and little pieces of prose that were not connected to a "plot." They were connected in the way that verses in a lyric poem were connected, or like sections in a long narrative poem. It's not a question of A to B to C to D to E. It's a question of these units existing by themselves, but having a certain vibration with the ones they are placed with.

Hancock: Did that create any technical problems?

Atwood: I wasn't doing them on purpose. I started writing them—fooling around. Then it occurred to me, at some point near the end, that this was probably a book.

Hancock: Michael Benedikt, who edited an anthology of prose poems some years ago, claims the prose poem never really settled down in the English language. That it was something exclusively French, Spanish, or Italian. Generally speaking, we don't see that many prose poems in English in Canada.

Atwood: It's unfortunate. I found they were excellent for readings. Some of them have enough of a plot that you don't have the problem you have with a poetry reading. You can't read very much poetry without people's eyes glazing over. The level of concentration required is so great you can't do it for an hour. I can't listen to a poetry reading for an hour, no matter how good it is. I just can't. My attention gets burned out in the first half-hour. Some of the prose poems are funny enough, or have another line that isn't lyrical, so they don't require the absolute kind of distilled concentration that an hour of lyric poetry requires.

Hancock: With *Murder in the Dark*, you come back to those concerns that the writer is a liar, that memory is unreliable, that fiction is a distortion, the unspecified narrator. Would I be stretching a point to say there is a connection between this book and *The Journals of Susanna Moodie*?

Atwood: Susanna Moodie was a specific person for me. I thought you were going to say *Surfacing*, in which the narrator lies and her memory is unreliable. Susanna Moodie doesn't lie. Nor is her memory particularly unreliable. She has two different sides to her personality. The narrator of the first eight chapters of *Surfacing* is much more an unreliable narrator.

Hancock: Are you interested in characters, their names, their psychology, their types?

Atwood: I'm very interested in their names. By that I mean their names don't always readily spring to mind. I have to go looking for their names. I would like not to have to call them anything. But they usually have to have names. Then the question is, if they are going to have names, the names have to be appropriate. Therefore I spend a lot of time reading up on the meanings of names, in books like *Name Your Baby*.

Hancock: What does your name mean?

Atwood: "Pearl." And "of the woods." It's an English name. Quite old. Probably fourteenth century or earlier. From *atter wode*. //

Hancock: When the stories of your characters are unfolding, do you look for that moment when their whole world changes?

Atwood: In a novel you hope there's more than one of those moments. In a short story there may only be one such moment. And it may not be their whole life changing. It may be one thing they've thought which they can no longer think. It may not be their entire life, it may be just an area. I don't have any thoughts about what *has* to happen in a story beyond the fact that *something* has to happen.

Hancock: Do you have to know more about a character than you can actually tell?

Atwood: I have to know more than I actually tell. Lots more. I get bogged down in detail. I try to tell too much. I try to tell everything about this person. I try to tell too many things about their underclothing and their breakfast foods. I often have to cut some of that out.

Hancock: When the something that is going to happen happens, what is it? Something as basic as an antagonist? Or a social situation?

Atwood: It depends on the story. There are hundreds of possibilities, and many ways of arranging them. That's what I was playing with in, for instance, "Happy Endings." You could start at any point in the story. You could start at the end if you wanted to, then go back and show how that end was arrived at. //

Hancock: Professor Elspeth Cameron has written in an essay on your work that your characters are "transformations of imagined persona around an inner self."

Atwood: What does that mean?

Hancock: In *Lady Oracle*, Joan Foster creates various personas and some- where in the midst of them all is "Joan Foster." Many of your stories, both long and short, are built around shifting identities, the various personas the characters create. You often organize your books around a split point of view. First and third persons, contradictions within the characters, fractured identities. Is that how you see characters?

Atwood: Well, maybe. I might see them that way. It would depend upon the character. But probably I do them that way because I get bored with writing in the first person, so I switch to the third. I get bored with writing in the present tense, so I switch to the past. I get bored with having just a single narrator, so I have three instead of one. A lot of this is trying to keep oneself amused, isn't it? I don't like to feel I'm doing the same thing over and over. I would die of boredom if I felt I were doing that. I like to try things that are hard for me. That's despite laziness.

Hancock: Do you think human beings are a species to be observed? Someone described you as "an anthropologist from another world."

Atwood: Most novelists do that in some way. They may treat certain forms of human behavior as something you should take for granted, more than I do. I find a lot of behavior very strange. Therefore, worth pondering.

Hancock: Do you find your various travels reinforce that?

Atwood: We have an unconscious assumption that the way we live is normal and average, and that everybody else is strange. I've never been able to buy that. I think we're strange, too.

Hancock: Do you keep notebooks when you travel? Photographs?

Atwood: Graeme takes the travel photographs; I would if he didn't, though. Right now I tend to go in for family snapshots—the birthday parties, the Christmas trees, and so forth. I used to take pictures of things like fire hydrants, but when you have a growing family, there is an urge to create future nostalgia. As for notebooks, I've tried, but I'm not good at it.

Hancock: Someone said that the center of your work is the power of language to transform our perception of how the world works.

Atwood: I'll buy that, I'll endorse that one! I've got to endorse something in this interview. Whoever said that, it's true!

Hancock: Are you interested in boundary lines? Is there a point where poetry and prose merge? Become something different? Prose looks a certain way, as do poetry and drama. Perhaps there's a point where they run together?

Atwood: Probably there is.

Hancock: I mention this because some place you wrote that in fiction you were "a curious bemused disheartened observer of society," but you felt differently when you wrote poetry.

Atwood: Probably I do. But I'm not very good at analyzing what I feel like when I do those things. Probably different parts of the brain are involved. If you could hook up somebody's brain while they are in the throes of composing a poem, and hook up the same brain while that person was writing a novel, I'd expect you'd find brain activity in different areas. I think poetry is written more on the right side of the brain, that is, the left-handed side. That side of the brain is sadder than the other side, according to researchers.

Hancock: I'd like to discuss layers and levels in your work. I'll let the explicators get into the depths of *The Handmaid's Tale*.

Atwood: They haven't got around to it yet. The book is still on the level of popular reaction. The explicators haven't had time to get in there and explicate it a lot.

Hancock: Are you glad?

Atwood: None of it has much of an impact on me, to tell the truth. If I were to obsessively read everything everybody wrote on me, I'd go nuts. You couldn't keep up with it and remain sane as a writer.

Hancock: Why do you suppose people want to write about you and your work? There's at least five books now, countless scholarly essays, graduate theses, and a clipping file I've seen is about two feet thick.

Atwood: You got me. Better to ask them. Why do people collect stamps? There is indeed an impressive amount of work. But I don't put them up to it. This is something they do on their own hook. So either they find it pleasurable, or they find it of interest. But it's not up to me to say why they do it.

Hancock: Some people might see you and your work as a nodal point, a focal point of all our interests and concerns.

Atwood: It has certainly been seen as that. But it's not something I did on purpose. Or put them up to doing. It's just one of those things. Maybe it's because of my horoscope. Jupiter in the tenth house—very lucky for a career.

Hancock: Do you follow astrology closely?

Atwood: I know how to do it. I can also read palms. I was taught all this by a Dutch art historian whose specialty was Hieronymus Bosch. She had to know these things because they are built into medieval works of art. A ring on a certain finger means something. When Hieronymus Bosch paints the Last Judgment with the stars in the sky in a particular pattern, the pattern means something. So there we were in Edmonton, during a winter when the temperature didn't go above zero F in a whole month; she lived downstairs, and we did this to pass the time.

Hancock: Do you want to talk about *The Handmaid's Tale*?

Atwood: When I first started thinking about it, I thought it was such a whacko idea I wrote it with some trepidation. It could have been the worst failure you could possibly imagine. I was afraid people would say it was stupid, silly. There was also the risk it would be thought feminist propaganda of the most outrageous kind, which was not really what I intended. I was more interested in totalitarian systems, an interest I've had for a long time. I used to read Second World War stuff in the cellar when I was twelve or thirteen, for instance.

Hancock: Did the idea that the book is about now, written as if it's the future, told in the past tense, complete with epilogue, create a problem? Do you think you might go in a further direction, like Russell Hoban's *Riddley Walker*, and create a new language for the future?

Atwood: I didn't think that language would be that different twenty years from now. I would never have written *Riddley Walker* because I don't believe after the big bang, supposing we have one, that there will be anybody walking around. I wouldn't have written a post-atomic-war book. So I didn't change the language much, because in the nature of things it wouldn't have changed much, except for the slogans, greetings, etc. Anyway, the character telling the story was brought up in *our* time, in *our* language.

Hancock: Could you tell me about the tape recording as a device in *The Handmaid's Tale?*

Atwood: I had to do it that way. The paper and pencil supply would have been quite limited. It also allowed for the discontinuous, episodic nature of the narrative.

Hancock: Could you tell me about your use of scenes as narrative units? Characters, suspense, tone of voice, thematic concerns are all compressed into short units. The gap is just as important as the text.

Atwood: You're dealing with a character whose ability to move in the society was limited. By the nature of her situation, she was very circumscribed. She couldn't communicate well with people. It was too dangerous. She was boxed in. How do you tell a narrative from the point of view of that person? The more limited and boxed in you are, the more important details become. If you are in jail in solitary, the advent of a rat can be pretty important to you. Details, episodes separate themselves from the flow of time in which they're embedded—a flow which tends to be monotonous—and become significant, luminous.

Hancock: The epilogue was interesting. It was back to splitting the point of view.

Atwood: I did that for several reasons. For instance, the character herself was so circumscribed that there were a number of things about the society she could not know. If she started telling us, the readers, about it, we would have thought, Balderdash, how could she know all this? The newspapers are censored, TV is censored, she can't talk to anyone, how can she know all this? So there were things the reader had to know that she couldn't tell us. Especially things that took place afterwards. Also, I'm an optimist. I like to show that the Third Reich, the Fourth Reich, the Fifth Reich did not last forever.

In fact, Orwell is much more optimistic than people give him credit for. He did the same thing. He has a text at the end of *1984*. Most people think the book ends when Winston comes to love Big Brother. But it doesn't. It ends with a note on Newspeak, which is written in the past tense, in standard English—which means that, at the time of writing the note, Newspeak is a thing of the past.

Hancock: *The Handmaid's Tale* is going to be turned into a screenplay.

Atwood: Harold Pinter is writing it, which is very interesting. If anybody can do it, he can. One of his specialties is scenes in which people don't say very much, but convey meaning anyway.

Hancock: Do you embed things in the fiction? I've noticed all these elements of folktales, Gothic tales, fairy tales.

Atwood: I sometimes embed private jokes. Or little sketches of people I know; they know I've done it, they get a kick out of it. Sometimes, like Alfred Hitchcock, I make cameo appearances. I put myself into *The Edible Woman*—I'm the female graduate student dressed in black, the one who appears at the party and talks about Death.

Hancock: Do you do that after you've got the story-line under control, and the characters are off to meet their destiny, wherever that may be?

Atwood: It's more an impulse towards whimsy. It's like the Gothic cathedrals, where the carvers put imps under the skirts of the angels. Those are my bits of "imperfection," I suppose.

Hancock: Are characters in a natural environment more religious or spiritual? Is that where you find the gods, or the goddesses, or the God?

Atwood: Not usually in church, you'll notice. I can't say the established religions have a terribly good track record. Most of them have quite a history of doing people in—not to mention their attitude towards women.

Hancock: Do you want to say anything about the religious and mystical side of nature?

Atwood: I don't know if there is one, any more than there is a mystical side to anything. The mysticism is in the eye of the mystic—not necessarily in the stone or the tree or the egg. Or let's say it has to be a two-way street. If we had a sacred habit of mind, all kinds of things would be "sacred." Most are not at present. We would be able to see *into* things, rather than merely to see things. We would see the universe as alive. But you're more likely to find such moments in my poetry than my prose.

Hancock: Where does your interest in prehistory come from?

Atwood: As kids, we were fascinated with the idea of things that existed before there were any people. We used to build little plasticine panoramas of dinosaurs. As for aboriginal people, and early inhabitants and lost caves, I think that was the fantasy life of children before there was television. //

Hancock: And your interest in museums?

Atwood: I used to attend the Saturday morning classes at the Royal Ontario Museum. Museums are collections of memories. Each one is like a giant brain. I used to go there with a little girl whose father was an archaeologist and worked there, so we used to wander all over the place, by ourselves, after hours.

Hancock: You like to work with closed spaces in your stories.

Atwood: Some stories do, some don't. It's more likely to be the inner space of the character that's enclosed, not the actual space. *Surfacing* takes place mostly outdoors.

Hancock: Are you comfortable with your style?

Atwood: I'm never comfortable with my "style"—by which I mean that I'm never sure I have exactly the right words in exactly the right order. But I don't think I have just one style.

Hancock: Would you perhaps take your language off into directions suggested by Nicole Brossard or B. P. Nichol?

Atwood: There's more than one way of exploring language. Why do something that other people have already been doing for years and years? If I did what they do, I'd only be imitating them. I sometimes do "experiments," but it's hard to sustain such things for a whole book-length without repeating Beckett or Joyce. I wonder if anyone ever asks Alice Munro such questions? Or do they ask B. P. why he doesn't write like me? People sometimes assume that because I have a larger audience than is usual for a literary writer, I must be writing non-literary books. You do get that form of snobbery from this or that manikin of letters. But the truth is that I am a literary writer who has acquired, Lord knows how, a larger than usual audience for such things.

Hancock: Would you risk losing that audience?

Atwood: Since I didn't go about acquiring it on purpose, and since I don't write down to the reader, and since I never expected I would acquire it, it doesn't really concern me. If I lose it, I lose it. Probably it would depress me if I wrote a book that was universally loathed. But you take that chance with any book, don't you? I've never been accused of talcum-powdering the reader.

Hancock: One final question: do you have an optimistic sense of resolution? Is there hope in art? In the bigger sense of comedy as life affirmation?

Atwood: Hope for what? Let's put it this way. When I finish a book I really like, no matter what the subject matter, or see a play or film, like Kurosawa's *Ran*, which is swimming in blood and totally pessimistic, but so well done, I feel very good. I *do* feel hope. It's the *well-doneness* that has that effect on me. Not the conclusion—not what is said, *per se*. For instance, the end of *King Lear* is devastating, as a statement about the world. But seeing it done well can still exhilarate you.

If you are tone-deaf, you are not going to get much out of Beethoven. If you are color-blind, you won't get much of a charge out of Monet. But if you have those capabilities, and you see something done very,

very well, something that is true to itself, you can feel for two or three minutes that the clouds have parted and you've had a vision, of something of what music or art or writing can do, at its best. A revelation of the full range of our human response to the world—that is, what it means to be human, on earth. That seems to be what "hope" is about in relation to art. Nothing so simple as "happy endings."

It's about other things as well, of course, and it's much more complex than I can begin to analyze. But what you're really waiting for, when you read, when you listen, when you look, when your write, is that moment when you feel, "Hot damn, that is so well done!" An approach to perfection, if you like. Hope comes from the fact that people create, that they find it worthwhile to create. Not just from the nature of what is created.

Using Other People's Dreadful Childhoods
Bonnie Lyons

Bonnie Lyons's interview was conducted February 13, 1987, in San Antonio, Texas, and originally appeared in *Shenandoah* 37 (1987). Copyright © 1987 by *Shenandoah*. Reprinted by permission.

Lyons: You mentioned yesterday, "I see myself as a writer who happens to be female rather than a woman writer."

Atwood: I'm a writer who is female and therefore I write a lot from the point of view of a woman. In other words I don't see myself as a woman who is writing to promote certain things. I'm a bit too old to be that. I started writing in 1956 when indeed it was a lot more difficult to be a woman writer. // I was not socialized the way a lot of women describe themselves as being socialized. I was not made to wear frilly dresses. I was not told I couldn't do things because I was a girl. I didn't have a mother who said, "You can't do this and you can't do that and you have to be careful of evil men who will rape you and jump up and down on your head." I didn't get any of that. I grew up in the North where women wore pants anyway unless they were stupid and foolish.

Lyons: So it wasn't just your family, the whole culture was not sexist.

Atwood: Well, I wouldn't say that it wasn't sexist. It wasn't sexist in obvious ways. And since I grew up mostly with just my family, with a mother who could use a gun, shot a bow and arrow, fished off the end of the dock, was left with two small children in the woods with nobody around for long periods of time. What with the bears and strange animals we're not talking helpless femininity. And I think that for their time they were really very enlightened in that way. When I couldn't do something it wasn't because I was a girl, it was because I was younger. I had an older brother, who bossed me around a lot because he was older, but he didn't say, "You're a girl and you can't do it because you're a girl."

In fact, if he had done that, a lot of the time he wouldn't have had anyone to play with. I was it.

As a result we ended up playing *his* games a lot of the time. It was none of the "Girls are inferior and they can't do things" kind of stuff. If anything, it was "Pick up your socks and perform." If there were going to be any excuses, they were going to be youth excuses.

But when I hit society, then there was some of that sexism coming about. But there wasn't any from my family, and I think that's important. Your primary image of yourself comes from your early years and from what your parents say you are and can do—all those things. And there was also this double sort of life whereby when we were in the woods we would be comfortably dressed, and in the city Mother would put on a dress to go out to events and that sort of thing. But one was very conscious that this was a costume that one could assume at will. It wasn't something that was built in and you didn't *have* to, you could do it if you wanted to. //

Lyons: Recently some women have suggested that real feminists should only study women writers. Do you agree?

Atwood: I don't believe this "real feminist" category. That's like real women, real men, real Jews. I have a friend who is Jewish. He doesn't agree with the policy of Israel. People call him not a real Jew. I just don't buy it.

Lyons: I noticed yesterday that you certainly talk about male writers as being formative influences on you.

Atwood: I read men. Why deny myself knowledge? I read Africans!

Lyons: Do you feel more affinity to women writers than to male writers? Or just individually?

Atwood: I think that when I'm reading a woman writer I'm reading something closer to home. Why be surprised? I have an immediate curiosity. I might have another kind of curiosity with a male writer. "So that's what they think, ah ha! This is interesting, I never would have expected that." When I'm reading a woman writer it's more like saying, "Yes, true, right."

Lyons: Is that also true with Canadian writers?

Atwood: Yes, it's closer to home. And things that are closer to home have the power to make you a lot more nervous and anxious than things that are more remote. I read American literature more for entertainment because it's not so close to me. I don't have to feel embarrassed when the characters do something typically American, but when they do something typically Canadian I squirm. I say, "Uh oh, that's me."

Lyons: What was it like for you to write *The Handmaid's Tale*? // Does it feel like a different mind-set that you have to establish?

Atwood: I set it in the States because I couldn't fly it in Canada. In other words I tried all kinds of possibilities. Could this happen in Montreal or Toronto? And none of them felt right. Because it's not a Canadian sort of thing to do. Canadians might do it after the States did it, in some sort of watered-down version. Our television evangelists are more paltry than yours. The States are more extreme in everything. // Our genius is for compromise. It's how we make our way on the French/English front and keep from being squashed between the two super powers. Canadians don't swing much to the left or the right, they stay safely in the middle. So that's number one. And I lived in Boston/Cambridge for four years. That's number two. And then they are my ancestors. Those nagging Puritans really are my ancestors. So I had a considerable interest in them when I was studying them, and the mind-set of Gilead is really close to that of the seventeenth-century Puritans. It's also true that everyone watches the States to see what the country is doing and might be doing ten or fifteen years from now.

Lyons: Another thing you said yesterday was that the difference between a novel and a poem was length. And I didn't know how seriously you meant that.

Atwood: Quite seriously. Novels are about time and about what happens to you when you are living, how you use your time. If the characters are the same at the end of the novel as they are at the beginning, then something has gone wrong because novels are about change, living in time. But poetry, lyric poetry anyway, is more likely to be about the out-of-time experience. //

Lyons: Yesterday you mentioned that your father was a biologist and that you first intended to be a biologist. I had known those two things before, but when I heard you yesterday, I wondered if the decision to become a writer was also a way of throwing off the paternal influence, or if it had nothing to do with it.

Atwood: I was equally good at both, if my high school marks are taken as a measure. In fact, I did somewhat better in biology because they didn't take off for spelling. And like the character in *Life Before Man* I could spell *diplodocus* or *archaeopteryx* quite well but not ordinary words like *weird*.

Lyons: Can you say anything more about the writers who influenced you?

Atwood: I could add that because I was educated in the English tradition I never got the idea that you couldn't be a woman writer. // In the nineteenth century you cannot avoid Jane Austen and George Eliot and the Brontes. They are very much in the center of the tradition. So I didn't get any idea that women couldn't write novels. I got the idea that Canadians couldn't write novels and that's a lot easier to overcome, because I think nationality is secondary to gender.

Lyons: In the sense of its formative influence?

Atwood: And also in its changeability. You know that if you want to you can move to Switzerland and become sort of quasi-Swiss. But unless you have a sex-change operation, you can't change from one sex to the other. When I started getting published and reviewed, *then* if they thought you were any good, you were an honorary man. If they thought you were bad, then you had too many female hormones. I think American women writers of my generation had a harder time in the gender area although an easier time in the national area. Everyone said, "Yes, there are great American writers—but none of them are women."

Lyons: In another interview you remarked that the book that influenced you most was *Grimm's Fairy Tales*.

Atwood: Probably, because I had pretty well memorized them by the time I was six. // One of the interesting things was that there were a lot of quite active female characters, whereas if you get the watered-down version, you just get Cinderella and Sleeping Beauty.

Lyons: Were these female characters active in positive ways? The last time I looked at them I thought the stepmother was very important but very bad.

Atwood: Yes, the stepmother is bad, but there are active princesses. And if anybody is passive, it's the prince. You know, he goes home and his mother casts some sort of spell on him, and the princess has to go through all these interesting machinations to get him back. She rescues him; she's the one that has the magic powers. She's the one with the magic cloak, and if you throw it down, it becomes a forest full of trees. And that just was not the cutesy versions at all.

Lyons: For me so much of the essence of the fairy tales is transformation, and I wonder if you link that up with your own interest in transformation in your fiction?

Atwood: Probably, but it comes from all directions. My father wasn't only a biologist, he was also an entomologist. And the most transformative thing you can study is insects. They change from one thing into another, and the thing that they change into bears no relation to what they were before.

Lyons: I particularly connect that to the change from fat to thin in *Lady Oracle* and her dancing costume as a mothball among the butterflies.

Atwood: You can't imagine how many letters I got about that, all saying, "This was exactly my experience at ballet school—I had to play a shrub." I think it's also true that women are much more conscious of the possibility of bodily transformation. Of course, when you're pregnant you're quite a different shape, and when you go from being a child to being a woman your shape changes much more radically than a boy's does. You get extra things—they don't just get bigger. You really change from one kind of thing to something that is radically different. And then there's the absolute obsession in Western society with the shape of women's bodies in terms of fatness and thinness. I mean, show me three women who think they are the right shape—they don't exist and there is no "right." // And they falsely assume that everyone cares how they look, which is untrue. People, in fact, don't notice each other very much at all. And when they do, they're certainly not making a lot of value judgments, unless there is something radically strange about the person.

Lyons: Yesterday you said that in the stories of *Bluebeard's Egg* there were portraits of your parents, which were kind of an answer to people who mistakenly thought the heroine's parents in *Surfacing* were pictures of your own parents. I was wondering, do you often include portraits of yourself or your family or your friends?

Atwood: No, hardly ever, but I thought I would do that. And they got a huge kick out of it. They're very nice people, as you can see from what I've said about them. I used to feel that it was a disadvantage to have nice parents, because here are all these books about people's dreadful childhoods, so I would have to use other people's dreadful childhoods.

Lyons: You said that you wrote *Life Before Man* as a homage to *Middlemarch*. I wonder if you could discuss that a little.

Atwood: In *Middlemarch* everything is middle—it's the middle of the nineteenth century, it's middle class, it's the middle of England, the religion of people is middleism. It's about life as lived by the middle and that's what *Life Before Man* is. It's the middle of Toronto, it's somewhat the middle of the twentieth century, the people are middle-aged. If you look at the book they don't go out—they all stay within one square mile.

Everybody lives within that area and the only person who goes out is a dead person. Chris goes out when he's dead. In that way it's claustrophobic and it doesn't have what some of my other novels have. And that is a supernatural dimension or, shall we say, another world or another area of the mind. People have dreams in it and fantasies, but Hamlet's father's ghost does not appear. They may think about it, but it is not actually there. So it's a novel novel in that sense, where some of my other works are more in the romance tradition, according to Hawthorne's definition. //

Lyons: A frequently debated question in this country is whether women writers have special problems if they choose to become mothers as well. That is, whether motherhood is necessarily in conflict with their writing or whether it is an enrichment of their lives and in fact of their writing.

Atwood: Everything is a conflict with your writing. If there were no conflict there would be no writing.

Lyons: Do you consciously try to limit those conflicts? To take on as little outside your writing as possible?

Atwood: It just depends on what I'm doing at the time. I mean, I make a mean chocolate-chip cookie. I don't think that I'm ruining myself as a writer by doing that. They're not comparable things—being a writer and being a mother. It's not an either/or proposition and to think that it is is another one of those because-you're-a-woman-you-have-to-deprive-yourself-of-having-a-child ideas which we were taught to believe by reading biographies of nineteenth-century women writers who lived in a closet like Emily Dickinson or died in childbirth. I don't think that's necessary any longer. For men there was the tubercular-genius idea and for women there was the idea that they were somehow damaged or warped or suicidal and if they weren't that, then they weren't real writers. It was almost die and prove yourself. And I protest. I enjoy being a mother. I did it on purpose. I saved that until I was rather old.

Lyons: Did you ever want to have a second one?

Atwood: I did, but I was already pretty old and it wasn't really possible for me.

Lyons: Did being a middle child have anything to do with your development?

Atwood: I wasn't really a middle child. The youngest one was born twelve years after me, so I was really the youngest until I was twelve, and then it wasn't like being a middle child. It was like being a surrogate mother. //

Lyons: In the epigraph to *Bodily Harm* you quote, "A man's presence suggests what he is capable of doing to you or for you. By contrast a woman's presence...defines what can and can not be done to her." In that novel do you think it is necessary that Rennie be seen as a woman or is it more woman as everyperson?

Atwood: Why does it have to be either/or? Certainly I wanted to take somebody from our society where the forefront preoccupations are your appearance, your furniture, your job, your boyfriend, your health, and the rest of the world is quite a lot further back. And so your planning is, What am I going to do next year and the year after that, and if I stop smoking now, I won't get cancer in twenty years. That's not the way people in those other countries think, because they can't afford to. They are thinking what is going to happen tomorrow or next week, how they will get through the immediate time. I wanted to take somebody from our society and put her into *that*, cause a resonance there. And the other thing is the sort of sexual kink and violence. For us it's just that, underground sexual kink. In other countries it is a political instrument, an instrument of control. It's not something weird sadists and porn fanciers do; it's something governments do to people to keep them under control.

Lyons: At the end of that novel, it seems to me that you make it deliberately unclear whether she will ever get out of prison or not.

Atwood: Your choice, reader's choice. I like the reader to participate in writing the book.

Lyons: Is that supposed to suggest that what is really important is the internal change, so that it doesn't make a difference if she gets out or not?

Atwood: That's right. It makes a difference in a way, but whether she gets out or not, she has still undergone an experience that has changed her way of seeing. //

Lyons: Food and eating and fatness seem to be central in several of your novels in different ways.

Atwood: As in human life. Not the fatness necessarily, but definitely the food and eating.

Lyons: Do you connect that with women or the female condition?

Atwood: In this country, yes; in other countries, no. It's a human activity that has all kinds of symbolic connotations depending on the society and the level of society. In other words, what you eat varies from place to place, how we feel about what we eat varies from individual to individual as well as from place to place. If you think of food as coming in various categories: sacred food, ceremonial food, everyday food, and things that are not to be eaten, forbidden food, dirty food, if you like—for the anorexic, all food is dirty food.

Lyons: They just collapse the categories?

Atwood: Yes, and for the Buddhist, all food is sacred. Why do we say grace? Because we are making food sacramental. It's an activity that has all kinds of symbolic connotations.

Lyons: I think you handle that particularly well in your work. It becomes for me a very central part of a number of your novels. In *Surfacing*, the heroine's changing attitudes toward what she can eat.

Atwood: She defines most food as forbidden food and some food as sacred food.

Lyons: And I think that is such a wonderful way to suggest how she is putting herself in touch with the sacred.

Atwood: If you want to have visions, starve yourself and eat plenty of funny mushrooms.

Lyons: Certain images seem to me to play off each other, from one novel to the next. Besides the food images, there are the hands.

Atwood: Hands are quite important to me. The hand to me is an extension of the brain. And if you read theory on the development of the human species, everybody says that the ability to use the two is central; they are part of one another. I don't think of the brain as something that is just in your head. The brain is also in your body. Because what are we? We have this brain that is kind of the center, where all the synapses and neurological connections occur, but that information is coming from an extended network of nerves that are throughout the body, so your brain is all over your body. It's just that you think of it as being in your head. And the brain is certainly in the hands.

Lyons: I suppose we feel that the hand is the connection point between the self and the other.

Atwood: It's *one* of the connection points.

Lyons: It seems to be me that certain symbolic hand gestures are central in several of the novels. For example, when Rennie touches—

Atwood: —the grandmother.

Lyons: Yes, and to me the breakthrough gesture is when she touches Lora. And when I read *that*, the image of the mother feeding the birds in *Surfacing* flashed through my mind. When you write, do you feel the resonances of the earlier novels?

Atwood: No. You don't think of these things when you're writing. You may think about these things before you write or after you write, but if you think about them while you are writing, where are you? You're just daydreaming. //

Lyons: Do you tend to begin a novel with a certain thing? For example, Joseph Heller, who was here recently, said he needed to hear a certain voice.

Atwood: I need the voice, quite true. I can have all kinds of images, but unless I have the voice, there's still a lot of fumbling around. It's very hard to say. Things build up and then you reach a critical point and then you start to write. And then it works or it doesn't. As I said, I've written a couple of novels that didn't work out.

Lyons: Were there more than those two—the one before *Surfacing* and the one before *The Handmaid's Tale?*

Atwood: There's only those two. There's one that didn't get published, but it did get finished. That's my first one. I wrote it in 1963 when I was twenty-three years old, and it is an interesting novel for a twenty-three-year-old. But I'm not going to publish it now. I wrote *The Edible Woman* the year after, when I was twenty-four, and there's a big difference. //

Lyons: Do you consider the first one juvenilia?

Atwood: The first one is definitely more juvenile. I was looking at *The Edible Woman* the other day, and it's really fairly good. I liked it. I hadn't read it for years, but I read along and I thought, You know, this isn't bad for a twenty-four-year-old.

Lyons: Was it somehow necessary to write those unfinished novels before you would go on to *Surfacing* or *The Handmaid's Tale?*

Atwood: I don't think that way. That makes the writing sound much more planned out—more like a business plan, that kind of thing.

Lyons: I thought that in retrospect you might have seen something.

Atwood: Oh, in retrospect. In retrospect, who cares? If I hadn't done this, I wouldn't have done that—I mean, we can all say things like that. At the time you really don't know what you're doing. That's the main thing to know about writing: you don't know what you're doing.

Lyons: Judging from the acknowledgements in *Life Before Man*, it looks as though you had to do a lot of research. Did you do research for any of your other books?

Atwood: *While* I'm writing a book, not beforehand. //

Lyons: What sort of research did you do for your other novels?

Atwood: What did the Brownies sing around the mushroom? What subway station? What phone booth is on the corner of Davenport and George? I like them to be quite accurate. If not, people will write me gloating, "You got it wrong. That's not what the Brownies sang."

Lyons: Did you have to do a lot of research about Gothic novels for *Lady Oracle*?

Atwood: I already knew a lot. But I also had a source—I have a friend who is a Ph.D. who mainlines these things. I was familiar with the Gothic tradition, but not the modern variety.

Lyons: When you look back at your novels, would you say that one changed more than the others?

Atwood: *Surfacing* changed a lot. *Bodily Harm* was a pretty fast write, *Handmaid's Tale* was a fast write, *Lady Oracle* took me a long time because there are so many people and it's complex. I think *Surfacing* changed the most from beginning to end. //

Lyons: You've said that you don't read the criticism of your work.

Atwood: I file it. I used to read it, but it used to bother me too much.

Lyons: You mean if it was negative?

Atwood: Noooo, you know how it is: they get this wrong, they get that wrong, they get the names of the characters wrong.

Lyons: Is it ever any use to you? Have you ever read anything that made you say, "Hey!"

Atwood: Let me put it to you this way, I write book reviews from time to time. Lord knows why, I find it very difficult, I swear. Any writer who writes reviews of another writer's work, unless they are terribly callous or mean, they know that any book has had a lot of blood go into it, whether it comes out well or not. You can't just be flippant or casual, and you can't just make jokes. Which is a temptation if you happen to have any kind of sense of humor. So I have to really watch it and try to be responsible. What I like to do in a review is bridge between the reader and the book—I like to place the book in the writer's work. I like to give some idea of what the book is about without giving away the plot. I hate reviewers who give away the plot. And I like to say in what ways I think it's good, because I don't like to review books that I dislike. And that would give the readers some idea about whether this book is for them. For example, if I say this is a book about stamp collecting, people may not be very drawn to it. But I like to give as accurate an impression of the book as I can and to make the review interesting to read. Not just have it drone on.

Lyons: And are those the things that you would appreciate in a review of your own work?

Atwood: That's what I appreciate in a review of my own work.

Lyons: And how about in more extensive criticism?

Atwood: I don't read it anymore. It keeps them off the streets. They enjoy it, or they do it to publish and not perish or for some reason that is known to them. But in some way once the book is out there, it's beyond me. It's like what you wore last year. It's like somebody commenting on your wardrobe of a year ago; now you're wearing something different. That was last year's hairdo. //
   I like to feel like I'm going to try something I've never done and this is going to be hard. It's going to be a challenge. I'm going to sweat, this is going to be difficult, I might not pull it off. That was *The Handmaid's Tale*. It could have been a total disaster. And the same with the movie. I'm very glad it's Harold Pinter who is doing the screenplay. Because it could be a sort of S & M exploitation, a sensationalist movie of the worst kind. //

Lyons: In *Survival* you said, "The reader must face the fact that Canadian literature is undeniably somber and negative." That certainly doesn't seem true of your work.

Atwood: Well, I was writing about classic Canadian literature, everything before 1970, and it was. Now there's been a lot of more jolly things come out since that time. The earlier books were produced by a colony, a colony without very much cultural self-confidence. It *was* somber and negative.

Lyons: So you think it's not just your work that's outside that mold? That much recent Canadian literature has changed?

Atwood: It's changed quite a lot. Particularly the artist's view of the artist, which used to be very isolated, very blocked. As I pointed out in *Survival*, a number of books about the painter who can't paint, the writer who can't write, with a very serious audience problem during those years—like no audience. And artists did feel very isolated. They didn't know one another. And that has changed enormously.

Lyons: What do you think is the cause of that change?

Atwood: It's happened in a number of ex-colonies. It happened in the United States, just earlier. We know that it took two hundred years in the United States to produce any literature which we now find readable. And that just seems to be the colonial experience. It's what Gabriel Garcia Marquez is talking about as well, and we don't have any problem with writers from African countries or from Latin American countries or from India, from New Zealand or from Australia or from the West Indies talking about this configuration, because they've all experienced it. It's only when you talk to people from England, France, or the United States that you have to explain this. A lot of the rest of the world knows about it. They've undergone the experience of being culturally dominated by another country, having to forge their own modes. How do you come to terms with that? Do you try to imitate the mother country as Washington Irving did, or do you try to create new forms as Melville did and then everybody jumps on your head and spits at you. Women have had this experience. This is where you can say to American women, "Do you try to write like a man and get praised for writing such a good novel or do you try to write like a woman and have your work dismissed as secondary and inconsequential and subjective and too female?"

Our writers used to have publishers say to them, "This is too Canadian. Can't you make it less Canadian?" At the same time they would say, "There is no Canadian literature." Well, if there was none, why was it too Canadian? There is no women's culture. This is too female. It's the same thing. Right now we're having Chicano culture undergoing the same process. "We want to write like Chicanos, but how do we get the mainstream to acknowledge the fact that we can be ourselves and also be good?"

It's a historical process. On the one hand, all over the world you have homogenization, you know, everybody wearing jeans. On the other hand, you have an awareness of difference. "We're wearing jeans, but who are we?" We no longer can say, "We're these people because we're wearing these native costumes." And you notice that when women started wearing pants they had to face these questions. Before that, they may not have liked some part of their condition, but they *knew* they were women. They didn't have to say, "What is a woman?" //

Waltzing Again
Earl G. Ingersoll

Earl G. Ingersoll's interview was conducted by mail in November 1989 and originally appeared in *The Ontario Review* 32 (Spring-Summer 1990). Copyright © 1990 by *The Ontario Review*. Reprinted by permission.

Ingersoll: Since as you know I've been working on a collection of your interviews, could we begin by talking about interviews? You have been interviewed very frequently. How do you feel about being interviewed?

Atwood: I don't mind "being interviewed" any more than I mind Viennese waltzing—that is, my response will depend on the agility and grace and attitude and intelligence of the other person. Some do it well, some clumsily, some step on your toes by accident, and some aim for them. I've had interviews that were pleasant and stimulating experiences for me, and I've had others that were hell. And of course you do get tired of being misquoted, quoted out of context, and misunderstood. You yourself may be striving for accuracy (which is always complicated), whereas journalists are striving mainly for hot copy, the more one-dimensional the better. Not all of them of course, but enough.

I think the "Get the Guest" or "David and Goliath" interview tends to become less likely as you age; the interviewer less frequently expects you to prove you're a real writer, or a real woman, or any of the other things they expect you to prove. And you run into a generation of interviewers who studied you in high school and want to help you hobble across the street, rather than wishing to smack you down for being a presumptuous young upstart.

Let's not pretend however that an interview will necessarily result in any absolute and blinding revelations. Interviews too are an art form; that is to say, they indulge in the science of illusion.

Ingersoll: You've said that when you began writing you imagined you'd have to starve in an attic without an audience sufficiently large to support your writing. Is there a Margaret Atwood who would have preferred the obscurity of a Herman Melville to whom you refer so frequently, or do you draw upon your readers' responses to your work? How much do you feel involved in a kind of dialogue with your readers?

Atwood: The alternative, for me, to selling enough books or writing enough scripts and travel articles to keep me independent and to buy my time as a writer would be teaching in a university, or some other job. I've done that, and I've been poor, and I prefer things the way they are. For instance, this way I can say what I want to, because nobody can fire me. Not very many people in our society have that privilege.

I did not expect a large readership when I began writing, but that doesn't mean I'm not pleased to have one. It doesn't mean either that I write for a "mass audience." It means I'm one of the few literary writers who get lucky in their lifetimes.

My readers' responses to my work interest me, but I don't "draw upon" them. The response comes after the book is published; by the time I get responses, I'm thinking about something new. Dialogue with the readers? Not exactly. Dickens could have a dialogue with his readers *that affected the books* when he was publishing his novels in serial form, but we've lost that possibility. Though it does of course cheer me when someone likes, appreciates, or shows me that he or she has read my books intelligently.

Ingersoll: Are you worried by self-consciousness as you write? Or is it an asset?

Atwood: Self-consciousness? Do you mean consciousness of my self? That's what you have to give up when writing—in exchange for con- sciousness of the work. That's why most of what writers say about how they write—the process—is either imperfect memory or fabrication. If you're paying proper attention to what you're doing, you are so absorbed in it that you *shouldn't* be able to tell anyone afterwards exactly how you did it. In sports they have instant replay. We don't have that for writers.

Ingersoll: *The Edible Woman, Lady Oracle,* and now *Cat's Eye* seem in large part *jeux d'esprit.* You give your readers the impression that you are having a good time writing—it's hard work, but also good fun. How important is "play" to you in writing? Do you have a sense of how much the reader will enjoy what you write, as you're writing it?

Atwood: I don't think *Cat's Eye* is a *jeu d'esprit.* (*Oxford Shorter*: "a witty or humorous trifle.") In fact, I don't think my other "comic" novels are *jeux d'esprit,* either. I suspect that sort of definition is something people fall back on because they can't take women's concerns or life patterns at all seriously; so they see the wit in those books, and that's all they see. Writing is *play* in the same way that playing the piano is "play," or putting on a theatrical "play" is play. Just because something's fun doesn't mean it isn't serious. For instance, some get a kick out of war. Others enjoy falling in love. Yet others get a bang out of a really good funeral. Does that mean war, love, and death are trifles?

Ingersoll: *Cat's Eye* strikes me as unusual in one especially dramatic way: it builds upon the most detailed and perceptive exploration of young girlhood that I can recall having read. Once we've read that section of the novel, we readers might think, we've had fiction which explores this stage of young boyhood, but why haven't writers, even writers who are women, dealt with this stage of a woman's development before? How did you get interested in this area of girlhood, from roughly eight to twelve?

Atwood: I think the answer to this one is fairly simple: writers haven't dealt with girls age eight to twelve because this area of life was not regarded as serious "literary" material. You do get girls this age in *juvenile* fiction—all those English boarding-school books. And there have been some—I'm thinking of *Frost in May.* But it's part of that "Man's love is of man's life a thing apart, / 'Tis woman's whole existence" tendency— that is, the tendency to think that the only relationships of importance to women are their dealings with men (parents, boyfriends, husbands, God) or babies. What *could* be of importance in what young girls do with and to one another? Well, lots, it seems, judging from the mail.... I guess that's where "dialogue with the readers" comes in. Cordelia really got around, and she had a profound influence on how the little girls who got run over by her were able to respond to other women when they grew up.

   I sometimes get interested in stories because I notice a sort of blank— why hasn't anyone written about this? *Can* it be written about? Do I dare to write it? *Cat's Eye* was risky business, in a way—wouldn't I be trashed for writing about little *girls,* how trivial? Or wouldn't I be trashed for saying they weren't all sugar and spice?

   Or I might think about a story form, and see how it could be approached from a different angle—*Cinderella* from the point of view of the ugly sister, for instance. But also I wanted a literary home for all those vanished *things* from my own childhood—the marbles, the Eaton's catalogues, the Watchbird Watching You, the smells, sounds, colors. The textures. Part of fiction writing I think is a celebration of the physical world we know—and when you're writing about the past, it's a physical world that's vanished. So the impulse is partly elegiac. And partly it's an attempt to stop or bring back time.

Ingersoll: The reviewer in *Time* said that "Elaine's emotional life is effectively over at puberty." Does that seem accurate to you now as a reader of your own work?

Atwood: That ain't the book I wrote, and it ain't the one I read when I go back to it; as I'm doing now, since I'm writing the screenplay. I don't think Elaine's emotional life is over at puberty any more than any of our lives are over then. Childhood is very intense, because children can't imagine a future. They can't imagine pain being *over*. Which is why children are nearer to the absolute states of Heaven and Hell than adults are. Purgatory seems to me a more adult concept.

There are loose ends left from Elaine's life at that time, especially her unresolved relationship with Cordelia. These things have been baggage for her for a long time. But that's quite different from saying she stopped dead at twelve.

Ingersoll: At the end of *Cat's Eye* Elaine has lost both her parents and her brother, and said goodby finally to her ex- and to Cordelia. She has a husband and daughters she loves, but she seems very alone. What do you make of her aloneness now as a reader of your own novel?

Atwood: Writers can never really read their own books, just as film directors can never really see their own movies—or not in the way that a fresh viewer can. Because THEY KNOW WHAT HAPPENS NEXT.

Elaine "seems" alone at the end of the book because she's on an airplane. Also: because *the story* has been about a certain part of her life, and that part—*that* story—has reached a conclusion. She will of course land, get out of the plane, and carry on with the next part of her life, i.e. her ongoing time-line with some other characters about whom we have not been told very much, because *the story was not about them*.

Why do authors kill off certain characters? Usually for aesthetic, that is, structural reasons. If Elaine's parents etc. had still been around, we would have to have scenes with them, and that wasn't appropriate for this particular story. *Cat's Eye* is partly about being haunted. Why did Dickens kill off Little Nell? Because he was making a statement about the nature of humanity or the cruelty of fate? I don't think so. He just had to polish her off because that was where the story was going.

Ingersoll: Related to that question, a reviewer in *New Statesman* has written: "The novel is extremely bleak about humanity.... Through most of the novel you feel distance, dissection: a cat's eye. It ends on a note of gaiety, forgiveness and hope: but I don't believe it." When you were writing the novel did you have the sense of painting a "bleak" picture of "humanity"?

Atwood: One reason I don't like interviews, when I don't like them, is that people tend to come up with these weird quotes from reviewers, assume the quote is true, and then ask you why you did it that way. There are a lot of "when did you stop beating your wife" questions in interviews.

For instance, what is this "gaiety, forgiveness and hope" stuff? I'm thinking of doing a calendar in which each day would contain a quote by a reviewer of which the next day's quote would be a total contradiction by another reviewer. I'll buy the forgiveness, sort of; but gaiety? Eh? Where? The jolly old women on the plane are something she *doesn't* have. You find yourself looking under the sofa for some other book by the same name that might have strayed into the reviewer's hands by mistake. Or maybe they got one with some of the pages left out.

Nor, judging from the mail I received, did readers "feel distance, dissection." Total identification is more like it. Maybe the readers were identifying with the character's *attempt* to achieve distance, etc. She certainly attempts it, but she doesn't get it. As for "bleak," that's a word that tends to be used by people who've never been outside Western Europe or North America, and the middle class in either location. They think *bleak* is not having a two-car garage. If they think *I'm* bleak, they have no idea of what real bleak is like. Try Kierkegaard. Try Tadeusz Konwicki. Try Russell Banks, for that matter.

Or maybe... yes, maybe... I'm bleak *for a woman.* Is that the key? Are we getting somewhere now?

Contributor Notes

Jo Brans is the author of three books: *Mother, I Have Something to Tell You*, on family dynamics; *Listen to the Voices*, from which her interview with Margaret Atwood was taken; and, most recently, *Take Two*, on dramatic life changes. For fifteen years a member of the English department at Southern Methodist University, Brans now lives and writes in New York City.

Kathryn Crabbe is Associate Dean of Undergraduate Studies and Director of Graduate Studies at the State University of New York, College at Geneseo. She has written on Tennyson, J. R. R. Tolkien, and children's literature. Her most recent publication is *Evelyn Waugh* (Continuum, 1988).

Jim Davidson is an Australian cultural historian (not a contradiction in terms, he adds) who edited the literary journal *Meanjin* from 1974–82. He currently lectures at Footscray Institute of Technology, Melbourne, and is writing a biography of Louise Hanson Oyer, founder of the music press and recording company Oiseau Lyre in Paris.

Cory Bieman Davies is Associate Professor of English at Huron College, University of Western Ontario, where she teaches eighteenth- and nineteenth-century literature, and children's literature. She has published articles on Robert Browning, T. S. Eliot, nineteenth-century women's issues, and many Canadian children's writers.

Gregory Fitz Gerald's stories, poems, essays, and books have been widely published in the United States and abroad. His most recent fiction, a novel, *The Druze Document* was published in 1989 by Cliffhanger Press. He is currently completing a science fiction novel, *The Hidden Quantum*.

Graeme Gibson is the author of several novels and the editor of *Eleven Canadian Novelists*, in which his interview with Margaret Atwood originally appeared.

Mary Ellis Gibson is Associate Professor of English at the University of North Carolina at Greensboro. Her books include *History and the Prism* *of Art: Browning's Poetic Experiments* and an anthology published in 1989 by University of South Carolina Press, *New Stories by Southern Women.*

Karla Hammond holds a B.A. from Goucher College and an M.A. from Trinity College. She has published poetry, fiction, essays, articles, and interviews in numerous publications in North America, Europe, Japan, and Australia.

Geoff Hancock is editor-in-chief of *Canadian Fiction Magazine.* His recent books include *Canadian Writers at Work: Interviews* (Oxford, 1987), *Invisible Fictions: Contemporary Stories from Quebec* (House of Anansi, 1987), *Published in Canada: The Small Presses* (Black Moss, 1990), and *Singularities* (Black Moss, 1990), an anthology of prose poems, fragments, and parafictions.

Earl G. Ingersoll is Associate Professor of English at the State University of New York, College at Brockport. He is a co-editor of *The Post-Confessionals: Conversations with American Poets of the Eighties* (Fairleigh Dickinson, 1989) and editor of the forthcoming *SF Talk: Conversations with Writers of Fantasy and Science Fiction* (Penkevill, 1990).

Margaret Kaminski is a librarian with the Detroit Public Library. Her poetry and prose have appeared in numerous journals, notably *Poetry Review* and *University of Windsor Review.* She is the editor of *Moving Out, a Feminist Literary and Arts Journal.*

Christopher Levenson has been teaching English and Creative Writing at Carleton University, Ottawa, since he came to Canada from the United Kingdom in 1968. He has published seven books of poetry, four in the United Kingdom and three in Canada, most recently *Arriving at Midnight* (Mosaic Press, 1986). He co-founded and edited the literary magazine *arc* from 1978-88, and founded and still directs the Arc Reading Series in Ottawa.

Bonnie Lyons, Professor of English at the University of Texas at San Antonio, has published interviews with Henry Roth and Tobias Wolff (with Bill Oliver), a book on Henry Roth, and many articles on American Jewish literature and women writers.

Elizabeth Meese is Professor of English at the University of Alabama. She has published on nineteenth- and twentieth-century American writers, Southern women writers, and feminist criticism. She is the author of

Crossing the Double-Cross: The Practice of Feminist Criticism (Univ. of North Carolina Press, 1986) and *(Ex)Tensions: Re-Figuring Feminist Criticism* (Univ. of Illinois Press, 1990), and co-editor (with Alice Parker) of *The Differences Within: Feminism and Critical Theory* (John Benjamins, 1989).

Beatrice Mendez-Egle is Assistant Professor of English and Coordinator of Lower Division Courses for the Department at The University of Texas, Pan American. She has edited two volumes in the Living Author Series, *John Gardner: True Art, Moral Art* (1983) and *Margaret Atwood: Reflection and Reality* (1987).

Joyce Carol Oates's most recent novel is *Because It Is Bitter, and Because It Is My Heart.* She is the Roger S. Berlind Distinguished Professor in the Humanities at Princeton University.

Catherine Sheldrik Ross is Associate Professor at the School of Library and Information Science at the University of Western Ontario. Her publications include articles on Canadian writers such as Isabella Valancy Crawford, John Richardson, Hugh MacLennan, Margaret Atwood, and Alice Munro, and interviews with Canadian children's authors such as Jean Little, James Reaney, and Dennis Lee.

J. R. (Tim) Struthers is a member of the Department of English at the University of Guelph and the author of various bibliographies, interviews, and articles on Canadian literature. He has edited *Before the Flood, a Collection of Criticism on Hugh Hood* and *The Montreal Story Tellers.* As publisher of Red Kite Press he has produced several books, including John Metcalf's *What Is a Canadian Literature?*

Alan Twigg is the author of five books, including *Strong Voices: Conversations with 50 Canadian Authors* (Harbour Publishing) and the publisher/editor of *B.C. BookWorld*, a quarterly publication about books which reaches approximately 50,000 readers per issue.

Susan Walker is the editor and publisher of *Negative Capability*, a professor of English at the University of South Alabama, a recipient of the Alabama Council on the Arts Individual Writers Fellowship, a poet and writer who has published poems, essays, stories throughout the United States.

Index

II. GENERAL INDEX